The Great Society

The Great Society

Lessons for the Future

EDITED BY

Eli Ginzberg and Robert M. Solow

Basic Books, Inc., Publishers

NEW YORK

CONTENTS

The Great Society

THE AUTHORS

ANDREW F. BRIMMER is a Member of the Board of Governors of the Federal Reserve System.

ANTHONY DOWNS, Chairman of the Board of Real Estate Research Corp., is the author of *Federal Housing Subsidies: How Are They Working?* and *Opening Up the Suburbs*.

ELI GINZBERG is A. Barton Hepburn Professor of Economics, Graduate School of Business, and Director of Conservation of Human Resources at Columbia University.

CHARLES V. HAMILTON is Wallace S. Sayre Professor of Government at Columbia University.

HERBERT E. KLARMAN, who was formerly Associate Director, Hospital Council of Greater New York, and Professor of Public Health Administration and Political Economy at Johns Hopkins University, is now Professor of Economics at the Graduate School of Public Administration of New York University.

ROBERT J. LAMPMAN is Vilas Professor of Economics at the University of Wisconsin. Currently he is a Visiting Professor at the New York State School of Industrial and Labor Relations at Cornell University. He is the author of *Top Wealth-holders' Share of National Wealth* and *Ends and Means of Reducing Income Poverty*.

LANCE LIEBMAN is Assistant Professor of Law at Harvard Law School.

EDMUND S. PHELPS is Professor of Economics at Columbia University and author of *Inflation Policy and Unemployment Theory*.

ROBERT M. SOLOW is Professor of Economics and Institute Professor at the Massachusetts Institute of Technology.

GILBERT Y. STEINER is Director of Governmental Studies at the Brookings Institution.

RALPH W. TYLER is Director Emeritus of the Center for Advanced Study in the Behavioral Sciences in Stanford, California.

LLOYD ULMAN is Professor of Economics and Director of the Institute of Industrial Relations at the University of California at Berkeley.

Introduction

ELI GINZBERG & ROBERT M. SOLOW

O<small>NE</small> of the staples of political argument in the United States—more so than in other capitalist democracies—is the question of the desirability and effectiveness of direct government intervention into economic and social affairs. Most of the time, therefore, opinions follow the lines of regional, class, or other factional self-interest, and the two political parties look pragmatically for positions that will assure them the support of the majority they need to enjoy the benefits of office. Only occasionally does the rhetoric of the leadership slip into ideological gear. That is why it came as such a surprise that the Goldwater campaign of 1964 went so far as to attack a longstanding consensus policy like the Social Security system, and to attack it as a matter of principle. When this happens, the debate often becomes acrimonious and facts merge with legend.

A similar, but only partially similar, debate is underway now. The Presidential campaign of 1972 and President Nixon's large majority have provided the occasion and the backdrop for a steadily mounting attack on the social programs and policies that were summarized in President Johnson's slogan, "the Great Society." The present episode has its share of ideological stridency, but it has another element as well: Opponents claim not merely that many large-scale social programs are improper, but that they can be (or have been?) shown to be ineffective. "Throwing money at problems" is obviously not a cool scientific description of the social legislation of the 1960's. But the implication intended by those who use this phrase is clearly that throwing money at problems doesn't work, not merely that it is wrong in principle. In fact, the belief that many or most of the Great Society programs worked badly or not at all is shared by some people who would still probably describe themselves as liberals or even liberal Democrats.

Frank Knight's version of Gresham's Law was "Bad talk drives out good." That is in danger of happening here, as ideology and political calculation mix with what, in principle, should be questions of evidence and judgment. There is no doubt that Presidents Kennedy and Johnson and their staffs were both vague and grandiose about the new society they claimed to be fashioning. And it is equally true that, by 1972, many in the Republican camp, joined by disappointed reformers whose expectations had been dashed, were making exaggerated counterclaims, this time in criticism of the same legislative programs. One of the difficult, but indispensable parts of any reasoned appraisal of this episode is to extract from the rhetoric an estimate of what might reasonably have been expected in the way of accomplishment from each bundle of legislation and a judgment as to whether the budgetary and organizational support actually provided were at all commensurate with the task. Only then is it possible to begin grading the degree of success or failure of any particular program. (Whatever the case with students, with legislative programs it is better to grade on a scale from A to F than on a Pass-Fail basis!)

The idea of this symposium originated with Mr. Robert Schrank of the Ford Foundation, as a start to the process of dispassionate evaluation of the social programs of the 1960's, before the operation of Knight's Law rendered it impossible. We shared his view and undertook to organize a group of papers. Mr. Mitchell Sviridoff, Vice President for National Affairs of the Ford Foundation, arranged for a grant to underwrite the project, in the hope that a critical evaluation of these programs might add to public understanding of the potentialities and the limitations of legislative reform. The Editors of *The Public Interest* agreed that its pages provide an appropriate forum for this contribution to a discussion in which the magazine has already played an important part.

Setting the stage

One could easily argue that the shape of American society in the 1960's and after was more powerfully influenced by federal government actions not discussed here—and most of all by the prolonged war in Southeast Asia—than by the explicit social interventions we have chosen to discuss. We are not trying to produce a complete social history, however, but merely the beginnings of a sound appraisal of the intentions and effects of a number of specific legislative packages. It did seem to us important, though, to complement these specific studies with essays on a few broader background themes: the role of law in social reform in a democracy; the conduct of macroeconomic policy; and the broadened participation of minorities, especially the black minority, in the political process. These issues provide a context without which—in this country, at least— it would be difficult to think sensibly about social policy.

The specific areas of federal social policy covered in the contributions to this symposium are health, education, public assistance, income redistribution, housing and urban renewal, manpower development, and the economic condition of the black population. Although a few other areas of policy have been slighted, we think we have covered most of the ground.

It goes without saying that we sought contributors who could combine scholarly detachment with a lively interest in public policy. There is obviously some conflict between these two desired qualities, but we hope they can be reconciled—indeed, have been reconciled—so long as detachment is not interpreted to mean neutrality on specific issues. We did, with forethought, deny ourselves the possibility of contributions from anyone who had filled a substantial political office in any administration since 1961. There is a clear loss in this decision, but we concluded that it was more important, so soon after the fact, to avoid evaluations from even experienced scholars with a large personal stake in the outcome of specific pieces of legislation.

Before yielding to the individual contributors, we think it might be useful to sketch briefly the general shape and magnitude of the episode of the 1960's. In thus setting the stage for the specific essays, we hope to call attention both to elements of continuity in the story and to the special circumstances that surrounded the social interventions of the 1960's.

It is interesting to begin with some of the events of the second Eisenhower Administration, especially because President Eisenhower consciously sought to avoid legislative and social innovation. His intention was to restore and maintain stability both at home and abroad. Yet it was in the second Eisenhower Administration that the dress rehearsal for the 1960's occurred. The importance of this paradox lies in its suggestion that strong forces inside the society were calling for action.

It was Eisenhower who ordered the troops into Little Rock to enforce school desegregation in 1957, and in the same year Congress passed the first Civil Rights Act since Reconstruction. Although deep-

ly opposed to the extension of the federal government into areas historically under the control of the states and localities, such as the
financing of education, Eisenhower nonetheless signed the National
Defense Education Act, which put the federal government into the
financing of higher education in a major way. (Here the motive
force was the alarm engendered by Sputnik.)

The Kerr-Mills Act of 1959 increased the flow of federal funds
into health care for the indigent aged, even if it was later adjudged
by Congress and the public to be too little, too late. Toward the
end of Eisenhower's second Administration, Congress passed two
bills for the relief of distressed areas that contained provisions for
federal financing of manpower training and retraining. While Eisenhower vetoed both bills, he did so because he objected to the large
number of claimant counties, and not on the ground that the federal
government should avoid the financing of manpower training.

Even in macroeconomic policy, the financially conservative Eisenhower was pragmatic enough to tolerate unbalanced budgets and
to refuse to be panicked by his antedeluvian Secretary of the Treasury into destructive retrenchment as the economy slipped into
recession.

The counterpart to the occasional innovative aspects of the Eisenhower period is the relative conservatism of the Kennedy Administration. Its only distinctively new piece of social legislation was
the Manpower Development and Training Act (passed with bipartisan support), an experimental program of limited duration to
which the states had to contribute, and which carried a budget
figure of less than $100 million annually during the first two years
of operation. The Kennedy Administration's true innovations occurred in macroeconomic policy, not social policy, and even there,
the tax reduction of 1964 was not passed until after the President's
death.

In the civil rights arena, Kennedy sent forward recommendations
for new legislation in 1963, but it is well to recall that he cautiously
did not press for action directed against discrimination in the work
place. The equal-employment provisions were added on the floor
of the Senate and slipped through the House because Judge Smith,
the Chairman of the Rules Committee, succeeded in broadening
the scope of the provision to preclude discrimination based on sex,
as well as on race, in the mistaken belief that the Congress would
balk at protecting women workers and therefore delete the racial-
discrimination clause as well.

The Johnson legislative record

The Great Society programs that provide the substance for this
symposium were, with two exceptions, passed within a two-year

period—1964 and 1965—as President Johnson mobilized the wave of emotion after the assassination to bring to fruition several of his predecessor's plans and programs, and then interpreted his own overwhelming popular and electoral victory of 1964 as a mandate for social reform. The Administration was explicitly determined to use the power and resources of the federal government to speed changes on the domestic front that would help those who were encountering difficulties in taking care of themselves in the competitive arena.

The significance of those two legislative years is suggested by the case of federal support for elementary and secondary education. The issue had first come to the fore in the last decades of the 19th century, and was lost when the South opted for fewer schools without federal intervention rather than better schools with a federal presence. It had failed in its second appearance, in this century, because of the desire of church-supported schools to be included in any program of broad-scale support. Now suddenly this problem was finessed and the legislation passed.

The issue of health insurance had also been discussed for some time. In the mid-1930's, President Roosevelt decided not to include it in the new Social Security system. After the end of the war, President Truman pressed for the enactment of the Wagner-Murray-Dingell bill, but after several determined efforts to secure its passage, he reluctantly concluded that Congress would not act favorably and he let it die. Instead, Truman proposed alternative health legislation, according to which the federal government would concentrate on financing medical research and on the expansion of medical services. When Kerr-Mills had failed to cope effectively with the burdensome health costs of older persons who, though not indigent, had limited resources, the Kennedy Administration tried for Medicare, i.e., the use of the Social Security mechanism to cover the principal medical care costs of older persons. The effort failed. But in 1965 Johnson secured the passage not only of Medicare but also of a new federal-state system of Medicaid aimed at financing basic health services for the poor and near-poor. Here was a second recalcitrant issue that suddenly yielded.

Housing represented a third major area of intensified action, after decades of relative neglect. The federal government first made a commitment to the support of low-cost housing in the late 1930's, but little in the way of resources was devoted to this effort. Instead, support for housing took the form of subsidizing mortgages for the middle class. But in 1965 Congress passed new legislation, and in 1968 it vastly expanded the federal effort and belatedly took up the question of housing for the poor.

As majority leader in the Senate, Lyndon Johnson had assumed responsibility for securing passage of the 1957 Civil Rights Act, but it was the 1964 Act that really put the federal government into the middle of the unsolved race issue, with provisions that affected public accommodations, voting, the administration of justice, and employment. A Southern President acknowledged that the black minority had long been denied their Constitutional rights and promised the full power and force of the federal government to help restore them.

Finally, and perhaps most novel in conception, the Economic Opportunity Act of 1964 made poverty itself, and not only age or physical disability, an object of government policy. Besides providing funds for programs intended to break "the cycle of poverty" (as the phrase was), the Act encouraged the famous "maximum feasible participation" of the poor in the design and operation of machinery aimed at assisting themselves.

The question of funding

Now, the making of a speech or the drafting and even the passage of a statute is at best the statement of an intention to do something about some problem. Sometimes, of course, it is not even that. Barring great good luck, the effectiveness of social intervention depends on a sound diagnosis and understanding of the underlying problem. If that is lacking, a pavement made of good intentions may lead elsewhere than to a solution. Even given the sound diagnosis, little or nothing will happen unless the resources devoted to a legislative program are adequately proportioned to the size of the defect that has to be remedied. When such a program is underfunded, one may doubt either the seriousness of the intention or the soundness of the diagnosis—or one may conclude simply that the political appeal of the program was enough to get a bill passed, but not enough to get an adequate budget voted. These are precisely the questions that this symposium addresses.

In this regard, it may be useful to present a broad overview of the size of the financial effort devoted to the major programs with which we are concerned. In 1965, the combined expenditures for education (including manpower training), community development and housing, health, and welfare (i.e., public assistance and services to the poor) totalled $7.6 billion, or 6.4 per cent of the federal budget. In 1970, the comparable figure was $29.7 billion, or 15.1 per cent of the budget. The quadrupling of outlays is in part illusory, because prices rose between 1965 and 1970. It is hard to know exactly how to correct this mixed bag of social expenditures for price changes; the price index for consumption expenditure on services, which may be a reasonable guideline for making this correction, rose by 20 per cent in those five years. That would still leave "real" expenditures in 1970 more than three times those in 1965.

(The price index for "general government"—primarily the wages of public employees—rose by 40 per cent, but even a calculation on that basis leads to a tripling of "real" social expenditures.)

One's first impression is that Congress was not only willing to authorize new ventures in federal activity but was also willing to back up its commitments with sizable appropriations. A quadrupling of the absolute number of dollars spent (though only a tripling in real terms) and a more-than-doubling of the combined share of these expenditures as a percentage of the total budget constitute a fairly impressive track record for a period of time that covered only six budgets.

But there is another view possible. By far the largest component of this combined increase in expenditures was accounted for by Medicare and Medicaid, which together totaled about $10 billion in 1970. Only a small percentage of this amount, approximately one third, represented a drain on general funds; the remainder was covered by additional Social Security taxes.

Support for elementary and secondary education reached $3 billion in 1970; funds for community development and low-income and moderate-income housing were slightly higher; and about $3 billion more was made available for welfare clients in 1970 than in 1965. In short, the Great Society programs in the four fields of education, health, housing, and welfare were each funded by about $3 billion in new outlays, once the Social Security tax payments for Medicare are deducted.

To keep the size of these programs in perspective, it helps to remember that the budget of the Department of Defense during this same period increased from $46 to $77 billion, or by an amount greater than the total combined expenditures for these new human resources programs. Although President Johnson had initially expressed the hope that the country could simultaneously fight the war and make progress on its domestic problems, time proved otherwise. By 1967, the budget squeeze resulting from vastly increased military spending and the President's refusal to seek a tax increase made it difficult to find additional money for social reform. The new programs had to get along without significant new financing, at least until the war wound down.

To see what happened, we can compare the 1970 figures with the budget for 1972, the last year of the first Nixon Administration. Expenditures were up in each of the four major areas: from $7.3 to $9.8 billion in education and manpower, from $3.0 to $4.3 billion in community development and housing, from $12.9 to $17.1 billion in health, and from $6.5 to $12.1 billion in welfare. The total had increased from $29.7 to $43.3 billion, or by about 46 per cent, in the space of two federal budgets. Once again, we must allow for the rise in prices during those two years—about 10 per cent in the index for consumer services and almost twice that for general government. The real increase in spending therefore was only about a third, with the largest rise coming in welfare and thus not entirely voluntarily.

Conservative counterattack and liberal disillusionment

Between 1965 and 1972 federal spending on these four social programs had multiplied almost six times. In real terms, spending in 1972 was between four and five times what it had been in 1965. It was predictable that so rapid and sustained an increase would evoke a political counterattack, the more so because the Nixon Administration was committed to the doctrine of a reduced role for the federal government in domestic affairs, especially the affairs of the poor and disadvantaged.

The attack on "excessive" government spending was intensified for a more or less extraneous reason. The Nixon Administration inherited an economy operating under strong inflationary pressures, which it found difficult to bring under control. That, and the worsening balance of payments, provided yet another reason for sound-money men to chafe at social expenditures. There is nothing surprising about the strong offensive launched by the conservatives against the social programs of the 1960's, except that it was so long delayed.

The more surprising development was the attack both from many in the liberal camp who had been in the forefront of the reform movement and from some of the beneficiary groups themselves. The riots in Watts, Harlem, Detroit, and other urban centers had been a warning to the Johnson Administration and to the American people that many blacks had lost faith in the country's intention to deliver on its long-delayed promises. At a minimum, they were tired of waiting. Constant harassment of blacks who sought to register and vote, the use of excessive force against black suspects, and the violation of their rights in the courts only convinced the activists that talk about civil rights and equality was hypocritical. And the excessively high rates of unemployment among black teenagers and adults, the persistence of a large gap between the incomes of black and white families, and intensified residential and school segregation, particularly outside the South, were additional evidence to many blacks that the Civil Rights Act of 1964 was in large part "inoperative."

The poor were equally disheartened. They were unable to see much, if any, improvement in the quality of the schooling available to their children. Even the slightly improved levels of welfare payments and services still left many of them trapped in poverty; the funds for community development and housing did not prevent the deterioration of neighborhoods or ease the plight of many who were looking for improved living space. And the welfare rights movement had done some consciousness-raising.

Even the very substantial sums that were funneled into health still left a large number of low-income families with limited access to essential services. The same leadership that had hailed Medicare and Medicaid as a major breakthrough began to talk increasingly of the national health crisis, emphasizing that on most objective indices such as infant mortality and longevity, the United States had a mediocre record despite its reputedly superior medical establishment.

The extent of disappointment, discontent, and disarray among the long-term protagonists of social reform was revealed during the long-drawn-out effort to reform the federal role in welfare. Most of the interest groups representing welfare clients and potential beneficiaries were so taken up with the shortcomings of the proposed legislation that they were unable to agree among themselves on any compromise that had a reasonable prospect of gaining Congressional approval and Presidential consent. One way to interpret the fiasco of welfare reform is to see it as the breaking point in a long succession of disappointments and failures with social legislation that had undermined the faith of activist groups and their leaders in the ability of the political process to achieve significant gains.

The foregoing reconstruction of the 1960's and its aftermath points up the complexity of the social history to which this symposium is addressed. We indicated first that the roots of the Great Society programs lie deep in American circumstances. Next we noted the major task of leadership assumed and discharged by President Johnson in the crucial two-year period of 1964-65, when most of the new legislation was enacted. We then called attention to the amount of resources that flowed into these new programs, substantial in absolute terms, but relatively modest when measured against the size of the problems and against the volume of military spending. We also observed that the expenditures for these human resources programs continued to grow during the first Nixon Administration despite the declared aim of the President and his staff to disengage the federal government from so direct and potent an influence on the lives of the citizenry. Hence the attack that was finally launched by the conservatives was if anything overdue. They claimed that whatever gains had been achieved could be ascribed to general prosperity and that the social legislation had been an expensive fiasco. To be sure, despite all the talk of "evaluation," there was little or no evidence presented for these inferences. But more surprising was the growing disillusionment and despair of many of the social architects of these intervention programs and of the constituencies for which they spoke. The attack from the Left is much more surprising and it may possibly be much more dangerous in the long run to the interests of the poor than the attack from the Right.

We hope that by calling attention to these major strands of recent American experience the symposium as a whole and its several parts will be set in perspective. We have limited ourselves to setting the stage. The effective dialogue must be between our authors and their readers.

*   *   *

The essays which make up this book first appeared in the Winter Issue, 1974, of *The Public Interest*. The substantial interest this issue of *The Public Interest* elicited in the press, among government officials, and in the academic world pointed to the desirability of making this evaluation available to a larger audience. The Ford Foundation, the sponsor of the symposium, saw merit in a wider distribution and facilitated the publication of both the hard cover and paperback editions. Irving Kristol, the editor of *The Public Interest*, was helpful in this, as in earlier phases of the project.

Eli Ginzberg and Robert Solow
EDITORS

March 1974

1

Social intervention in a democracy

LANCE LIEBMAN

Born in the Enlightenment, the great age of making men good through the structure of social institutions, America has always sought justice and happiness through collective agreements. A proper constitution, John Adams wrote, "causes good humor, sociability, good manners, and good morals to be general . . . and makes the common people brave and enterprising." Thus it is wrong to say, as Charles Schultze and his Brookings associates do, that only recently has the American government sought "to change fundamental behavior patterns of individuals and institutions." Although some of the national crusades in the 1960's were different from most bread-and-butter New Deal programs, seen as a whole the 1960's were merely the latest phase of a two-century-old series of American obsessions and efforts. Nevertheless, they were a phase that revealed new aspects of the old ideas.

During the 10 years since Lyndon Johnson proposed a war on poverty, two main themes have dominated domestic politics. One is the question of man's ability to master his world. The moon trip—delivered as promised, almost like Babe Ruth pointing to the bleachers before a home run—was man's most dramatic feat in taming nature. Unlike Lindbergh's trip, it required thousands of participants, in a vast collection of orchestrated bureaucratic heroisms. There were also less overwhelming signs of human progress: the success of the Kennedy tax cut in priming the economy, the victory over polio, the development of cheap and safe jet transportation.

These and other successes stimulated the traditional hubris: We have done much, therefore we can do anything, therefore we shall do it. The domestic promises Lyndon Johnson made between 1963 and 1967 were not only expressions of a grandiloquent personality, or reflections of the institutional fact that Congress must be asked for everything before it will give anything. They were valid statements of one strain in the national mood, the dominant strain, at that moment, among the educated, professional, managerial classes. The idea was both that institutional arrangements could be imagined (indeed, could be selected by reason) which would produce whatever social circumstances were desired, and that technology had infinite capacity to produce the good life, at low cost.

The last decade has witnessed the steady tension between this powerful confidence and its antithesis: the idea that nothing works, that large organizations can serve only their own interests, that man has fallen and cannot be raised by conceptions of his own devising. *The Public Interest* has often been a forum for the espousal of what might be called the negativist reaction to the Promethean fallacy.

A second theme is closely related to the first. This is the tension between commitment to the economic market and dissatisfaction with the market's product. By 1960, economists had agreed on a party line: The market is ideal for allocating resources, for determining what should be produced, from what raw materials, and for whose consumption. Performance of this task by the market is value-neutral, and except for an occasional obligation to deal with "externalities" (costs or benefits that the market cannot easily consider), all deviations from market allocation are mistakes, for which consumers must pay. But, the economists were quick to add, the market's distributions—its determinations of how much of the social product each family should receive—deserve no such respect. Indeed, they must be tested by theory or philosophy or religion (by some standard, that is, outside the economist's competence), and should be speedily revised, by public redistributions, to fit the arrangement dictated by morality.

The discrediting of the market

Over the last 10 years, this simple position has crumbled. Environmentalism expanded the small problem of externalities into a major challenge to the validity of market decisions. Emphasis on industrial concentration suggested that large segments of the economy did not obtain the benefits of competitive allocation. Awareness of the power of television challenged the notion that consumer preferences are independently derived. Finally, distribution—who gets what share— came to be seen not merely as an outside variable to be adjusted in order that the market can respond to the preferences of those with money to spend, but as intimately connected to all other decisions of production and consumption. The words that have emerged are power and influence. The new recognition is that power and in- fluence flow from the fabric of social and economic institutions and ideas, and cannot be calibrated and redistributed as easily as disposable income. Therefore a mandate to alter the distri- bution of influence can be the authority to disturb all institu- tions, even purely economic ones, and conversely, attempts to alter influence without dealing with economic institutions are likely to be futile.

The new pessimism that exists concerning the human capacity to achieve social ends and the debate over the market's strengths and failings are closely related. Because the market is imperfect, every sort of corrective is necessary: interventions to achieve distributional improvements in an otherwise unfair labor market (minimum wage laws, strong unions, redistributive taxation, affirmative action, wage controls, pension reform) and interventions to improve allocation (price controls, environmental rules, foreign trade restrictions, farm subsidies, depletion allowances). But if nearly every intervention to perfect the market is theoretically justifiable, have we the intellectual and institutional ability to undertake these interventions success- fully, to come reasonably close to achieving what is sought and promised? This only poses the question, raised earlier, of human capacity to shape history.

When the economic market is rejected as a mechanism for trans- lating individual decisions into collective ones, it can only be replaced by a political market, supplemented by bureaucratic implementation. To pose the problem in simple terms, it is much easier to reject an economic market which places no value on pollution from a smoke- stack than it is to decide how much consumers of the factory's product should be forced to pay for a cleaner production process. Similarly, it is easier to reject the distribution of income that would result from a free labor market than it is to invent either a theoretical standard of distribution commanding wide assent or a satisfactory political process for making a decision on "proper" distribution periodically.

The essays that follow evaluate domestic reform in the 1960's in particular areas of federal activity. But that decade was also im- portant because of new efforts to improve processes of social choice, so that the economic market could be improved or replaced by satisfactory political arrangements. This article will focus on those efforts.

Explaining the failures of the 1960's

It is convenient to categorize the standard explanations for the failure of domestic reform in the 1960's. They fall into four overlapping categories:

1) Things improved, but not enough to meet the rise in expectations. This, the Banfield thesis, recently amplified by Wattenberg and Scammon, is certainly true with regard to some physically measurable physical amenities such as the percentage of families with indoor plumbing or a refrigerator.

2) There are things we do not know how to do. Teaching poor children to read competently may be an example. There may simply be no public program, at any cost, that can achieve this result.

3) The instrumentalities that deliver urban public services are inefficient. For example, New York City spends $49.00 to collect a ton of garbage while private carters do it for $17.50. Civil service unions, legislated pensions, poor wage bargaining, and inadequate supervision contribute to this higher cost.

4) Adequate resources were not provided. This means money, which was in insufficient supply because of the Vietnam war but also because the middle class resisted taxation. And it means more than money. Some policy goals—greater influence for the poor in local decisions, or more jobs on the police force for blacks—would have been costly to persons and groups benefitting from the status quo. Resources of some sort were needed to overcome their objections, and these resources were not forthcoming.

There is, of course, no inconsistency among the four "reasons." What was promised in the 1960's was partly an absolute increase in the level of goods and services: housing, schools, hospitals, jobs. But this promise was often interpreted to mean something else—that the percentage distribution would be altered, that some would have more and others less or the same. When the redemption of promises began, it turned out that offers that had seemed redeemable without taking from anyone in fact required significant seizure or sacrifice. Cheaper housing meant ending building-trade inefficiencies that were valuable to carpenters and electricians; dispersed housing meant travail for neighbors; and, most important, if the Phillips curve required five per cent unemployment, jobs for blacks or the poor meant layoffs for some people who would otherwise have been working.

And yet, despite the difficulty of these undertakings, the national government of the United States embarked in the 1960's on even grander and nobler missions than the mere increase of material well-being. It sought not only to upgrade quickly the education, health, and housing of a large part of the population, but also to alter the way many people thought about themselves, their community, and their society. Attempts were made to end attitudes of superiority among whites and of inferiority among blacks; to stop the poor from feeling alienated and powerless; and to encourage individuals raised in a culture of poverty to go off each morning to a job, do an honest day's work, and spend their wages prudently.

But there was even a third category of objectives, related to the first two but distinguishable from them: the national effort to alter the distribution of power and influence over local public processes (and, in so doing, to bring a changed set of influences to bear on Washington as well).

Social change and interest-group politics

These latter classes of objectives raise the most interesting questions about the role of the liberal interest-group state in seeking to alter the society to which it responds—to alter it, necessarily, in the direction of some theoretical model of justice. In approaching these questions, it is well first to note that the explanations set out above for the failure of the government to build housing and employ blacks apply as well to the inadequate progress made toward altering individual attitudes and redistributing local power.

1) *Expectations.* A lot was done. Racism remains, but no one who remembers the early days of the sit-ins can deny vast change. It is now reasonable for black children to believe that if they live a straight and studious childhood, a place in the middle class is attainable. The Voting Rights Act led to dramatically increased black political power in the South, where blacks have voted in large numbers, although not in the North, where they have not. These achievements, however, are now generally viewed in the context of higher goals that so far are unattained.

2) *Knowledge.* Some efforts remained beyond the state of the art. For example, the Model Cities program was based on the premise that while physical slum-clearance projects and social service programs were each of some value, combining the two—targeting physical and social improvements on the same individuals—would have benefits beyond the sum of what the separate expenditures normally achieved. This synergistic effect did not occur, and in retrospect there seems no reason except hope for having believed such an effect could be brought about.

3) *Urban service machinery.* Governmental efforts required public agencies to function in ways that were at odds with the sophisticated personal alterations they were now expected to bring about. Because of the kinds of workers whom the agencies employed, the way they had operated in the past, and the manner in which their employees were paid and supervised, the possibility of effective performance toward the new goals was practically doomed from the start. After

all, how could "welly workers" achieve the human liberation mandated by the 1962 Welfare Amendments?

4) *Resources.* Perhaps the major barrier to the achievement of
these goals was that the stated commitment to them was rarely
followed by the allocation of sufficient resources. Change was sought
not only in procedures and attitudes that were plainly inefficient,
unfair, and unpatriotic when judged by some aggregate national
welfare function divinable in Washington, but also in ways of life
that were comfortable, profitable, and reasonable for the individuals
told to change. In that situation change is not impossible, but it is
expensive—expensive in resources hard to mobilize by a government
inherently responsive to precisely the individuals and groups who
were the targets of change.

When viewing the government interventions of the 1960's, it is
entirely possible to be both surprised by how much was done and
aggrieved by what was not done. Learning from those years requires
a more complicated and sophisticated evaluation.

The importance of political structures

Four current issues suggest the extent to which we have learned
from the attempts, successes, and travails of the past decade. The
first of these, the significance of structure, has roots as deep as
the Constitution. The 1960's witnessed a resuscitation of the naive
18th-century view that changed rules of public process can
produce better citizens. Indeed, some of the domestic programs
of the Nixon Administration—the New Federalism, for example
—are based on the related notion that a tidy structure will produce,
if not citizens worthy of a "New American Revolution," at least
efficiency and stability.

The Johnson Administration's great adventure in structural tinker-
ing was the Model Cities program. Walter Reuther's original plan was
to rebuild two cities, Detroit and any other. Robert Wood's Task
Force proposed significant reconstruction of 66 poor neighborhoods.
But by the time Congress had finished authorizing and appropriating,
Model Cities chiefs Ralph Taylor and Walter Farr were left with
150 cities and $212 million (for the first planning year). Not sur-
prisingly, their emphasis turned to coordinating the entire federal
effort in their chosen cities: Much rhetoric was expended about
coordination; the President declared HUD the "lead agency" for
urban activities; new institutions were established, such as the Washington Interagency Coordinating Committees (WICC's) and Regional Interagency Coordinating Committees (RICC's); cabinet members said helpful things to their subordinates; and Joe Califano made
cooperative phone calls from the White House whenever someone at
Model Cities could get through to him. But money did not move

into the control of national or local Model Cities personnel—not from other HUD sub-units, and not from HEW or Labor or OEO. Substantial forces stood in the way of such fund transfers: statutory language; Congressional substantive and appropriations subcommittees devoted to the categorical programs from which funds were sought; Washington bureaucracies whose existence depended on these programs; state or local units through which the funds were flowing; recipient organizations, often private or quasi-private "provider" agencies fearful of losing their share. What power could Taylor and Farr command against these enemies?

We have certainly learned that structural alterations are more easily proclaimed than instituted. But we have also acquired some skepticism about the connection between a given structure and the specific public actions that result from it. Thus we must ask whether it would have been valuable to give Taylor and Farr the control they sought over federal activity in model neighborhoods.

The United States government pays for a great many interventions in cities, but few of its dollars go to the purchase of specific categorical services. Of the $1.316 billion in federal funds in New York City's 1970-71 Expense Budget, for example, over 75 per cent was for direct or indirect payments to individuals. Another $117 million was education money limited only by the broad Title I guidelines. Less than five per cent of the money the city received was restricted in any serious way as to use. And even in regard to these specific programs, duplicate or contradictory expenditure is a minor problem. It rarely happens that the federal government pays twice for the same act, or that it pays through one program for goal A and through another for goal anti-A.

Instead, the real problem is a lack of elegance and tidiness. No single political process, local or national, determines which activities are most in need of money, or exactly how much they need. Rather, a messy federal process, Congressional and administrative, combines with crazy local processes, political and bureaucratic, to make these decisions. Yet it is not easy to imagine a system that would spend the available money so that a great deal more happiness would be purchased.

In other words, emphasis on the inefficiency of the system by which government intervenes for social ends has probably been misplaced. Our approximation of a process for choosing a national welfare function—for deciding how much of particular public goods (including those strange goods, the improvement of attitudes and the redistribution of influence) to purchase—is unesthetic. But structure is power more than it is efficiency. (The true significance of special and general revenue sharing is that they represent a forswearing of federal efforts to have the money spent differently than the local political process resolves. That is itself a political decision, to be praised or condemned depending on whether one likes or dislikes the local distribution of influence.)

If it is a problem that recipients and providers of particular services are empowered by circumstances of the political process to obtain production of the goods they prefer in quantities deemed excessive by someone else, then resources must be found for diminishing or overcoming that power. Structural changes may allocate influence differently, and may be sought or opposed on the basis of predictions about their substantive consequences. But it is futile to aim for structures that are somehow neutral in this regard, or that significantly reduce the overhead of the entire operation.

Changing the distribution of local power

There is a basic incongruity in federal attempts to change the pattern of local power. If the government is nothing but a machine for filtering aggregated private interests—a conception at the heart of contemporary political science—then what business is it of government to set out to alter those influences? There are two possible solutions to this dilemma, one simple and the other more complex.

In the first place, national government, in response to national influences, may seek to lessen the influence of locally powerful but nationally less powerful groups. It is easy to argue that federal action on behalf of blacks in the South can be explained in this way.

The more complex argument would hold that the extent to which government is merely an interest-balancing machine may be limited by an obligation to behave in accordance with theories of justice—at least in regard to certain public actions at certain times. American political theory has always seen the legislator as both the agent of his constituents and the interpreter and applier of higher law. With a written Constitution, which every official swears to uphold, there is no theoretical doubt that the legislator or the executive official, like the judge, is obliged to place his interpretation of the Constitution's requirements ahead of his own temporary preferences, or those of his constituents or his President.

Certainly, the Constitution sets out fair procedures for making public decisions. On its face it is essentially a procedural code. And beyond its specific words, it is a document that imposes minimal restrictions on the distribution among the citizenry of influence over public affairs.

Reapportionment, voting rights, and perhaps even community action can be justified on this basis. Yet difficult, perhaps impossible, questions remain. The purest "one person, one vote" rule (in 1973 the Supreme Court quietly shifted from the sexist formulation, "one man, one vote") will give no power at all to groups that are widely scattered, and therefore are a minority in every district.

To what extent must government positively encourage persons to assert themselves? Is it enough merely to abolish discriminatory barriers to political activity? Is it acceptable for the system to reward expenditures, and so decide issues in favor of those who can afford to pay?

While it is not easy to interpret the Constitution's standards for the distribution of access to government and influence over the decisions of government, as a general basis for national action the concept of some minimum right to political access is unquestionable—and its acceptance is responsible for a long line of reforms including emancipation, women's suffrage, and the National Labor Relations Act (NLRA).

Voting rights, community action, and Model Cities were all programs of this sort. Community action sought to develop political effectiveness in the poor, so they would fare better in future political contests. The goal of Model Cities was different. It sought urban political processes in which (a) an effective mayor could achieve more of his purposes, less hampered by the obstructions observed in what seemed to be Dickensian city governments; and (b) the poor, and especially the black poor, would fare better in local distributions, because one part of the local pie would be specifically directed to them, and institutions would be mandated to share decision making power over that part with representatives of the poor.

Using the system to change the system

Observe the central contradiction of this attempt: using the system to change the system; altering the distribution of power through machinery responsive to today's power; seeking substantive outcomes tomorrow by exerting influence today that is assumed to be insufficient for obtaining those outcomes now. This is surely why endeavors such as community action and Model Cities have a youthful, *American* spirit to them.

But similar programs have worked in the past. The National Labor Relations Act transferred influence to workers by lending public sanction to their efforts to become organized. The Voting Rights Act gave blacks influence over Southern political processes by removing obstacles to their exercising the franchise. The OEO legal services program achieved changes in statutory law and administrative practice by making judicial challenges possible on behalf of persons previously without access to the courts.

The differences between these successful interventions and the community action and Model Cities failures are important. First of all, NLRA, voting rights, and legal services were theoretically simple: The transfer of influence would result from uncomplicated alterations in federal behavior. The Model Cities conception of city politics, on the other hand, is intricate. Second, the problems of implementation are vastly different. It may be hard to regulate labor relations, or supervise voter registration, or supply lawyers. But spending money so as to encourage a proper transformation of political power in each of thousands of neighborhoods around a large country is much harder. Third, the extent of the challenge to traditional ideology was different. By 1937 there was wide acceptance of a right to organize. The rights to vote and to sue have deep roots. But claims of a right to influence that is not sanctified through traditional electoral institutions, and claims of opportunities for some that are not generally available to all are more difficult to defend.

Finally, and most important, changing the distribution of influence through the system requires that at some point the beneficiaries of the change achieve the means to hold their own against other interest groups. Unions became rich, and had mass membership sometimes amenable to electoral suggestion. The unions therefore could take a place at the interest-group bargaining table. In the South blacks registered, voted, and therefore could negotiate. In Northern cities they did not register, did not vote, and could not bargain. By definition, the deprived underclass consists of those members of the society who cannot assert themselves effectively. Perhaps, therefore, no temporary federal assistance can get them to the point of protecting themselves through politics. Perhaps opportunities given to that group will be like ropes dropped into a pit, on which those who do not belong in the pit will climb out (those with energy and skill—for example, blacks mired by racism rather than by lack of capacity to perform in society). They climb out, of course, as champions of their neighbors, but to some degree also at their neighbors' expense. Perhaps the worst-off members of the society cannot benefit by efforts aimed at process and influence, but only by direct assistance that assures them some minimum level of goods and services.

Direct government assistance

The first glimmers may be visible of a new theoretical restriction on the functioning of the interest-balancing liberal state. Government labored in the 1960's to create and strengthen groups able to speak for individuals that were previously "underrepresented." It acted to encourage individuals to participate, and to alter local political institutions so that selected groups would gain more of the rewards. But government also acted to aid individuals directly. It expanded the range of services made available with federal funds: Medicare, Medicaid, housing subsidies, rent supplements, legal services, child care, public television, and symphony orchestras. It improved the coverage and amount of federal income-support payments to the aged, the blind and disabled, and families of dependent children. In addition, it made certain changes in the tax system beneficial to those with low incomes.

These changes must be explained partly as responses to organized pressure, but also partly as steps taken out of a belief that they were just and necessary. Old age benefits are increased because present and prospective recipients are a potent and aware constituency. Some programs, such as housing subsidies, are powerfully sponsored by those who profit from delivering the public good. But despite substantial middle-class pressure against benefits for the poor, it is fair to say that significant concern over the extent of poverty, over shortages of what are regarded as essential goods, and over the unfair distribution of income and wealth has been expressed regularly by political leaders and has influenced legislative action beyond the extent to which it could bring political benefit.

These actions have not been mirrored judicially. While Justices Douglas, Brennan, and Marshall, and sometimes Justice Stewart, have been willing to impose on Congress and the state legislatures obligations to meet minimum standards in the distribution of goods and services (they have usually spoken of an obligation not to impose certain burdens on the poor), the problems of definition and of line-drawing have kept the other five Justices steadfast in avoiding such holdings. Nevertheless, it is not entirely inaccurate to interpret at least some legislative action as being influenced by the attempt to determine what the fundamental law of the society requires.

The movement toward theoretically justified standards for the distribution of money and goods has suffered to some degree from the rapid growth of programs which distribute public benefits of high quality and expense to a small part of those who would like to receive the benefit. Because there has been no progress toward defining the content of a minimum "bundle" of services, legislators who consider a service tend to authorize its delivery in the standard middle-class quality, and the administering bureaucracy proceeds accordingly. Whether the service is "meals on wheels" or seeing-eye dogs, the argument for its being "needed" is usually overwhelming and the case for restricting free delivery to the very poorest of those in need seems weak. (Why exclude those slightly better off, who nonetheless share the particular need?) The problem of total cost is left to the separate appropriations process. The result, for program after program, is an appropriation of one per cent to 25 per cent of what full delivery would cost, and the creation of artificially valuable "political" goods: the power of deciding which hungry old person, or which blind person, will be benefitted. Whether distribution becomes a matter of arbitrary bureaucratic rule or of political favor, the outcome is unfair in the extreme.

The income strategy

The paths for escaping this problem are clear, if not always nego-
tiable. First there is the income strategy, which focuses on the disposable income of each family, and thus brings families up either
to some selected level, or by some selected amount. The individual's
welfare is most efficiently raised, because he and not a paternalistic
government determines the object of his expenditures. Daniel P.
Moynihan gives a significant place in the catalog of reasons for the
defeat of the Family Assistance Plan to the difficulty of reconciling
the assured-payment scheme with existing in-kind benefits available
unequally around the country and within communities. That is, the
new payments must either replace allotments of food, medicine,
housing, and so forth, in which case some persons would be worse off
after than before the new legislation, or they must be made in addition to in-kind benefits, thus putting the recipients in much better
circumstances than unassisted working people. There are, of course,
as Moynihan recognizes, other problems with an income strategy.
Taxpayer-voters, who regard themselves as donors, would rather give
goods to the poor than money that might be drunk away or smoked
up. They also tend to believe that if the goal is greater opportunity
and a better environment for the children of the poor, then money
given to the parents may not be a very effective instrument for
achieving it.

Assuring money also raises the same difficult question posed by
assuring goods and services: How much should be provided? An interest-balancing theory avoids the question by contending, for example, that the right level for Social Security payments is the level
that the Congress and the President approve. But as soon as some
theoretical basis is urged as justification for larger benefits than
result from the workings of politics, the question of amount becomes
critical.

The list of possible theories is remarkably short: 1) equality; 2)
Professor Rawls' "difference principle"—equality except where deviations are so productive as incentives that every member of the
society is better off for their being awarded; 3) some arbitrary relationship—for example, no one is to have less than one third of the
largest share; 4) what the economic and political markets distribute,
but with certain minimum levels assured; 5) what the markets distribute.

The fourth theory, which received its most serious and sophisticated defense from Professor Frank Michelman, is undoubtedly
closest to the present state of the American consciousness. It holds
that no one deserves equality, or even a specified relationship to the
top or the middle, but that everyone has a right to *some things*—to
some minimum bundle of goods whose possession is a necessary condition of true citizenship and human dignity. The theoretical problem

is that once this mandated level is higher than what is physically necessary to keep a human being alive, there seems to be no objective principle for determining the size and shape of the bundle. Food? How much meat? Housing? How many rooms are "decent" for a family of four? As Michelman recognizes, the minimum obligation takes its content from the levels that have become common in the society. That is to say, it quickly becomes a relative matter, thus again raising the question: If not equality, then what percentage?

But although questions of line-drawing remain, it is important to observe that the terms of discussion have changed. Today, unlike 10 years ago, the majority seems to recognize some public obligation to provide certain things. Questions are sometimes put in the form: What is the decent minimum owed to an American family? And as a result of this change in attitude, the absolute circumstances of both the bottom tenth and the bottom quarter of the population have been improved significantly.

Distributions to groups

If the economic market is rejected as a satisfactory machine for distributing the society's rewards, if changes in the operation of the political market imperfectly improve that market's results, and if the search for theoretically justified distributions to individuals poses the issues too starkly, then one alternative is distributional arrangements that award fair aggregate shares to subgroups of the population. Distribution according to group identification is common when individuals are seen primarily as members of a group and when there is no accepted "just" method for determining who should receive some benefit. For example, the European Common Market has a formula for hiring employees by which each member country is assured a negotiated percentage of the jobs. Undoubtedly, this is a convenient and necessary arrangement. In the early stages of multi-nationalism, no version of "merit" hiring would be trusted if the final results seemed to reward one country or penalize another.

In America, emphasis on identifications of race, ethnic ancestry, religion, and sex has recently increased. Meanwhile, more and more matters have become the subject of standardless political distribution. How then can results be measured except by whether subgroups obtain their appropriate share?

Reliance on group shares as an instrument of mandated social change has occurred in three different but overlapping contexts. First, it has been an enforcement tool. If, for example, there has been illegal discrimination against blacks in hiring, there may be no way of verifying that acceptable criteria are now being employed except by evidence that appropriate numbers of blacks are now being hired.

In a milder enforcement use, a focus on group shares may identify those situations in which procedures and policies require careful investigation, or may shift burdens of proof. Second, there is distribution by group in order to attain the benefits of integration. Racial or economic integration might be required in a subsidized apartment house because the proximity of families from different backgrounds is thought socially desirable. Third, groups can be given shares because the commodity is somehow inappropriate for distribution to the highest money bidder. Using a lottery to pick those who must serve in the army is based on this sort of idea. There is certainly deep support in the American tradition for the view that if some schools educate better than others, it is wrong to let the ability to pay be the basis for allocation of places at the desired school. If the government sought only to increase the housing stock, it would construct new units and sell or rent them to the highest bidder. But because it seeks to give some of the poor better housing than their resources can command in the market, the government rents the apartments for less than they could bring, and then clears the market with rules restricting the eligibility to low-income families.

Distribution by share has been ordered by courts recently for school assignments, jobs, and housing. Denver will probably have to implement widespread redistribution of school assignments in order to balance the ratios of blacks, Chicanos, and whites in its schools, because prior school boards during the 1950's and 1960's sought racial segregation in drawing district lines in one section of the city. The largest industrial and commercial enterprises consider themselves obliged to increase significantly the ratio of blacks in their work force at what they regard as some short-term sacrifice in production efficiency. State and municipal zoning and housing officials have been ordered, on the basis of federal statutes and the Constitution, to distribute subsidized housing among neighborhoods and to adjust zoning rules to permit construction of multi-family buildings. In all these situations, there is a disjunction between past illegality and present remedy; the individuals who were mistreated in the past do not now benefit, and the individuals who formerly misbehaved or made unfair gains do not now pay the price. In all of them there is also an inability or an unwillingness to define individual entitlements (to schooling or work or housing). And in all of them the selection of which blacks or which poor persons obtain benefits must be made by political or bureaucratic processes, which are at best arbitrary and are at worst susceptible to corruption.

Quotas: dangers and benefits

It is easy to list the dangers posed by national intervention in local or private affairs that uses the mechanism of conferring entitlements to some limited good on certain subgroups of the population. First, there is the problem of determining who belongs to each subgroup, and whether an individual (e.g., a black woman) may belong to more than one of them. Second, one need not overestimate the regularity and legality with which public institutions function in order to recognize that private groups show much less. Yet if private groups are to possess significant delegated public authority, must they not be open, regular, and fair in ways that are both unpoliceable and inconsistent with their nature and purposes? The Atlanta branch of the NAACP was willing to give up busing to obtain leadership jobs for blacks in the school system. The national NAACP thought this was a bad settlement. But if the *right* to busing belongs to Atlanta blacks as a group, must there not be some recognized process for their asserting, compromising, or waiving it? Third, individuals should not be forced through the ringer of private associations, or forced to affirm their membership in a subgroup of the population, in order to obtain their due from government. There is a large distinction between an individual encouraged to participate in a group by the fact that his chances of obtaining standardless allocations will be magnified and an individual granted rights in the form of shares given to a group whose rules he must follow or whose games he must win if he is to get his part.

On the other hand, it is easy to see the circumstances in which emphasizing the share received by various groups becomes an enticing device for intervening to change unsatisfactory arrangements. One such circumstance is wide dissatisfaction with the distributional consequences of the current order; another is an inability to define satisfactory consequences in terms of individual shares; and a third is lack of confidence in the likelihood that procedural changes would lead to the desired outcomes. The perceived ill is precisely that blacks do not have enough and that they should have more, not that some individual black person or family has received too little. Therefore, the intervening authority—whether Congress, a court applying the Constitution, or a court interpreting freely from an ambiguous statutory mandate—seeks to obtain more for the deprived group. It may well be that group shares constitute the only midpoint between acceptance of the status quo and some future consensus on individual shares. For example, the agitation over affirmative action that surely lies ahead may be immensely useful in spreading the awareness that, rather than dividing too few jobs between black and white claimants, society should be guaranteeing work to all as individuals. But even if temporary, necessary, and unavoidable, the creation by Congress and the acknowledgment and creation by the courts of collective rights belonging to racial, ethnic, and sexual groups is offensive and dangerous, and should be treated as a challenge to overcome rather than a solution to preserve.

Prospects for the 1970's

During the past decade American public discourse has moved a long way toward confronting real issues of social circumstance: questions of hierarchy and ownership, of manipulation and choice, and above all of distribution—of who gets the society's scarce benefits, and with what claim of right. Discrediting the economic market as a magic guarantor of the rightness of resource allocation and benefit distribution has been and will be painful. Destroying that market's mystique means that intervention can always be justified theoretically. But intervening successfully in practice is much harder: first, because devices of politics and bureaucracy that can do the work of the economic market are poorly developed and perhaps of inherently limited potential; and second, because agreement on intervention—on what will be changed, at what cost to those benefitting from present practices—is far more difficult than the rhetorical proclamation of programs and goals. The consequence of the experience discussed in the following essays is surely a new realism concerning social commitments. But more important still, recent experience may have brought new attention to theories of the proper functioning of society. If that is so, we may soon come to be not only more hesitant to promise change without having the resources to accomplish it, but also more ready to diagnose and thus to reject the present. This, however, would breed instability in a country that has always shown strong tendencies toward order and against theory. The story of the 1970's may well turn on whether the need for stability can repress theory and ideology now that the market's veil has become transparent.

2

Economic policy and unemployment in the 1960's

EDMUND S. PHELPS

C ERTAINLY it would be a mistake to interpret the experiments in governmental economic intervention made in the 1960's as a quantum change in the country's theory of the role of government or its attitudes toward inequality and redistribution. From the times of Bentham and Bismarck to the New Deal and Fair Deal there has been increasing government intervention on behalf of various groups, including those that are poor or disadvantaged. The policies and programs begun in the past decade, mainly during the Presidency of Lyndon Johnson, are another important episode in that history. My own guess is that, to the extent that the 1960's differ significantly from other periods of social change and experiment, they will be characterized by the widened assertion of various natural rights ahead of the public convenience, and even above equalitarian notions of fairness or "equity" in the distribution of economic benefits.

Whatever the 1960's were, the Great Society programs that were an important feature of them have since become the object of sweeping criticisms. Many of them are viewed as failures. There seems to be a diminished confidence in the effectiveness of the government generally to achieve its announced objectives and a heightened sense of the fallibility of the social knowledge, if any, that serves as the basis of government action. The record of the Nixon Administration, itself a leader of much of this criticism, has done little to abate the loss of confidence.

There is a short story about a writer who begins an essay with "Certainly . . ."—as, for fun, I began this essay—and then cannot type any words to follow it. Human knowledge is uncertain, at least knowledge that goes beyond observable facts. It will be the recurring theme here that our social knowledge, our economics and sociology of how things work and will respond to a government action, is especially unreliable. That proposition is perhaps daringly platitudinous, but it is not very well understood and easily slips our mind.

Some criticisms of some of the programs of the 1960's are undoubtedly informed and disinterested, though that does not guarantee their being right. It will be good if the public's enchantment with the tendency in government to claim mastery, despite almost total ignorance, is lessened as a result. But much of the criticism is surely unwarranted by theory and evidence. The socio-economic theories of some critics are no more to be taken seriously than those they attack. The criticisms of some programs are as disingenuous as were the overblown claims made for them by their proponents: In view of the hard choices among costly alternatives, anything that would "work" in the eyes of these critics they would declare to be "too expensive."

Herewith are an economist's reflections on the evaluation of two programs in the Johnsonian "war against poverty." One of these programs was "macroeconomic": the adoption of fiscal and monetary policies to create an environment of greater job opportunities and higher employment in which, presumably, low-income workers would fare better, both relatively and absolutely, than in the Eisenhower-Martin economic slack. The other program was "microeconomic": the welter of expenditure schemes to invest in low-income workers for the purpose of raising their relative earning power.

Romantic Keynesianism and its consequences

The macroeconomic policy of the Johnson years was the long-awaited expression of the romantic strain in Keynesian thought. The Keynesian primitives of two decades earlier had held that fiscal and monetary stimuli should be applied to the economy until unemployment had vanished from every hamlet and slum in the land. After the experience with cost inflation in the late 1950's, few economists believed in the 1960's that "maximum employment," let alone zero unemployment, would be desirable. What the romantics among the Keynesians believed, however, was that *within wide limits* the norm of "full employment" was what the nation wished to make it. The economy could be managed to produce its natural, demographic growth rate under "low-pressure" monetary and fiscal policies which stabilized the unemployment rate around, say, 5.5 per cent of the labor force. Or the economy could be made to grow at its natural rate under "high-pressure" monetary and fiscal policies that caused the unemployment rate to center around 3.5 per cent, for example. In each such steady state, there would tend to be some corresponding *steady* rate of inflation. The lower the average unemployment rate enjoyed in the steady state, the higher the average rate of inflation that would be experienced. Selecting the steady state that we would be happiest living in was a matter of balancing the advantages of a lower average unemployment rate against the advantages of a lower average inflation rate.

It was with this conception of the choices before them that the Kennedy and Johnson economists settled on their objectives. The Kennedy-Johnson objective in macroeconomic policy, the objective that prompted the tax cuts in the 1964 Revenue Act, was the reduction of the unemployment rate to an average level of about four per cent. This was the interim target, pending improvements in the functioning of the labor market and the skills of its low-wage participants. No precise prediction was offered of the inflation rate that would tend to result if that unemployment target were realized. The impression given was that any inflation in such a state would lie generally within the limits of the nation's post-War experience—not more than two per cent per annum—and that such an inflation rate would exist more in the indices of measured prices than in the reality of the consumer satisfactions that a dollar would buy. (Not that any respectable economist worried much about whether the inflation rate would be two or three per cent; the worry was more about how the public would worry.)

Thus did the best and the brightest—if not in the set of all economists, then in the subset of romantics—set up a testing ground for one of the grandest experiments in social theory of this century. The macroeconomic developments from 1965 to 1972 are largely the aftermath of (and the basis for reflection upon) the 1960's experiment in high-pressure macroeconomic policy.

As it turned out, the economy reached the four per cent unemployment mark by the end of 1965, and did better than that for the rest of Johnson's term. In both 1966 and 1967, unemployment averaged 3.8 per cent; it averaged 3.6 per cent in 1968. If these figures were off target, they were not off significantly. The real surprise lay elsewhere: The same pressure of aggregate demand that produced these unemployment rates also produced a concomitant inflation that was much swifter than had been anticipated. By the end of 1968, the inflation rate had reached six per cent per annum. It was widely suspected by then that if aggregate demand were to maintain the unemployment rate at its existing level, the rate of inflation would quite probably go on to much greater heights. Thus 1968 was a year of recognized disequilibrium. It would not be possible to maintain unemployment at 3.6 per cent for very long. Even the viability of the four per cent unemployment target came into question.

Perhaps historians will label the rise of prices in the long period of 1966 to 1970 the "Vietnam inflation." Economists, however, generally doubt that the Vietnam build-up made so extensive an inflation inescapable. The monetarists argue that the rise of output and employment that occurred in this period would not have taken place if the Federal Reserve, after initial resistance, had not accommodated the Vietnam impetus to aggregate demand by permitting faster growth of the money supply. The non-monetarists argue that the Congress could also have offset the rise in Vietnam spending with a prompter and larger tax increase, had there been a determination to check the Vietnam boom. The failure of monetary and fiscal policies to hold more closely to the four per cent unemployment target may have been due in part to the unexpected pace at which government and private spending grew. Nevertheless, the weakness and lateness of the stabilizing actions actually taken suggest a reluctance to jeopardize the gains in employment that the Vietnam boom was tending to produce. Many of the Johnson economists felt that it was merely the speed with which unemployment had reached 3.8 per cent, not the level per se, that was responsible for much of the rise in prices in 1966 and 1967. Only when the force of the inflation momentum imparted by the boom had become more apparent did there begin a serious reappraisal of the unemployment objectives that had steadily been espoused.

The Nixon response

Enter Richard Nixon, inheriting the economic disequilibrium. The Nixon men did not make the mistake of supposing that the rate of inflation could be contained while the economy was being held in a disequilibrium state of four per cent unemployment or less. They also supposed—classically and sensibly, I believe—that what could go up in one disequilibrium could be made to go down in another equal and opposite disequilibrium. The anti-inflationary policies undertaken (after some hesitation) by the Federal Reserve in 1969 predictably threw the economy into a slump at six per cent unemployment during most of 1970 and 1971. But the Game Plan greatly overestimated the speed and reliability with which inflation would shrink at the six per cent unemployment level. Though assuredly the matador could eventually kill the bull, the crowd was growing restive at the gory and clumsy spectacle. Moreover the contest for re-election drew nearer. The four-year Presidential term would not be long enough for the Game Plan to erase an inflation of such proportions.

Here begins the program of controls with its innumerable phases. The relatively firm and comprehensive program that was Phase I looked promising. At least it would set back the whole time schedule of general price rise in the same way that a train temporarily detained never makes up all the time lost. The freeze might also cause expectations of inflation—which were responsible for the important anticipatory element in price hikes—to dwindle. And there would be no great economic damage from shortages and misdirected production in view of the substantial slack still prevailing in late 1971. But in a series of Kafkaesque moves, the Administration loosened the controls before they had much time to help.

The experience with these controls strongly suggests a continued underestimation by the Administration of the upward pressures on prices and wages that were already built into the 1972 situation, as well as a failure to anticipate new forces of an exogenous character (coming mainly from international developments) that could not easily have been foreseen. During 1972, the post-Phase I bulge wiped out most of the deferral of price increases effected by Phase I. Nonfarm prices and wages rose at about the same rate in 1972 as they had been rising in the 12 months before Phase I. Phase II does, however, appear to have helped hold back some profit margins when account is taken of the strong upward pressure on prices exerted by the expansion in 1972, a boom that the Nixon Administration was anticipating, hoping for, and using monetary and fiscal measures to assist. In the first half of 1973, price rises were generally greater than a year earlier and wage increases continued to exceed seven per cent per annum. Students of Phase III contend that it allowed profit margins in the non-farm corporate sector to rise significantly, more than was promised on the installation of this new phase.

Many of the Nixon men have since averred that Phase II was abandoned too soon. Yet even the tougher Phase II controls would not have been adequate to hold the wave of commodity price rises resulting from the worldwide boom that developed in 1972-73, a reduction of farm supplies due to bad weather, the better terms demanded by the oil-supplying countries, and, most notably, the marked depreciation of the dollar against most foreign currencies, following the decisions of foreign governments and international speculators to revalue or bid up most foreign currencies against the dollar.

Lessons in humility: moving targets

This record shows evident miscalculation and bad luck. Must we also conclude that forces have been at work that are beyond the power of existing economic theory to explain? There are some puzzling phenomena in the recent record. Our facility at listing the important causative factors that have been at work gives no assurance that these explanations add up to a quantitatively accurate account of past events. Many thoughtful economists are despairing of any theoretical explanation of the summer of 1973 run on the dollar. The rises in some metals prices are also difficult to account for. Yet these phenomena may prove to be only aberrations, the random deviations that every science copes with. It is not obvious that the economic record reviewed here has turned up anything so fundamentally anomalous or paradoxical that an alteration of economic theory would be required to explain it. The experiments in macroeconomic policy since 1965, by providing us with some rather spectacular evidence not available before, have encouraged the enrichment and deepening of mainstream economic theory, not its abandonment.

The miscalculations that have beset macroeconomic policy making since 1965, I would argue, arise from the treacherousness of the empirical inferences that have to be made in the prudent design of macroeconomic policies. It is largely a story of the poverty of econometrics. The conclusion is not, of course, that all statistical inference is useless, only that its usefulness is limited and that perhaps there is a tendency toward its misuse. Nor should it be concluded that ventures in meliorative social policy had best be abstained from in favor of the status quo, however that might be defined. There seems to be no meaningful alternative to purposeful social action, with all its attendant risks.

There are three types of difficulties confronting the designers of any social program that I shall mention here. The plainest of these difficulties, one that we are all aware of, is that the world does not stand still. And usually we glimpse how it has changed only well after the fact. Even if the social planner knows which one of several candidate targets he would like to hit, and he is a perfect marksman (so that his arrow always reaches the spot aimed at), he may be in the dark as to how the desired target has shifted. A pertinent example is the magnitude of what has been called the equilibrium unemployment rate. The notion here, undoubtedly too simple a notion but satisfactory for our purposes, is of that rate of unemployment which, if maintained, is consistent with an unchanging rate of inflation. Students of the post-World War II period were apt to infer that unemployment in the neighborhood of four per cent would be consistent with equilibrium at a fairly negligible rate of inflation. It may very well be, however, that demographic and technological changes in the economy over the past 20 years combined to increase substantially the equilibrium unemployment level. If so, the Johnson economists' interim target of four per cent unemployment spelled disequilibrium, and greater disequilibrium than they had realized or desired. Correspondingly, the Nixon economists' effort at a corrective disequilibrium of low employment may have produced a much smaller amount of disequilibrium than they had intended. A similar difficulty for macroeconomic policy makers rose in the 1970's when it came to be suspected by some observers that the rate of growth of productivity had fallen below expectations. The worry resulted that the use of GNP as an approximate target for monetary and fiscal policy might produce strains on available capacity and labor supplies that would be much greater and occur much sooner than intended.

"How could we have known, having to loose our macroeconomic weapons in the darkness of night, that our targets had moved?" There are some who regard this type of explanation of the miscalculations of the 1960's as altogether too convenient and self-serving. Even now we do not know how much weight should be accorded this appeal to a rising equilibrium volume of unemployment. Casual observation of the sensational price rises accompanying quite unsensational unemployment rates during the boom of 1972-73 has greatly added to the impression that the "full-employment unemployment rate" is worse than it was in the post-War years. But some econometricians say they can fit their models to the facts of unemployment and inflation without resort to any assumption of a worsening equilibrium unemployment rate since the mid-1950's. Whatever the consensus that emerges on this narrow question, it is a good bet—having asserted nothing is certain, I will not say "certain"—that the problem of shifting targets is far from the whole story. There are other pitfalls of econometric policy making that help to account for the record of macroeconomic miscalculation compiled in these years.

Control problems

The second type of difficulty in macroeconomic decision making is the same problem of "statistical estimation" that confronts acousticians, ecologists, chemotherapists, and other engineering practitioners in the natural sciences. Even in normal circumstances, with so much happening at once, it is hard to "read" the economic data reliably enough to predict with much accuracy the course that the economy will take under this or that stabilization policy. The difficulties of empirical estimation are especially thorny in the area of stabilization policy because there one is concerned not just with the ultimate effects of a policy step now—in the long run a whole class of policies may lead to the same end result—but with the time-shape of the effects over a couple of years.

One of the "control problems" resulting from these long and fickle lags is that a choice of the appropriate step today must depend upon an estimate of the size of the effects of previous policy steps not yet felt. A function of the research department at the Federal Reserve, it has been remarked, is to remind the Board of Governors that the effects of monetary policy occur with a lag, so that some of the effects of previous policy actions may still be *en train*. Another control problem arising from the presence of lagged policy effects could arise even if the time-shape of the lagged effects were perfectly known. If the effects of present policy actions are stronger in the future than in the present, an attempt during each "period" to approximate some economic target as nearly as possible—to take each day as it comes—would generate a spectacle of ever widening stop-go alternations worthy of the Keystone Kops. Perfect stability of the economy is therefore unattainable and dangerous to strive for.

Nowhere are the problems of control more applicable than to the Federal Reserve's manipulation of the money supply. Economists regularly berate the Fed for tightening or easing too late or too soon, and sometimes it is attacked from both sides at once. As an aloof and secretive institution run by 14 Governors with no known competence in matters monetary, it is no wonder that the Fed is every economist's whipping boy. Still, it is abundantly clear *ex post,* and it was tolerably clear even before the fact, that the Fed erred three or perhaps four times over the period of the above narrative. The good Governors let the boom go much too far in 1968-69 and bizarrely repeated the mistake in 1972-73. With Nixon safely re-elected, and virtually every indicator pointing toward rapid growth and already strained capacity, why did the Governors not apply the brakes firmly in late fall 1972? The misjudgment must presumably be laid to misestimates of the lagged effects of current and past policy actions. By summer 1973, however, the Fed had tightened to an unprecedented degree and was tightening further despite mounting storm signals that a growth-recession, with unemployment rising beyond 5.25 per cent, was already a likelihood within the next year. Whether the silent Fed was hatching another Game Plan of contrived recession in another compulsive contest with inflation, or whether it was inadvertently overdoing things once again, no one on the outside could say. The situation would have produced outrage, had not the resources of righteous indignation already been spread so thin.

The factor of public expectations

The first type of difficulty in macroeconomic stabilization that I cited arises from the motion of the desired target and our consequent ignorance of its current location. The second class of difficulties, which arise even when the target is visible, encompasses the problem of control or guidance under incomplete knowledge of the environment and especially the relevant dynamics. The third difficulty for macroeconomic policy making that I shall discuss is posed by the presumption that the behavior of the actors in the economy is based on their surmises of future government policy. In particular, the response of the "private economy" to a governmental action is apt to depend very much on the "world," especially the governmental policy environment, in which they believe themselves to be living. Therefore, the way the economy reacts to a government move may depend critically upon whether, in the eyes of the public, it signals a fundamental shift in government policy or whether it is just another vicissitude in the world as lately known.

This policy perplex possesses the basic features of a *game*. An alteration of the government's strategy will cause its opponent eventually to perceive the change and to adjust his own strategy accordingly. True, the government's interests are not inimical to its opponent's—let us suppose the government is merely trying to serve the public—but this makes no real difference. It would be very stupid of the government's econometricians to predict the consequences of a shift in policy under the assumption that the public will not now or ever adapt their behavior to their own perceptions of that policy shift. The econometrician, however, does not find this admonition very helpful, for he has not had the opportunity to study the behavior under those conditions.

The economics of fiscal policy provides an example of this policy difficulty. That an increase in income tax rates will reduce consumer demand is a Keynesian canon. The magnitude of the reduction, however, can be supposed to depend upon consumers' expectations of the duration of the tax rate increase. The econometricians were in a poor position to predict the effectiveness of the avowedly temporary tax surcharge introduced in 1968 because most of their data represented observations of consumer responses to avowedly permanent tax changes in the past. In fact, the effectiveness of the fiscal brakes applied in 1968 appears to have been less than the Johnson economists had anticipated. It is generally conceded now that countercyclical fluctuations in tax rates have a far weaker impact upon consumer demand than secular shifts in the degree of fiscal austerity over the business cycle. But we can only guess how much weaker this effect is unless and until such countercyclical jiggling of tax rates is actually tried.

The classic example, already classic, is the belief held by the Kennedy and Johnson economists that, to reduce poverty and raise prosperity, it would be possible to "trade off" an increase of the rate of inflation in return for a lasting reduction in the (average) rate of unemployment. The belief that a lasting reduction in the average unemployment rate could be "purchased" in trade for an increase of the average inflation rate was based on no more than an empirical regularity, a positive statistical association between inflation and employment known as the Phillips Curve. This statistical relationship was derived, it should be noted, from epochs in which a level trend of prices was the norm of macroeconomic policy.

The curious fact is that there was absolutely nothing in economic theory that would have lent significant support to such a belief. Indeed, various papers appearing in the years 1947 to 1967 by Abba Lerner, William Fellner, Milton Friedman, and myself adopted the hypothesis—more or less on the principle of insufficient reason—that a high rate of inflation, once built into the expectations of consumers and investors, would be associated with the same levels of production and employment that would prevail in a regime of zero inflation where consumers and investors expect a level price trend. The theorists' presumption that the equilibrium unemployment rate is a number that is independent of the inflation rate when people have been anticipating that rate of inflation and are expecting it to continue has come to be called the *natural unemployment rate hypothesis*. According to this hypothesis, if the government steps up the inflation rate to a higher level and the public adjusts its expectations accordingly, there will result at best a temporary, short-lived decline of the unemployment rate for as long a time as it takes the public generally to adapt their expectations to the change in the government's inflation target.[1]

In the amiable contest between the aprioristic theorists and the empiricists that ensued over the permanency and usability for policy of this Phillips-type relationship, the theorists largely were willing to play the empiricists' game. First, when rudimentary efforts to "control" for adjustments in inflation expectations were introduced, much ground had to be conceded to the natural rate hypothesis: The terms at which increased inflation could purchase a lasting reduction of the unemployment rate appeared to be much less favorable than had originally been thought by those who had first proclaimed the possibility of a trade-off. Further, technical papers by Robert Lucas and Thomas Sargeant argued that the prevailing empirical tests were biased in favor of confirming a Phillips Curve trade-off even when none existed. They made concrete the point that one past policy epoch constitutes one and only one "observation" and is thus insufficient by itself for any extrapolative prediction of the consequences of another policy regime.

Is "politics" in the way?

So much for this catalog of the pitfalls faced in macroeconomic policy making. Mercifully for the reader, I have not even asked myself whether it is tolerably complete. It is already long enough, however, to prompt the question: Is the explanation of the disappoint-

---

[1] Some critics have travestied the hypothesis by imputing to the "naturalists" the belief that the equilibrium unemployment is an intertemporal constant, something like the speed of light, independent of everything under the sun; but clearly the hypothesis asserts nothing about the determinants of the natural rate and its drift over time.

ments and failures of macroeconomic policy since 1965 then primarily technical? In other words, is the explanation essentially a matter of the uncertainty inherent in econometric knowledge plus occasional pilot error?

Economists frequently talk quixotically of what would happen if somehow they could cease being underlings and install the first Economist King. It often does seem that the introduction of some sound economic policy—some policy action that would surely be approved by an impartial ethical observer and by a well-informed electorate—is stymied by the interest group whose ox would be gored. The interest group adversely affected hires lawyers and economists to dramatize the damage that is threatened and to explain solemnly that the group affected is a linchpin in the Republic, essential to the welfare of all.

There is a school of skeptical thought which asserts that the economic policies selected tend, at least in the long run, to be "efficient" in this technical sense: It is never or only exceptionally the case that the economists' advice will produce policies which *all* will see as preferable to the old policy. Similarly, for a long time many political scientists have held the position that the "pluralism" of contesting interest groups, through a process of vote trading in legislatures, tends to reach an efficient outcome, as if led by an invisible hand.

The falseness of the analogy with the invisible-hand theorem of classical welfare economics is that the latter analysis supposes perfect markets and thus perfect information costlessly possessed by all about all prices, wage rates, and the rest, now and in the future. Clearly the real-life political system, and real-life markets too, are shot through with ignorance and misinformation. An interest group often has the incentive to conceal information and to spread misinformation about the character of its effect on the economy. In such an environment, the group may not always know what its own true interests are. The public-interest economist plays the useful role here of combatting error and misinformation—useful insofar as his knowledge and information is correct. Perhaps one of the inefficiencies of the system is that it produces an under-demand for public-interest economists. Economists like to think so at any rate.

A related defect of the political system is that it takes up policy proposals in a piecemeal, sequential fashion, since there is not enough time in the day to do everything at once. The result is that it is difficult or impossible to achieve a cooperative arrangement among the interest groups by which each group can accept some losses for the sake of larger gains. This is where the rationalist social compact theory of civil obligations and self-enforced restraint comes in; but that theory now seems to have fallen by the wayside, or by the Watergate.

There is plenty of room, I would thus maintain, for arguments that macroeconomic policy makers would do much better were it not for political flaws in the system, which occasionally prevent the policy makers from doing the right thing. Fiscal policy may sometimes have been a victim here. Everyone seems to oppose a tax increase on the worried assumption that his tax will be raised more than others'. Would it be less satisfactory to have a system in which the AFL-CIO determined the corporate tax rate and the NAM determined wage-income and employment taxes?

Nevertheless, the flaws of the political system and their exploitation by pressure groups seem not to have been crucial to the conduct of countercyclical *monetary* policy. After the fashion of "radical" social analysis, one might flirt with the theory that it is the banking industry which lies behind the Fed's attraction to recessionary game plans and its anti-inflationary stance, on the ground that they profit from the Fed's tight-money methods to keep inflation down. The trouble with this theory is that the banks would almost certainly gain more, in high interest earnings, by a permissive regime of steady and substantial inflation. The bankers' economists, at least, certainly believe that.

A similarly perplexing case occurred last year. When George McGovern proposed a scheme that would have raised the incomes of the bottom half of the population, it appeared that he was going to lose votes in the bottom half because of it. It made one wonder about the theory that people vote their self-interest. Evidently, their ideas are their interests. Ideological doctrines and habits may constrain economic policy as much as imperfections in the political system of government decision making.

Pulling up our socks

What can be done to improve macroeconomic policy in the future? We ought at least to endeavor not to repeat past mistakes. We should not encourage the idea that moderate inflation can do much to brighten job opportunities for the poor. At the same time, we can insist that inflation at four or five per cent per annum is not so bad that it is worth engineering a prolonged recession to reduce or eliminate it. We should acknowledge that no one has yet put forward a program of permanent wage and price controls—formal or informal—that plausibly promises a significant reduction of the average or equilibrium unemployment rate that would be associated with the monetary and fiscal policies in use. We might usefully continue to press the Congress for more flexible use of tax policy, while recognizing that this flexibility will not be a panacea against the largely unforeseeable economic disturbances that produce cyclical fluctuations in employment and inflation rates. We should try to teach the public that better stabilization of output and employment may require the acceptance of greater fluctuations in interest rates, exchange rates, and perhaps prices, and that (up to a point) it will be worth it.

Beyond that, we should continue the everlasting struggle toward a deeper understanding of business fluctuations and alternative sorts of stabilization policy. A new breed of theorists well trained in stochastic processes, statistical inference, dynamic games, and the rest, are already turning their attention to this subject. I doubt, however, that there ought to be a crash program that would divert analytical talent away from other equally or more important analytical problems in social policy. Despite the increasing sophistication of our understanding and its gradual translation into policy, it must be expected that from time to time there will be novel problems of policy making which have not and could not have received adequate theoretical and econometric research beforehand. Difficult times are likely to lie ahead for stabilization policy. However, the unprecedented stability in unemployment since World War II, and especially in the past 10 years, suggests that a great deal of progress has occurred in our knowledge of how to stabilize unemployment.

The microeconomic program

Stabilization policy cannot hope to provide the country with an average unemployment rate over the next 10 years that is much different from five per cent of the measured labor force. This is the estimate of the equilibrium unemployment rate which emerges from recent econometric models of the relation between employment and inflation. Now that these estimates are based on experience with a wider range of inflation rates than was heretofore observable, I believe that these estimates are worthy of credence. In fact, some of these models would suggest that the equilibrium rate is somewhat worse than five per cent.

The meaning of this equilibrium concept is that if monetary and fiscal policies and eventualities were to produce an unemployment rate significantly lower—say, 4.7 per cent on average over a period as long as a decade—there would almost surely be a significant rise in the inflation rate from beginning to end. The monetary and fiscal authorities are not likely to let this happen, if they can help it. So it is a pretty safe bet that American unemployment will not average much below, if at all below, five per cent of the labor force over the next 10 years. Even if a 4.5 per cent unemployment rate, not to say a four per cent rate, were in fact sustainable without ever-rising inflation, the now widespread belief that it would not be sustainable, that it would court the danger of rising inflation, pretty well insures that we are not likely to see a lengthy experiment with those rates of unemployment in the foreseeable future.

Corresponding to the five per cent aggregate unemployment rate, unless the "structure" of the labor market changes, will be an unemployment rate in officially designated "poverty areas" of about eight per cent, and an unemployment rate among non-whites in these poverty areas of about 10 per cent. These unemployment rates are higher than those that occurred during the boom of 1966-69 and the boom of 1955-56. So the unemployment rate among poor (especially non-white) persons, already greater than that among the non-poor, will be higher in the future than in the best years of the past two decades. It is in this bleak light that any appraisal of the record and prospects of the Johnson Administration's structural or microeconomic programs for improving the job opportunities of low-income workers should take place.

It used to be said by social workers that the various manpower programs inaugurated by the Great Society would do little good if the economy were not booming so as to display gaping shortages in the supply of skilled labor, Apparently, the intended implication was that the manpower programs would not be worthwhile, would be a misallocation of public money, if macroeconomic policy could not keep up the Johnson boom of 1966-68 or do better. This is a little like assuming that if Johnny is discovered by his teachers to be slower than the others, he should receive less attention than the others. The reasonable decision may be to give him more attention (though not necessarily so much more that he finally performs as well as the others). Nowadays we do not hear so much wishful thinking about what the effectiveness of manpower programs would be in some infeasible or unsustainable state of the economy. Increasingly the social worker seems ready to say, "I accept the universe." To which the macroeconomist is tempted to add, "By God, he'd better."

The classical mechanism by which manpower training programs open up increased employment at skilled jobs that pay better than unskilled jobs has nothing to do with shortages, imbalances, disequilibrium, hyperinflation, and all of that. The story is that governmental training of the unskilled will drive down the wage rates of skilled workers by increasing the supply of skilled workers wanting work, thus inducing profit-seeking businessmen to hire more skilled workers. This substitution among inputs drives down the pay to the more substitutable factors of production whose supplies have not changed. Thus, wages of already skilled workers tend to fall. Because they are nearest to the program's point of impact, they are, so to speak, its victims. The wages to those left unskilled may rise or fall, depending upon the particulars of each case. But some factor reward must go up. If it is not the wages of the unskilled, then perhaps it will be the rentals going to capital. It is a classical proposition that the sum of all factor incomes must go up by the amount of the "marginal product" of the skills created. Society as a whole gains that much extra consumable output over future years. But society in the present must also foot the bill, in lost consumption, for the resources devoted to the training of the unskilled.

The problem of evaluation

Other doubts about the promise of the manpower programs spring from impressions or examinations of the results, and the comparison of these findings with intuitive expectations of what the results would be. Some of these appraisals have focused on the micro data of particular programs in particular places. I would not comment on these sorts of appraisals except to say that it is unclear what standard of performance should be regarded as the boundary between success and failure. Other impressions of the performance of the manpower programs as a whole have been macroeconomic. There has been no calculable reduction in the unemployment rates of poor persons relative to the unemployment experience of the population as a whole. Similarly, there is no widespread impression of a significant gain in the earnings of unskilled workers as a whole relative to the earnings of the skilled over the past five years. No leap forward in productivity during this period has been evidenced by the data on output per man-hour.

This intuitive pass at a quantitative appraisal of the manpower programs ignores that the expenditures made by them, while seeming large to the taxpayer, are dwarfed by the national income. Manpower expenditures were about $4 billion in 1972 while the Gross National Product was about $1200 billion. If we think of the manpower programs as directed at the bottom 10 million workers in a population with 70 million workers, they amounted to $400 per worker in that bottom group of earners. Viewing it from another angle, if one thinks of the manpower programs as typically making an investment of $8,000 in each young worker enrolled in them, the budget of $4 billion can reach just half a million workers each year, or about three quarters of one per cent of the labor force. The same observation, however, suggests that if the manpower programs make a lasting difference for the earnings and unemployment of those enrolled in them, then their continuation at some steady level will have a growing cumulative effect upon the distribution of earnings and unemployment until the beneficiaries eventually leave the labor force. Even in a controlled experiment where there were no socioeconomic trends countering or reinforcing the cumulative effect of the manpower programs, only the statistical "noise" contained in all economic data, it would still take time for the manpower programs to register significant effects on the macroeconomic data of unemployment, earnings, and their distribution over the population.

Still another objection to the manpower programs is that we do not know what we are doing. In truth, there is no widely understood and accepted theory of poverty, of the distribution of earnings, and of happiness. No wonder, then, that hypothesized remedies offered by our social apothecaries command little agreement as to their promised effectiveness. It is even being suggested these days that education may have as little to do with productivity as, say, tournaments in jousting; schooling is merely our medium for signaling will and stamina. Education theory refers to how-to-think techniques for the adaptive solution of new problems; not much education is necessary for stable, routinized jobs; and so on. If we would like to improve the earning power of low-income workers, however, it would not be illogical on the face of it to respond to our ignorance by diversifying our experiments in manpower training, trying many different programs run by rival agencies, and even perhaps expanding our investment in these programs as a hedge against disappointment in the rate of return on the aggregate investment.

We come finally to what may be the most perplexing evaluative problem of all. Suppose, though it can never be so, that we knew with certainty the consequences of each manpower program, actual or contemplated. On what basis should we decide that any such program was working well enough to warrant continued support? We have no agreed-to standard of success or failure against which to measure the results of these manpower programs—unless, of course, the results be nil or pernicious. Asked whether a manpower program is doing well, one has to answer, like the man asked about his wife, "Compared to what?" There is no clear rival program making alternative use of the public funds that would naturally provide a criterion of performance.

Defining our basic objectives

The economist cannot devise a performance criterion without some notion of what society's basic aims are. If our objective is to raise the earning power of some group of low-income workers, subject to certain budgetary and other constraints, the performance criterion to be employed may involve comparing one manpower program against another. If our objective is generally to help those in greatest distress, the criterion will involve comparisons with a much wider range of alternative government programs. In evaluating the effect of the manpower programs on poverty in general, we might worry about the New Poor: people who are sick, economically deprived, emotionally disturbed, physically disabled, mentally retarded, and so on. If the reduction of the most acute distress and deprivation were our basic aim—I do not affirm or deny that it is—the economist would point to the opportunity costs of the manpower programs in the form of income not provided the destitute, food not given to the hungry (at home and abroad), psychotherapists not trained, kidney machines not built, and the rest.

It may be, however, that such reflections mistake the true nature of the Great Society idea. Perhaps the "war against poverty" should not be interpreted simply as a bundle of pragmatic instruments having the fundamental purpose of achieving a fairer, less unjust distribution of human satisfactions. The Old Left did not identify the industrial worker as "poor"—his immiseration was a theoretical projection into the future—so much as "exploited" (and hence entitled to redress). The New Left has expanded the list of victims (farm workers, students, and so on) and the variety of injuries. Similarly, many defenders of capitalism, having admiration for what they regard as its "meritocratic" competition for prizes, have been increasingly willing to see to it that all participants in the foot race have equal access to adequate training before going to the starting line. In both these views, there is the assumption that workers have certain natural rights that ought to be accorded to them regardless of the size of the resulting gains to workers and regardless of the costs to competing social claimants that are possibly worse off. From this viewpoint, it would be simply anomalous to ask: Are the manpower programs worth the cost?—just as it would be jarring (for the liberal) to be asked whether freedom of speech benefits the poor.

3

Reform
follows reality:
the
growth of welfare

GILBERT Y. STEINER

THE Administration that came to
power in 1961 and looked forward to being in power for eight years
did not dare nor wish to deal with public assistance as its predecessor
had during its last years—by holding on to the status quo and hoping for the best. A policy fashioned in the 1930's and 1940's particularly for the aged simply would not self-adjust in the 1960's to cope
with the needs of unmarried and deserted mothers and their children. The changing shape of the welfare population presaged high
costs without political benefits, the worst of all situations. Accordingly, formulating plans to cope with the needs of dependent families constituted a built-in, unavoidable challenge to the new
Kennedy Administration just as it would have to a new Nixon Administration then, and as it did to a new Nixon Administration eight
years thereafter, and a Johnson Administration in the interim.

In the key aspect of the first Presidential message exclusively
devoted to public welfare ever sent to Congress, Kennedy unfortunately depended on the experts. He proposed an emphasis on
psycho-social services, to be offered with a gentle touch by skilled
professionals. After a full five-year run, Congressional skeptics and
Johnson's systematic thinkers evaluated that emphasis, found it
wanting, and displaced soft social work therapy with a tougher

posture that focused on economic incentives for working, on job training, and on child care. But economic incentives had the effect of extending welfare eligibility; job training did not lead to jobs; and child care was more complicated and more expensive than had been expected. So, in 1969, welfare reform took on a third face, a family assistance plan that at least reflected reality: Families with absent, unemployed, or underpaid fathers could be neither soft-serviced nor hard-serviced away. They require a minimum and assured level of cash assistance.

If the three waves of social interventionists proposing welfare change in the 1960's had different ideas about how to get from here to reform, their expressed goals coincided. All three spoke of restoring dignity and independence to clients and of saving money in the long run. Alas, by the end of the 1960's, public assistance clients were still without dignity and independence. Their numbers, however, had increased by 4.5 million; and rather than diminishing, payments had increased by $4 billion. Nor has the long run yet appeared. Both costs and clients continued to escalate even more sharply in the 1970's: Recipient totals are up another three million and annual money payments are up another $3 billion. Since cost increases are precisely what the reformers sought to avoid, it is a mistake to conclude that welfare policy in the 1960's represents the extreme case of deliberately throwing money at a social problem in hopes that it would go away. It is also a mistake to conclude that failure to meet the stated goals of the various reform efforts means that there has been no welfare reform. Admitting more of the needy poor to the relief rolls, no matter how reluctantly, rather than keeping them off, no matter how ingeniously, is the quintessence of welfare reform.

The inheritance

John F. Kennedy's Administration inherited a welfare system based on the theory of a reciprocal relationship between Old Age and Survivors' Insurance (OASI) and public assistance. While the system had been tied to that theory for almost a quarter of a century, it simply did not hold when applied to dependent children. Old Age Insurance (OAI) might eventually drive out Old Age Assistance (OAA), but Aid to Dependent Children (ADC), the public assistance category in which there had been little interest when the Social Security Act was written, was well into a sharp, persistent, and expensive growth cycle.

Between the end of the War and the Kennedy inauguration, imaginative state efforts to hurry the deterioration of public assistance by demeaning or repressing the client were more likely to be tolerated than damned in Washington. Those state efforts focused on publicity, on the pursuit of absent fathers, on punishing apparent promiscuity, and on residence requirements inhibiting interstate movement of the welfare poor. Together with other restraints, and with a prevalent view of welfare as a privilege rather than a right, they served to discourage poor people from seeking help.

None of the efforts to help the system expire had had the desired effect. For example, when Congress acceded to a demand from the Governors' Conference and made it permissible for states to provide public access to the rolls, it did more for the states' rights cause than for the cause of welfare reduction. By the mid-1950's, 21 states had opened their rolls for public inspection. In subsequent years, few public inquiries were made, and there was no material effect on the case loads in those states to distinguish them from the loads in other states. Comparable disappointment resulted from the so-called NOLEO amendment, a requirement of notice to law enforcement officials when desertion or abandonment resulted in ADC dependency. States and localities found that tracking down a deserting father is expensive. They found, too, that even if he can be found, a deserting father is unlikely to be able to support his family—which is often why he deserted in the first place. Again, the "suitable home" test, invented to halt support to unwed mothers who continued to bear children, did allow Louisiana temporarily to reduce its ADC load. That one, however, was too much for the departing Eisenhower Administration. As a *quid pro quo* for approval, it insisted that other provisions be made for the children affected. But it left long-run solutions to its successor.

Most politicians who had been present at its creation found the 25th anniversary of the public assistance system more to be regretted than celebrated. "I remember," said Senator Lister Hill early in 1961, "when we passed the [Social Security] Act in 1935, the thinking was that the public assistance grants were being only for more or less of a temporary period, that soon everybody would be under OASI and you would not have any need for public assistance grants." Alabama's venerable Senator had resurrected the social insurance blueprint used by the New Deal in 1935 and 1939 as the design for a system to offset prolonged dependency resulting from old age or from absence—then assumed to mean death or incarceration—of a father. An assured social insurance income for the aged and for dependent survivors was to be financed through an earmarked federal tax imposed equally on employers and employees. The accompanying public assistance system, jointly financed by federal and state governments, would give relief to the needy aged and to needy children prior to the growth of universal social insurance. Complementary programs of disability assistance and disability insurance were added in 1950 and 1956, respectively. In all three categories—old age, dependent children, disability (APTD)—it was expected that good social insurance would ultimately be able to drive out bad public assistance.

By 1960, Social Security coverage had been widely extended: in 1950 to most urban self-employed persons, to regularly employed agricultural and domestic workers, and on a voluntary group basis to employees of non-profit organizations and of state and local governments. Coverage was further extended in 1954 to about 10 million persons with some earnings as farmers or in domestic service and to additional groups of state and local government employees. In 1956, military service and 850,000 other jobs were included. Despite this growth in social insurance, and despite the repressive measures that characterized the 1950's, the need for public assistance had given signs of deteriorating only in the aged category. To be sure, without a mechanism for periodic and systematic Congressional review of the relief apparatus, with bureaucratic attention focused on discharging only a ministerial role, and with the political atmosphere of the 1950's not conducive to expansion of federal responsibility for the poor, only those few policy specialists who were paying close attention knew the system was in trouble. The Congress was almost entirely out of touch, since authorizations to spend and actual expenditures on public assistance were automated rather than subject to renewal at periodic intervals. The Social Security Act did fix the limits of federal financial participation in assistance payments to individuals and did require participating states to submit state plans. It did not impose any limit on total federal spending, nor establish an expiration date, nor impose positive conditions for approval of state plans. Effective control over benefits and eligibility decisions was left to the states and localities. Once a state plan was filed, the federal role became that of a disbursing and auditing clerk—finding the money to pay claims presented to it by the states, and taking occasional exception to a doubtful payment.

Misplaced optimism

Responsible officials in the Truman and the Eisenhower periods helped sustain the concept of public assistance as a declining business that could safely be left to wither away. During all the years before 1961, they had neither expressed doubts about the reciprocal relationship between insurance and assistance, nor emphasized interstate inequities in both old age assistance and aid to dependent children, nor pinpointed ADC as a high-risk category. "If we have a comprehensive contributory social insurance system covering all of these economic hazards to which the people are exposed, I believe that in time the residual load of public assistance would become so small in this country that the states and the localities could reasonably be expected to assume that load without federal financial participation," said Social Security Administrator Arthur Altmeyer in 1949. Five years later, the Republican Secretary of Health, Education, and Welfare sounded typically optimistic: "It really happens much faster than you think," said Mrs. Oveta Culp Hobby, "as the federal Old Age and Survivors' Insurance system really begins to do its job, the need for public assistance would deteriorate." And, as late as 1958, the Eisenhower budget message spoke confidently of "modernizing the formulas for public assistance with a view to gradually reducing federal participation in its financing."

This optimism obscured trouble with the aged category as well. If the number of aged recipients was inching downward, and if, unlike ADC, OAA was not provoking sanctimonious orations on immorality, each category had a serious problem of irrational inequities in benefit payments. Categorical assistance had not been required of the states, but represented an offer from the national government to the states to assist in meeting benefit payments. The formula for sharing imposed limits on federal contributions; it did not tell a state how small or how large a benefit to pay. Differences among states in average payments were unconscionably wide from the outset. In OAA, for example, California and Colorado pre-War benefits were four times those of Arkansas and Georgia. By 1960, the high-benefit state of Connecticut paid $109 compared to Tennessee's $42. Although it might have been expected that the richer states would provide more generous benefits than the poorer states, a state's wealth actually provided no sure clue to its likely level of support for its indigent aged. Of the top quintile of states in average per capita income for 1959-1961, only two, California and New Jersey, were in the top quintile when ranked according to average monthly OAA benefits. Seven of the states in that OAA top-benefit quintile, on the other hand, had average per capita incomes below the national average.

There was no sign either that a low proportion of recipients to total aged population led to relatively higher benefits, or that a high proportion of recipients to total aged population was a trade-off for skimpy benefits. Oklahoma, with the fourth highest recipient rate in the country, was paying an average monthly benefit of $92, but Georgia, with the fifth highest recipient rate, was paying only $55. Hawaii and Alabama both paid average monthly benefits around $68, but Hawaii's went to only 3.6 per cent of its aged population while Alabama payments went to 39.3 per cent. Louisiana paid an average of $84 to 49.8 per cent of the aged there, yet rich Delaware's average payment was $63 and only 2.8 per cent of its aged population received benefits.

Comparable irrationalities were to be found in the operation of ADC. The perverse behavior of that category was mystifying in several respects. First, it gave no sign at all of responding to the growth of survivors' insurance. Late in 1957, the ADC recipient totals, rapidly on their way up, passed the OAA totals, which were slowly on their way down. In the Eisenhower years alone, ADC recipient totals increased more than 50 per cent, to the point where the number of ADC recipients passed three million in 1960, with payments that year for the first time exceeding $1 billion.

Second, interstate differences in ADC benefit payments, like those in OAA, baffled students of state expenditures. High ADC recipient rates were shown to be associated with state characteristics of urbanization, low incomes, and low levels of employment, but no satisfactory economic explanation could be provided for differences between states in average ADC payments. Neither the relative size of the ADC population nor the relative wealth of a state provided that explanation. For example, Texas and New Hampshire, with virtually identical ADC recipient rates (1.5 per cent of the population under age 18), made average monthly payments per recipient as different as $19 in Texas and $40 in New Hampshire. Again, average payments in the two states with the country's highest per capita incomes, Delaware and Nevada, were only $30 while the relatively poor state of North Dakota was paying an average of $42 per recipient.

Whatever the explanation for the growth of ADC or for benefit levels that varied wildly in both the aged and the family categories, President Kennedy was concerned about an immediate, practical problem: how to help the hungry people he remembered seeing in West Virginia during his campaign. Accordingly, the Administration pushed a three-point program. It proposed enactment of temporary legislation, particularly aid to dependent children of the unemployed, designed to extend federal help to that previously uncovered category. It directed the people it assumed to be most concerned and most knowledgeable about public welfare to review the scene and to suggest appropriate action. And it arranged for a "quick fix" by stepping up food relief.

Food stamps: a quick fix

Concerned about hunger, yet too inexperienced to challenge the whole public assistance system immediately, Kennedy quickly set in motion a pilot food stamp program that ultimately became a separate welfare system, in part overlapping public assistance, in part reaching a different clientele. Reinstituting food stamps—a comparable program had existed between 1939 and 1943—was a way of increasing federal financial participation in and imposing a national floor under relief benefits without overhauling the formulae spelled out in the Social Security Act. As a separate program for which income was the sole condition for eligibility, stamps could reach needy people who did not fall into a public assistance eligibility category. If lesser amounts of money could be traded for stamps of greater value by those outside the ambit of categorical assistance—unemployed household heads, childless couples, and single individuals—as well as by those with inadequate benefits from OAA or ADC, and by many OASI beneficiaries, a minimum public benefit, virtually universal in coverage, would be accomplished. Only the tiny fraction of the population lacking even the cost of food stamps would be excluded.

Stamps were an old Democratic cause. Indeed, in the last of the Eisenhower years, the Democratic Congress gave him unwanted and unused authority to set up a limited food stamp program. Eisenhower stuck to direct distribution of surplus commodities, and there was not even much of that. While Kennedy's first executive order, signed the day of his inauguration, liberalized and expanded the surplus commodity program, less than two weeks later he announced a pilot stamp operation. Since, as a Senator, Kennedy had sponsored a food stamp bill, bureaucrats responsible for evaluating the pilot program could be expected to look especially for its strengths.

Those strengths were easier to discern if stamps were compared to the alternative food relief program, distribution of surplus commodities, rather than to cash income supplements. Surplus commodity distribution involved giving away selected government-owned products purchased under a price support program. The products available for distribution might or might not coincide with the needs of the poor. Available for distribution, moreover, did not mean universal availability. Some counties chose not to participate at all, and others to accept only selected products for distribution. Needy clients could be seen lined up, soup kitchen style, with their own containers, for what was usually a month's supply—an impractically large amount— of cheese, cornmeal, dried milk, or whatever product was involved. Compared to that, a booklet of food coupons redeemable for any domestic food product appeared to be an advance in both dignity and efficiency. Throughout the years of the Great Society, however, almost 80 per cent of potential stamp users did not participate.

At the end of the decade, another administration was looking for ways of its own to advance dignity and efficiency in public relief. Its family assistance plan would have cashed out food stamps. By then, however, after the media and a Senate committee had focused on hunger in America, an aggressive campaign to encourage the use of stamps was finally taking hold. Cashing them out at the income guarantee level being proposed would have disadvantaged large numbers of beneficiaries. In short, accepting a return to an anachronistic relief-in-kind system, because it seemed quickly attainable, led to a separate federal welfare program that has come to reach 11 million people, and has become virtually impossible to eliminate. Less demeaning and more practical than commodity distribution, stamps for the user are more demeaning and less practical than cash. Yet, in fixing a floor under family income, a straight substitution of federal cash for federal food stamps produces intolerable complications. Under existing cost schedules, such a substitution would push the family assistance federal guarantee beyond acceptable limits or would leave some working poor, and some welfare clients in generous states, less well off under the reform program than they presently are. Neither is an acceptable alternative. While the return to in-kind relief with stamps may have been a quick fix for a weak relief system in the early 1960's, stamps are a second-best arrangement for clients and a formidable obstacle to the development of a universal system of family assistance.

Rehabilitation instead of relief

Instead of attending to the restraints and restrictions on client behavior that had been allowed to grow during the 1950's, and instead of dealing with the *sine qua non* of public assistance, the benefit payment, Kennedy's welfare consultants floated before the politicians the dream of welfare cost reduction under honorable conditions. The politicians dreamed the impossible dream, and continued to do so throughout the 1960's, even as the Great Society's anti-poverty program and the civil rights movement furnished evidence that public assistance had a far larger market of eligible clients than it had ever reached.

After promising a thorough review and investigation of federal welfare law, Abraham Ribicoff, Kennedy's first HEW Secretary, met in May 1961 with representatives of the National Association of Social Workers. It was a first move toward what would become an unfortunate overdependence on social work professionals. When, shortly thereafter, Ribicoff created an Ad Hoc Committee on Public Welfare, 23 of its 24 members turned out to have attachments to schools of social work or to welfare agencies, while its principal consultant was the dean of a school of social work. Ribicoff followed this with the appointment of the Director-Designate of the New York State Department of Welfare as a consultant to propose administrative and program changes in the federal role. The ultimate and not entirely surprising result of the official advisory efforts, strengthened by a concurrent foundation-financed study of public welfare under the auspices of the New York School of Social Work, was a proposal to put more social work into public assistance. Bypassing analysis of the changing causes of ADC dependency, Ribicoff and Kennedy thereupon embraced a legislative package that would, it was claimed, "bring a new spirit in our public welfare program . . . a long overdue change in the direction and philosophy of our welfare programs. . . ."

The new spirit was to be a spirit of rehabilitation that would sub-stitute for the old spirit of relief. Its method was to be psycho-social services, its instrument was to be professionally trained social work-ers. Ribicoff characterized the new program as one that could move some persons off the relief rolls entirely, enable others to attain a high degree of independence, encourage children to grow strong in mind and body, and train welfare workers in the skills needed to help make these achievements possible.

Without ever making the point explicitly as they unveiled the serv-ices approach, its proponents interred the old idea of a reciprocal relationship between survivors' insurance and ADC. Continued dependence on the old theory was unrealistic because death of the father no longer was an important cause of ADC dependency. Sur-vivors' insurance had done its job. By 1961, only 7.7 per cent of ADC dependency was attributable to death of the father; 66.7 per cent was attributable to absence of a live father from the home. In those cases, survivors' insurance was irrelevant, just as it was for the five per cent of the cases attributable to unemployment.

A social services emphasis in public relief was a new concept. The problem was with its relevance rather than with its novelty. Public assistance recipients were not typified by those whose success stories were conveniently drawn from 10 demonstration projects and used to buttress the case for services instead of support, and rehabilitation instead of relief. Could "mature, experienced workers" make a dif-ference when, in 1961, 8.7 years was the median number of years of education of an ADC mother, a bare 15 per cent were high school graduates, and 55 per cent had no high school at all? When almost three quarters of all ADC mothers were either incapacitated, needed as homemakers, or had no marketable skill? The philosophers of the New Deal legislation had been thinking about the widow and children of the coal miner killed in a mining accident, and not about the deserted young mother in Cleveland or Chicago who was the apparent model for the 1961 welfare planners. Survivors' insurance (and a strong United Mine Workers union) ultimately did take the widows off public assistance. Psycho-social services might help the deserted Cleveland mother understand why she had been deserted and what special problems her children faced, but unlike insurance payments of death benefits, such services bought nothing.

The experts

In yet another respect, it took an anxious-to-believe frame of mind to accept the case for social work training as a specific for public assistance. Through the years, professionally trained workers had shunned public welfare work.

While President Kennedy and Secretary Ribicoff were urging

support for training social work professionals, the Department of Labor was reporting that even allowing for the inclusion of supervisors, administrators, and other non-direct service personnel, less than four per cent of the more than 35,000 social workers then in public assistance work held an advanced degree in social work. Over 2,000 such degrees were awarded annually, but with the private agency offering both a salary advantage and the opportunity to work with a diversity of social and emotional problems, trained social workers scorned public assistance as semi-professional employment at best. Federal support for social work training could produce more social workers; most of them would not wind up working in public assistance. Those few who did were to find that their skilled services might be a welcome supplement to adequate cash relief, but not a substitute for it.

To be fair, there was no easy way for Kennedy and Ribicoff to know that many welfare advisers of the early 1960's were more self-serving than expert. Advice giving in this field was non-competitive; public assistance experts were in short supply. At the time, there were no knowledgeable staff members for the responsible Congressional committees (Ways and Means in the House and Finance in the Senate), no organized client groups save for one in California concerned with old age assistance, no academic specialists outside the schools of social work, no policy evaluation units in the federal agency. There was no system anywhere for assembling and analyzing public assistance information. Information gathering agencies in Washington and on the campuses either avoided the role entirely or provided only selected case information to reenforce preexisting convictions of those who neither needed to be persuaded nor had control over public policy. Until the middle 1960's, public assistance specialists could have organized as a club with only a few dozen members, and an inner circle of half a dozen, most of them veterans of the writing of the Social Security Act. But it was their last hurrah. The 1962 Public Welfare Amendments were underresearched and oversold. They were foisted on an administration concerned about human need, but either reluctant or unable to acknowledge that in relief there is no substitute for money.

Reviewing the reforms

New methods in public assistance in the form of skilled casework services to clients were the first social reforms to be tried in the 1960's. It was their fate also to be the first reviewed, and the results were plain: Casework services produce no economic miracles for poor people. While that conclusion was disappointing enough, especially to the original proponents, the timing was especially unfortunate. The five years between 1962 and 1967 encompassed the period of Congressional approval of legislation dealing with civil rights, federal aid to education, health care, economic development, and poverty. After the euphoria of 1965, there came the second thoughts of 1967. Having exhausted itself with what seemed to be a massive response to the problems of the poor, Congress was in no mood to shrug off the apparent failure of the 1962 "rehabilitation instead of relief, services instead of support" amendments when the program approached the end of its five-year authorization.

The 1967 amendments—the second big crack at welfare policy in the 1960's—turned out to be a mixed bag. Psycho-social services were discredited, yet the theme of services instead of support was not abandoned. The June 1966 report of the Advisory Council on Public Welfare, a council created by HEW Secretary John Gardner pursuant to statute, had urged still more social services, in the manner of the 1962 program. It found no supporters. By now, planning and evaluation activity within HEW was competing with the experience and good intentions of the Department's outside advisers. Realizing that the principal cause—75 per cent, up from 66.7 in 1961—of AFDC dependency continued to be the female-headed family with a live but absent father, Congress and the HEW policy evaluators jointly concluded that modern paths to self-destruction of public relief were hard services: tracking down fathers who had deserted; educating poor females—married and unmarried—on how to avoid conception; testing for employability; job counseling and referral of AFDC's adults; and caring for their children.

Self-destruction has come no closer to accomplishment after five years of hard services. Instead, the operation of the 1967 legislation provides evidence that while work may be a way to supplement welfare for some of the AFDC population, work cannot substitute for welfare for most of that population.

In the middle of 1967, when the House Ways and Means Committee was in executive session considering welfare legislation, aid to families with dependent children (ADC had by then been so re-named, a change that bothered no one, helped no one, and neither strengthened nor weakened the program) recipient totals reached five million, up 1.5 million from 1962. Ways and Means turned its attention to the absent father syndrome. Dead fathers, incapacitated fathers, jailed fathers, unemployed fathers were not able to support their families. Whether absent fathers could provide support was unknown. The Committee's Chairman, Rep. Wilbur Mills, had been a willing sponsor of the 1962 program. Now, he was troubled by unchecked AFDC growth, and particularly by state failure to locate and obtain support from absent fathers. "In 1962, we gave them options," he explained to the House, but "it takes requirements on the states to reverse these trends."

Actually, Congress unwittingly had done more for the states than give them options. State government officials were not up in arms about welfare costs pressures because their troubles had been eased by a seemingly unimportant floor amendment added to the Medicare-Medicaid legislation in 1965. The preexisting federal-state cost-sharing formula in AFDC provided for federal assumption of five sixths of the first $18 of average payment plus between 50 and 65 per cent (varying inversely with state wealth) of the next $14. All sharing had stopped after $32, a figure that was exceeded by 30 states in mid-1967. (In the three adult categories, the comparable cost-sharing figures were $31 of the first $37 plus 50 to 65 per cent of the next $38.) Under Senator Thomas Kuchel's amendment, which was passed off as primarily a bookkeeping convenience for his state, those states operating an approved medical assistance (Medicaid) plan had the option of using the federal medical assistance percentage—varying from 50 to 83 per cent with no maximum—for the federal share of all public assistance categories also. The option became especially attractive for industrial states whose benefit levels exceeded the statutory maximum for sharing. Its use surely served to dull temporarily what otherwise might have been intense pressure to reduce relief rolls or to effect drastic fiscal changes in the federal-state public assistance relationship.

Soft services and hard

In 1967, however, Mills gave the states a requirement they could not accept: a freeze on federal matching funds for AFDC cases attributable to desertion or illegitimacy. In addition to the high monetary costs to the states of such a freeze, the implication that a financial penalty would overcome alleged state foot-dragging troubled some state welfare officials whose experience suggested it was not cost-effective to pursue absent fathers. In too many cases, those fathers were likely to be unskilled and low-paid or already supporting another family, or both. Other groups, including the newly organized National Welfare Rights Organization, viewed it as palpably discriminatory to single out from the whole class of dependent children those with a parent absent from the home. After very considerable hesitation, President Johnson delayed the freeze. President Nixon was to delay it again, and ultimately the Nixon Administration wisely and quietly arranged for its repeal. Wilbur Mills's freeze on federal payment was less a rational than an emotional reaction to continued concern about absent fathers. The concern and the reaction are understandable in view of the apparent growth of the particular phenomenon. That cooler heads overcame the emotional reaction is also understandable. What ultimately became a non-freeze nevertheless had important symbolic significance. By legislating it in the first place, Congress acknowledged unmarried and deserted mothers to be the critical welfare problem and implied that the states could solve the problem. By backing away from imposing the fiscal penalty on the states, two administrations acknowledged that the states had not carelessly ignored a solution, but that there was no solution.

Other aspects of the Great Society's legislative response to welfare growth, as embodied in the 1967 amendments, stemmed more from rational calculation than from emotion. Self-support of AFDC clients was the point of departure for these calculations. An HEW Task Force on Services for Self-Support of AFDC Recipients was plugging away on the self-support theme even as Ways and Means brought its hard services bill to the House floor. As if to underscore the Department's decision to adopt a new approach to dependency, HEW's Welfare Administration itself was reorganized out of existence, superseded by a Social and Rehabilitation Service whose director accepted with pleasure a *Wall Street Journal* characterization of her as "a diligent disciple of work." The Congressional committee reports may have sounded a little harsher than the bureaucrats in HEW might have liked, but there was no basic disagreement between Congress and the Administration over the self-support principle.

Self-support as reform

Self-support became the welfare reformers' theme in 1967 after the hapless program adopted five years earlier had run its course. While the latter had no particular effect on who got how much relief, the former, by reducing the 100 per cent tax on earnings of AFDC clients, itself contributed to an expansion that has finally brought public relief benefits to most low-income, female-headed families.

In pursuit of the new self-support goal, the 1967 legislation broke with the keep-mother-in-the-home tradition that had been adhered to as an act of faith in AFDC from its beginning. Instead, a no-nonsense work-incentive program (WIN) was adopted as the wave of the future. As the original ADC program undertook to substitute support for starvation, and the 1962 Kennedy-Ribicoff welfare amendments hoped to substitute social services for support, the 1967 program emphasized self-support rather than social services. After 30 years, employment incentives for AFDC mothers and day care for their children were to be installed as hard-line approaches to family dependency. According to the new wisdom, since as many as 13 per cent of AFDC mothers were employed part time or full time without an emphasis on employment services, a substantially larger number should be employable after job counseling, training, and referral. As for children, care outside the home might even be advantageous for them. Witness Head Start, then at the peak of its popularity.

And the whole process would be sweetened by requiring the states to disregard a portion of client earnings—the first $30 a month and one third of all other earnings—in computing benefits, so that there would be a real economic incentive as well as a supposed psychic advantage to working.

Once again, the hoped-for welfare decline proved elusive. Counseling, training, and referral aspects of WIN had virtually no depressing effect on the relief rolls. As the 1970's began, nearly 1.5 million welfare recipients had been screened for possible referral to the WIN program. Only 20 per cent were found appropriate for referral, three fourths of whom were actually referred. Just 10 per cent of those referred were employed. Early explanations for the failure of WIN spoke to different interpretations among the states of "appropriate for referral," and to conflicts of philosophy between HEW and the Department of Labor. After perfecting amendments designed to settle those problems by limiting exceptions to the general requirement to register under WIN as a qualifying condition for AFDC, and by putting the Labor Department in control, WIN still continued to falter. Subsequent explanations ascribe WIN's failure to rigid Labor Department regulations covering wages, hours, and health and safety standards; to preoccupation with planning for the Nixon Administration's family assistance legislation; and to the perennial absence of coordination.

Since the AFDC population is composed of women with children and without skills, it is hard to believe that any of these implementation problems are as significant as either the absence of jobs at the end of the line or the presence of children in need of care. Neither could be considered an unexpected complication, but neither appears to have been thought through and faced squarely in the early WIN period, let alone before its enactment. A study by the Auerbach Corporation, Labor's own outside evaluators, found that there was little investigation of the labor market to determine where and how jobs could be obtained, how many jobs were available, and how many jobs were likely to become available for WIN enrollees. As Leonard Goodwin's subsequent social-psychological study of work orientations suggests, under these conditions WIN may be counterproductive: Work-oriented enrollees seize the opportunity for training, terminate from WIN only to find that there are no jobs, abandon both the hope and the hunt for employment, and accept welfare more readily than they did before WIN enrollment.

Long before they had a chance to be discouraged by the absence of jobs, some WIN trainees were discouraged by the absence of child care arrangements. Day care was far from a flourishing industry when the self-support amendments gave it an important place in welfare reform. A half-hearted effort incorporated in the 1962 amendments had had no effect. Because it was half-hearted, however, it allowed self-support proponents in the latter years of the decade to seize on the history of Congressional underfinancing and on HEW's ambivalent attitude toward day care as explanations of past failures. As to underfinancing, the $25 million day care authorization adopted in 1962 eventuated between 1962 and 1965 in only $8.8 million in appropriations, none of which was for facilities. Doubts about the HEW commitment to day care were also legitimate. The Children's Bureau was the agency responsible for day care policy and it did not encourage making day care a routine aspect of public assistance. Even after high-level bureaucrats began to accept responsibility for failing to face reality in day care needs, the lower echelons were insisting that the day care decision should be shared by a mother and her social worker, that a mother's desire for the service in order to go to work is not adequate justification for providing it.

Child care and the welfare problem

Head Start changed the nature of the problem by enlisting child development groups on the side of supporters of day care expansion. The dilemma facing welfare reformers was whether to push efforts to move younger mothers—with highest potential for success—toward self-support and ignore opponents of wholesale day care, or to concentrate on older mothers with less chance for success but where the day care issued might be muted. By 1967, two years of experience with Head Start put in jeopardy the old-line insistence on caring for children only in their own homes. Head Start was combining the newest findings in educational psychology with the then current community action philosophy of political liberals. Its beneficiaries were three to five year old children of the poor. What happier arrangement than for mothers to work or to be trained for work while their children were being provided Head Start's important pre-school services, and school age children were being provided comparable after-school services?

But the Head Start model cut two ways. While it increased the attractiveness of pre-school care out of the home, it also introduced expensive components in the form of educational, health, and nutritional benefits. If additional welfare mothers were to be freed for work, benefits for their children could be no less "developmental" than those provided poor children enrolled in Head Start. Any plan to provide less came to be referred to as "merely custodial" care, judged bad for children and an act of discrimination against the poor. Once welfare reform day care picked up the "merely custodial" label, the tie between welfare-policy reformers and child development proponents dissolved. Both groups lost enthusiasm for day care as an element in welfare reform as the absence of safe and sanitary facilities became apparent, as a study by the Westinghouse Learning Corporation cast doubt on the permanence of Head Start gains, as developmental day care programs undertaken as experiments by federal agencies showed costs to hang around the $2,000 per child per year level, and as plans to develop WIN day care simply could not be put into effect. When the Nixon welfare reform program was under scrutiny by the Senate Finance Committee in June 1970, the actual WIN child care total was 61,000 compared to a target of 188,000. Only one fifth of the children in care were in a day care facility, half were cared for in their own homes, one tenth in a relative's home, and the balance were in "other" arrangements—including self-care. Effecting a revolution in parent-child affairs clearly would take more than a manifesto from HEW's policy analysis group.

Those who were skeptical about day care plans embodied in the 1967 amendments had no misgivings about the so-called "30 and a third" earnings disregard in the same legislation. Theretofore, a 100 per cent tax had obtained on virtually all earnings of adult AFDC recipients, a provision dating to the 1930's when it was needed to protect the federal treasury and clients in all categories against political favoritism accorded some clients. First the blind, then the aged category, had been allowed an earnings disregard as a matter of compassion. Later, states were allowed to disregard earnings of AFDC children and allowed to disregard adult income set aside for future needs of a dependent child. Before 1967, however, neither the Administration nor Congress had shown an interest in mandating an AFDC adult disregard. Now it was adopted as an indispensable step along the route to regular employment and self-support. Welfare rights groups embraced the disregard as a provision that could do the client no harm and might make it possible for some AFDC families to live a little better.

In practice, the latter expectation has been confirmed. Sponsors of the disregard simply overestimated the potential of the welfare population. The emphasis on self-support combined with the earnings disregard did not reduce either the numbers or the costs of AFDC, but had the reverse effect. To disregard a portion of earned income means to accept the principle of aid to the working poor. The number of eligible clients increased as small amounts of client earnings were ignored in computing benefits. At the same time, federal pressure pushed states' needs standards closer to actual minimum living costs. Reporting small earnings did not jeopardize welfare benefits. In short, the disregard brought some of the working poor onto the assistance rolls for the first time, and kept on the rolls some clients who might otherwise have been forced off because of self-help efforts. The mandatory disregard was actually no less than a state-administered negative income tax for the AFDC category with state-by-state variations in the minimum guarantee.

Welfare rights and family assistance

So the self-support amendments of the Great Society period helped open the door to welfare growth without being designed to do so. The door opened wider as welfare rights groups spread the message of welfare as a right; as mayors and governors decided to accept the new liberalism rather than chance the consequences of the new militancy; as the legal services movement successfully challenged state efforts to limit eligibility; and as a departing HEW Secretary late in 1968 fired off liberalizing regulations that his successor ratified. The annual rate of growth of the AFDC population rose from a mildly steep seven per cent in 1967 to a staggering 28 per cent only four years later. In the meantime, Daniel P. Moynihan sold Richard Nixon a seemingly more radical proposal for welfare change than anyone had sold either John F. Kennedy or Lyndon Johnson.

Confronted with a choice between passive acceptance of continuing cost increases in the old public assistance program, and aggressive pursuit of an imaginative alternative, Nixon accepted the latter. To preside over uncontrollable increases in a multi-billion dollar domestic program that was invented and nourished by past Democratic administrations, and whose beneficiaries were likely to vote Democratic was a cheerless prospect. "I fear in four years time you really won't have a single distinctive Nixon program to show for it all," Moynihan wrote the President in June 1969. "Therefore I am doubly interested in seeing you go up now with a genuinely new, unmistakably Nixon, unmistakably needed program, which would attract the attention of the world, far less the United States." The program that Nixon later sent up to Congress did attract the attention of the world. In the early days of the battle over family assistance, nothing delighted the President's men more than to quote the London *Economist*'s characterization of the plan as one that ranked in importance with the Roosevelt Social Security proposal of the 1930's. The praise seems somewhat fulsome. Family assistance would have been the logical extension of the income disregard provision already in effect. It would have increased that disregard slightly, fixed a national minimum guarantee level in lieu of separate state standards, and extended income protection to all families with children rather than just those able to qualify for AFDC. But the extended coverage and the improvement in the benefit level in many Southern states would have been dearly bought. Nationally, family assistance, for all the rhetoric, would have left 80 per cent of the AFDC recipients no better off than they already were.

Too little for most liberals and too much for most conservatives, family assistance was out of phase politically: a proposal with which the Great Society would have been comfortable, offered instead by its enemies, and offered after the bloom was off the Great Society. But the loss of family assistance mattered less in 1970 than it would have in 1960, because by 1970 welfare realities were overcoming the need for reform. The explosion of the welfare rolls was at hand, and the explosion of the rolls, as Richard Cloward has put it, was the reform.

Welfare growth as social reform

Transformation of public assistance during the 1960's from a low-paying, restrictive program that, after 25 years, reached only a fraction of poor families without fathers to a program providing improved benefit amounts to most single-parent families in need and to a substantial number of families with incapacitated or unemployed fathers was less the result of systematic intervention in welfare policy than it was the indirect consequence of intervention in other areas of social policy. Within the limits of public assistance policy itself, the earnings disregard did make it possible for some clients who might previously have worked themselves into ineligibility to stay on the rolls and enjoy a higher total income. But the massive additions that brought AFDC recipient totals up from 4.4 million in 1965 to eight million in 1970 to 11 million in 1973 have their explanations in other social and social policy developments: civil rights, civil disorder, legal services, medical services, community action.

The welfare poor became a major beneficiary of the militancy of the 1960's without contributing appreciably to that militancy. As a direct outgrowth of the civil rights movement, for the first time in the program's 30 years AFDC clients were organized. Moreover, the relatively small number of activists mobilized by George Wiley's National Welfare Rights Organization surely would have been ignored or dispersed if mayors and governors had not been so fearful of civil disorders. In fact, welfare clients did not riot, loot, or burn; but no big-city mayor could be confident enough to act on that belief. When welfare rights leaders asked for what the statutes authorized, most political leaders in the late 1960's found it judicious to comply. Both earlier and again more recently, they were wont to plead municipal or state poverty, and to call for zero welfare growth.

The very fact of client organization, without regard to tactics, itself contributed to growth. For the first three decades of public assistance, welfare status was a badge of shame. While it would be foolish to argue that client organization changed that judgment even among recipients themselves, organization facilitated open discussion of benefits, of eligibility status, of arbitrary and capricious administrative behavior, and of remedies. Some who were denied benefits learned to appeal. Some who had never known of AFDC learned from friends and neighbors. Some who had migrated to the cities in search of self-support opportunities they never found were guided to the welfare department rather than the bus stations.

The economic opportunity program, not constructed with the AFDC client as a planned major beneficiary, nevertheless led to important welfare expansion through its legal services program. Direct challenges were mounted to such federal, state, and local barriers to welfare eligibility as residence requirements and man-in-the-house rules, challenges that achieved an extraordinarily high rate of success. Outreach—the active search for potential beneficiaries of a public benefit—resulted in growth of the public assistance rolls. Do-it-yourself welfare information pamphlets ("Your Right to Welfare") were prepared at legal services centers and distributed through both local welfare rights groups and community action agencies. Had there been no civil rights movement and no Economic Opportunity Act, there would have been no expansion of public assistance in the 1960's, just as there had been none in the 1940's and the 1950's.

Public assistance flourished in the 1960's, in the sense of embracing much more of its target population than had ever before been the case, partly because it was in place and ready to benefit from the new wave of social concern for the disadvantaged. No effort had to be expended in framing a legislative package and in moving it through the Congress. Aid to dependent children did not have to be adopted as an acceptable federal purpose as model cities and depressed area development and aid to education and medical care for the aged had to be so adopted, with consequent heavy expenditures of political capital on just passing the bill. Similarly, the public assistance administrative apparatus was in place, readily able to move more checks to more people if so instructed.

But building on a program-in-place turned out to produce complications as the Nixon Administration sought to rationalize relief policy with, as Moynihan put it, "cold cash." The "discovery" of hunger in the 1960's had led to revival of the dormant, but previously used, program of food stamps. Slower than AFDC in its initial expansion, the food stamp program accelerated directly with the growth of social concern over hunger and malnutrition. The Department of Agriculture responded to its critics by mounting a massive food stamp campaign. Ultimately, stamps developed an independent constituency and an independent life. That separate relief system stands as an unplanned major barrier to welfare simplification.

The lesson is that reform follows reality. To the extent that welfare reform involved perfecting a mechanism that would simplify the system and minimize the costs of public charity, virtually all welfare-policy change since 1961 has been counterproductive. To the extent that welfare reform involved recognizing and relieving dependency, policies pursued in the 1960's effected that purpose. Paradoxically, the latter occurred in the face of persistent efforts to achieve the former. While the planners are frustrated, the welfare poor are better off.

4

What
does it do for the poor?
— a new test
for national policy

ROBERT J. LAMPMAN

J OHN F. Kennedy's slogan was, "Let's get the country moving again." He sought to reduce unemployment and increase the rate of economic growth without causing inflation or a deficit in the balance of payments. His emphasis was on efficiency and, although he did press for such New Deal-Fair Deal measures as civil rights, health insurance, and aid to education, his Administration placed higher priority on an investment tax credit, research and development outlays, and, above all, a Keynesian tax cut designed to spur economic recovery.

Lyndon B. Johnson's vision of a "Great Society" emphasized equity. He foresaw a nation where no one would have to live in poverty and all would have sufficient money income, public services, and civil rights to enable them to participate with dignity as full citizens. It would be an affluent society, but also a compassionate one, one that called for sacrifice by the majority to bring out the talents and willing cooperation of previously submerged and disadvantaged minorities.

It is right to call the war on poverty—first enunciated in President Johnson's State of the Union message and promptly endorsed by Congress in the Economic Opportunity Act of 1964—a logical extension of Franklin D. Roosevelt's Social Security Act and Harry S.

Truman's Employment Act. It is also correct to identify it as in the general pattern laid down by the more advanced welfare states of Western Europe. But no other President and no other nation had set out a performance goal so explicit with regard to "the poor." No one else had elevated the question, "What does it do for the poor?" to a test for judging government interventions and for orienting national policy.

This question served as a flag for the great onrush of social welfare legislation commencing in 1965 and the consequent expansion in the role of the federal government. When poverty became a matter of national interest, Washington moved into fields where state and local governments had held dominant if not exclusive sway up to that time. This movement was manifested by the enactment of such measures as Medicare and Medicaid, and aid to elementary and secondary education. It led to uniform national minimum guarantees in the food stamp program, in cash assistance to the aged, blind, and disabled (under the title of Supplemental Security Income), and in stipends for college students in the form of Basic Educational Opportunity Grants—all adopted in the first Administration of President Richard M. Nixon. Other interventions—notably equal opportunity legislation, the provision of legal services for and on behalf of the poor, and "community action"—made little impact on the budget, but reflected new efforts by the federal government to be an integrative force in national life.

Measuring poverty

The scope of the American poverty problem and ways to measure progress against it were originally stated in terms of income. "Poverty" was quite arbitrarily defined as pre-tax money income below $3,000 in 1962 prices ($4,300 in 1973 prices) for a non-farm family of four. Perhaps this is no more arbitrary or unreasonable than the official definition of "unemployment," and like the latter, it enabled a quantification—in this case, of the changing number of poor people and hence of progress toward the goal of eliminating poverty. No target date was ever set for reaching this goal.

In the late 1940's, over 45 million persons, almost a third of the population, had incomes below the poverty line. This number was reduced in the period 1950-1956 by about one million per year. It stood, then, at about 39 million through the late 1950's and early 1960's. After that period of recurring recession, the more favorable developments of 1962-1969 brought the number in poverty down by almost two million per year to under 25 million persons (about 12 per cent of the total population), where it stands today. The typical family in poverty has a "poverty income gap" of $1,000 (i.e., its cash income falls about $1,000 below the poverty line); the gaps of all poor families add up to $12 billion, which is less than one per cent of the gross national product.

Some neo-conservative critics have faulted the anti-poverty theme as committing the government to an unattainable goal. As Aaron Wildavsky phrases it in a recent article in *Commentary*, "Part of the secret of winning, as any football coach knows, lies in arranging an appropriate schedule. Governmental performance depends not only on ability to solve problems, but on selecting problems government knows how to solve." However, eliminating income poverty, as defined, may be rated a "set up" on the schedule, since it was reasonable to believe in 1964 that increases in per capita real income, stable unemployment, and an evolving set of cash transfer programs would all contribute to achievement of the goal. As of 1973, the goal is virtually achieved. The "poverty income gap" will be reduced by the Supplemental Security Income plan, which goes into effect in January, and could be further cut by merely "cashing out" the $2 billion worth of food stamp benefits that are in the current budget.

Unfortunately, the measure of poverty employed was not well articulated with the larger vision of a Great Society and the several components of policy directed toward its building. There is a hiatus between the measure and the policy in that expenditures targeted to the poor, but taking the form of non-cash or in-kind benefits (e.g., food stamps, health care, or education benefits), do not show up in family money income. It is more unfortunate that the goal with respect to these in-kind benefits was never made precise. Was it simply more for the poor than they had been receiving, or was it access to (or consumption of) a per capita quantity of selected goods and services equal to the national average? Or was it—and here the goal would be most expansive—the achievement by the poor of health (as indicated by morbidity and mortality experience) and educational attainment (as indicated by school test scores) in line with norms for the non-poor population? We will comment later on the fact that such goals—which would require compensatory expenditures and new and untried methods—were read into the several programs by both proponents and opponents. We will also return later to a third anti-poverty goal, namely increased political participation by the poor. But more to the point here is the failure to establish definitions of "health care poverty" and "education poverty" and the like in any way comparable to the income poverty definition.

The rise in social welfare spending

We can say that if the import of the anti-poverty theme was to expand the broad set of "social welfare expenditures under public programs" and to get more cash and in-kind benefits for the poor, then it must be identified as a huge success. Social welfare expenditures are defined by the Social Security Administration as those for health, education, welfare services, and income maintenance. Such expenditures by the federal, state, and local governments went up almost fourfold between 1960 and 1972—from $52 billion to $193 billion (see Table 1). They were 10.6 per cent of GNP in 1960 and 17.6 per cent in 1972. By far the greater part of this rise happened after 1965. The average annual increase in real terms was only five

TABLE 1. *Social Welfare Expenditures Under Public Programs (Federal, State, and Local)*[1]

	1960	1965	1970	1972
	(IN BILLIONS OF DOLLARS)			
Total	52.3	77.2	146.0	192.7
Social insurance	19.3	28.1	54.8	75.1
Public aid	4.1	6.3	16.5	25.6
Health and medical programs	4.5	6.2	9.8	12.4
Veterans programs	5.5	6.0	9.0	11.5
Education	17.6	28.1	50.8	61.1
Housing	.2	.3	.7	1.4
Other social welfare	1.1	2.1	4.4	5.7

[1] Source: Alfred M. Skolnik and Sophie R. Dales, "Social Welfare Expenditures, 1971-72," *Social Security Bulletin*, December 1972, Table 1.

per cent between 1960 and 1965. Since 1965 that rate of increase has been nine per cent. To keep this in perspective, it should be noted that social welfare expenditures have risen more rapidly than GNP in every decade. The post-1965 record is one of unusually sharp transition toward a "mature" welfare state. Perhaps the full measure of this trend is that public *and* private spending now devote 9.0 per cent of GNP to income maintenance, 7.6 per cent to health care, 6.8 per cent to education, and 1.4 per cent to welfare and other services—a grand total of about 25 per cent of GNP. (This contrasts with about eight per cent for the military.) A rising share—now 40 per cent—of all public and private social welfare expenditures is funded via the federal government, and a considerable part of the private spending is encouraged by income tax exclusions (e.g., employer contributions to health insurance) and deductions.

It is, of course, impossible to say what part of the acceleration of social welfare expenditures would have occurred without the marking out of the poor as a target for federal attention. The declaration of war on poverty coincided with the realization that federal budget revenues were rising faster than projected expenditures for ongoing programs. So there were annual "fiscal dividends" to be claimed for tax cuts, general revenue sharing with the states, or new programs. In the event, some of these dividends were claimed by the military; some went to federal tax cuts (particularly in 1964, 1965, 1969, and 1971); but the great bulk of them went to social welfare programs. Yearly federal outlays for older income maintenance programs went up from $28 billion in 1963 to $75 billion in 1973, while spending on new Great Society programs went up from $2 billion to $36 billion. Of the latter total, $20 billion provided goods and services directly to people and $16 billion was in the form of grants to state and local governments and non-profit institutions. These increases came in large part out of forgone tax cuts, although Social Security payroll tax rates and state and local tax rates were raised. This meant that overall the nation's tax system became somewhat less progressive. The new federal programs claimed only part of rising incomes and few families experienced direct cuts in their standard of living because of them. Almost everybody was better off and almost nobody was worse off—truly, a Great Society!

By no means all of these increased expenditures went to families in income poverty, or even to families who would be poor without receipt of benefits. Out of the 1972 total public social welfare expenditures of $193 billion, only $25 billion was income-tested in a way designed to confine it to poor families. Many of the non-income-tested benefits, however, go to poor families. Eighty billion dollars of the total was in the form of cash transfers to persons. A rough guess, based on a 1967 survey, is that about $35 billion of this $80 billion went to the pre-transfer poor. In the earlier year, cash transfers went to 40 per cent of all households and took 6.1 million households out of income poverty. The pre-transfer poverty income gap was $24.3 billion; post-transfer it was $9.7 billion. These cash transfers are heavily weighted, of course, toward the aged and disabled and do little for the poverty of families headed by able-bodied men under 65.

Of the $193 billion of social welfare expenditures, $113 billion takes the form of goods and services. If 10 per cent of the education services, half of the health services, half of veterans services, and most of a wide range (totaling $14 billion) of housing, social services, and food stamps go to the poor, then about $32 billion of non-cash benefits can be credited to the poor. As we noted earlier, none of these non-cash benefits are counted in the income measure of poverty, and no increases in them or in direct taxes to pay for them figure directly in the recorded reduction of poverty. It is of at least related interest that the pre-transfer poor have about three per cent of "original" income, but after all social welfare expenditures and off-setting taxes are taken into account, they have about eight per cent of "post-tax money and in-kind income."

Poverty and income inequality

We have asserted that two anti-poverty goals have been accomplished. The number of people in income poverty has been reduced, and public social welfare expenditures carrying disproportionate benefits for the poor have been substantially increased. Numerous critics claim, however, that these two achievements are relatively insignificant and that a "real" war on poverty would aim for far greater victories. Let us consider two of these claims: first, that inequality of income should be substantially narrowed; and second, that benefits for the poor must be not simply large but also "effective" in meeting the needs of the poor.

Some economists and others have wanted to set the poverty line equal to a constant fraction (say, one half) of the national median of family incomes. By that standard there has been virtually no reduction of poverty in recent decades. Setting such a standard is essentially the same as saying the goal should have been to increase the share of total money income received by the lowest fifth of households—which is about five per cent—and thereby to narrow the overall inequality of income. By this measure, inequality has failed to decline in the United States since the end of World War II and is higher than in several Western European nations.

To change the lowest fifth's share of income from five to, say, 10 per cent of total income is a demanding goal and would require strong measures. Senator George S. McGovern's $1,000 per person refundable tax credit, which called for a thoroughgoing change of the income tax base with all income subject to a 33 per cent tax rate, would only have changed the share of the lowest fifth by about two percentage points. Those points would, of course, have had to be offset by reducing the post-tax income share of the top 80 per cent of families from 95 to 93 per cent. Increasing governmental outlays for the poor and assuring them new rights to jobs and political participation mean that some of the non-poor have to give something up, and many discussions of the poverty program are flawed by not being explicit about this. In practice, some violations of vertical and horizontal equity do occur. Some of the pre-transfer poor have more combined money income and in-kind benefits than do some of the non-poor. This kind of leap-frogging of poor over non-poor in income ranking—and some unhappiness with poverty programs because of it —might not have happened if the total income distribution had been more clearly in view.

However, comprehending the distribution of money income and its dynamics is a bewildering challenge. It is remarkable that this distribution shows little change over the decades (see Table 2), in spite of staggering changes in the size and composition and geographic location of the population; the size and role of the family (with the decline of the three-generation extended family); the pattern of participation in the labor force (with men starting to work later and retiring earlier and more women working away from home); the decline of farming and self-employment and the rise of service industries, government employment, and professional and

TABLE 2. *Shares of "Total Money Income" Received by Fifths of Families, Ranked by Income*

FAMILIES	1950	1970
Lowest fifth	4.5	5.5
Second fifth	12.0	12.0
Third fifth	17.4	17.4
Fourth fifth	23.5	23.5
Highest fifth	42.6	41.6

technical occupations; a rise in the median income of black, relative to white, families; the increase in taxes and government spending; the growth of fringe benefits; and the conversion of ordinary income into capital gains. The explanation must be that some of these changes offset others in such a way as to sustain a constancy in the shares of the several fifths, but we have no good explanation as to why the offsetting changes should balance out so neatly.

The intricacies of income distribution

One matter confusing to many people is that, although there has been no shift in the distribution over time, there is a considerable amount of redistribution every year. That is, there is a spread between the lowest fifth's share of earnings and property and their share of total income after taxes and transfers. Ben Okner at the Brookings Institution calculates that federal income and payroll taxes and cash transfers alone raise the share of the lowest fifth from 1.7 per cent of "original" income to 6.3 per cent of "income after redistribution." In spite of—and to a certain extent because of—this rather extensive redistribution in one year, inequality has not lessened over time. We say *because of* since there can be no doubt that social security and public assistance benefits have enabled old people and women heading families to withdraw from the labor force and to live and be counted separately as low-income households.

It is not clear that the percentage shares of "total money income" going to fifths of "families" measure faithfully whatever changes in economic inequality may have taken place. Consider all the things left out of account—home production, imputed rent from owner-occupied housing and consumer durables, non-money benefits from employers and governments, realized and unrealized capital gains and losses, leisure, direct taxes paid, work expenses such as child care costs, and disamenities experienced as a worker and as a consumer. Numerous adjustments to the crude income data would have to be made to get a true ranking of "richer to poorer" persons. These might include adjustment for family size, number of workers, part-year workers, variability of income, and net worth. Tax and welfare policies are often keyed to highly refined and adjusted definitions of "income" and "family," which take account of legislative determination of "reasonable classification" in ways that the crude income rankings do not.

The 12 per cent of the population now counted as being in income poverty are quite different in composition from the persons in the lowest fifth of families. The latter group now includes all those with incomes under $5,500. As an example of the difference, aged couples with $3,000 or more of income are not below the poverty line, but many of them are, of course, in the lowest fifth. A large family with $6,000 is not in the lowest fifth but is below the poverty line. It is a matter for judgment as to whether the poverty ranking, which makes adjustments for family size and holds to a constant market-basket of goods in setting the income cut-off, yields a more acceptable target group for governmental policy than does the lowest fifth. In any event, it would not be easy to get a consensus among experts on how best to measure overall income inequality and what targets should be set for changing it. The income poverty measure and goal doubtless have more public support than would any particular measure and goal which start from the thought that government should "manage" the whole income distribution.

Perhaps some of the difficulty arises from lack of awareness of the facts of income distribution. Few people seem to realize or accept their actual ranking in the income distribution. How many people with combined family incomes of $30,000 realize that they are not "middle class," but are actually in the top five per cent of the distribution? Although economists are wont to look to an index of inequality of income shares in comparing the fairness of result of one political economy with that of another, this particular measure has never had any standing among political leaders. None has rallied political troops with a plan to change the shares of the several fifths in a stated way. Concern with income inequality has been more indirect; the focus has been on "fairness" in taxation, relief for those "unable" to work, replacement of income lost without fault, sharing the cost of extraordinary expense, and helping people get a minimum provision of "essentials" in order to assure "equality of opportunity." It is interesting to note that advocates of such schemes as progressive income taxes and social security often deny that they are concerned with income redistribution. These have been more acceptable political approaches to equity questions than have wide sweeps to "correct" the distribution of income as such. The goal of eliminating poverty is a modest addition to the array of apparently politically useful rationales for redistribution.

Economic inequality among persons is immensely complicated. This explains why it is possible for people to reach contradictory conclusions about what is happening on the inequality front in America. In the last 10 years there was no significant change in the distribution of "total money income" as it is conventionally measured, but there *was* a great drop in the percentage of people living in "income poverty." There was no increase in the progressivity of the overall tax system, but there *was* a considerable increase in public money for the poor. Further, there *was* some narrowing of inequality in the consumption of food and medical care, and perhaps of housing, educational services, and public recreational facilities as well.

Thus, many critics have contributed to the feeling that the anti-poverty goal and programs in pursuit of it have been unworthy because they did not seek a more fundamental change in the distribution of income. Another group has fed the belief that poverty programs have failed because they did not meet new standards of "program effectiveness" that were introduced after 1964. The poverty theme and program-planning methodology both came into the social programs part of the federal budget at the same time—and both with the enthusiastic support of the same high-level appointees of President Johnson. It is ironic that the evaluations and cost-effectiveness studies and experiments started under the Johnson Administration have been used with some success by President Nixon to support his decision to cut back on certain parts of the poverty program.

The escalation of standards

It can be argued that a poverty program is "effective" if it simply channels more money or standardized goods or services to the poor, and thereby brings the level of income and consumption of the poor up to some stated minimums. To the extent that this was the goal of the President and the Congress that enacted the set of related measures, the budget shows considerable success in reaching the goal. But as individual programs came up for budget review they were judged against quite different goals.

Any program will, of course, get a low score on a cost-effectiveness basis if the goals are set high enough and the constraints (or side-effects to be avoided) are numerous enough. So the key to understanding what a low score means is to look at the goals and where they come from. Charles L. Schultze, Edward R. Fried, Alice M. Rivlin, and Nancy H. Teeters comment on this topic in their Brookings publication, *Setting National Priorities: The 1973 Budget*:

> It is no longer enough for politicians and federal officials to show that they have spent the taxpayers' money for approved purposes; they are now being asked to give evidence that the programs are producing results. . . . In the 1960's . . . people began asking more of the federal government. First, a variety of new programs were enacted, many of them designed to provide direct services to people, especially poor people. Poverty was to be reduced not just by giving people cash income but by providing medical care, pre-school programs, job training, legal

services, compensatory education, and opportunities for community action. . . . Along with the new activities came the gradual development of new and far more ambitious standards for judging federal programs. For the first time, federal officials—indeed all government officials— were being asked to produce "performance measures" as evidence that their efforts were achieving results. Administrators of education pro- grams were asked, not just to show that money was spent for teachers' salaries or books or equipment, but for evidence that children were learning more. . . . Even transfer programs were judged in a new light. It was not enough to distribute food stamps to a specified number of people. Attention was focused on measurement of nutrition or malnu- trition. It was not enough that Medicare and Medicaid paid medical bills for the poor and the aged. Attention was focused on the quality of care and the effect of the federal programs on the price of care for the rest of the population. (pp. 449, 451).

This is an intriguing statement by key members of the Johnson Administration. Schultze was Director of the Bureau of the Budget and Rivlin was Assistant Secretary of Health, Education, and Wel- fare. In those roles they were foremost among those asking for "performance measures" as evidence that the programs were "achiev- ing results." "Results" meant not simply that the poor were getting the same quality of educational and health services as the non-poor, but that these services were meeting some new tests of effectiveness that had never before been applied. In this exercise, the poor served as pawns in contests to reform all governmental policies, contests in which the best became the enemy of the good. Appraisals of the budget against poverty became entangled with discoveries that the links between educational spending and learning, and between medical care outlays and health, are not too clear.

Special circumstances in the development of the war on poverty may explain some of this escalation of standards. At the outset the policy was one of "let many flowers bloom," since there was no firm methodology as to what poverty—other than income poverty—was, and no consensus on preferred methods for dealing with it. The Office of Economic Opportunity (OEO) was charged with re- sponsibility for evaluating the role of existing anti-poverty programs, devising alternatives, encouraging innovation, demonstrating and experimenting with previously untried schemes, and advising the President how best to allocate given levels of anti-poverty funds. This meant that more programs were initiated on a tentative, pilot, and small-scale basis than could be funded nationwide. Hence some programs had to be shot down.

The statement of rigorous goals and new methods for evaluating performance specified by the Program Planning Budgeting System were built into the new governmental programs more readily than into the old ones. R. Sargent Shriver manned many key OEO positions with experts from the Department of Defense and its satellite Rand Corporation, where program-planning budgeting had flowered. Furthermore, as time went on, the evaluators developed their own preferences for inclusion in the anti-poverty budget and were comparing a range of rival programs against a perhaps untried ideal. Thus some reached the conclusion that the Aid to Families with Dependent Children program was a "failure" because a negative income tax was a better alternative. Aids to existing schools were found to be unsatisfactory because a radical transformation of education via a voucher system was envisioned as more desirable. This kind of competition, which was built into the operation, no doubt encouraged the public to view anti-poverty programs as uniquely questionable. Perhaps the verdict would have been more favorable if a new set of non-tentative programs could have been established at one blow and put into operation—as was the case with the Social Security Act of 1935—before program-planning budgeting was brought in, so that critical evaluations could have been produced more even-handedly across the complete range of government operation.

It is important to make the distinction between "effective" programs and "efficiently managed" programs. An effective program is one which achieves a stated purpose, sometimes in spite of a degree of mismanagement. Some efficiently managed programs fail to achieve a stated purpose (i.e., to be effective) because they are not well-designed or because no design would achieve the purpose. Nothing we have said above is meant to condone corrupt, sloppy, slow, or misguided execution of government programs. The introduction of a considerable number of separate programs with novel purposes—some of which involved several federal departments, state and local governments, and private contractors—stretched the skills and powers of managers. Some observers see the problem as more fundamental than lack of management skills. They conclude that the federal government cannot satisfactorily reach poor families via such cumbersome intermediaries. If poverty is a national problem, does not its amelioration require direct federal administration? Alternatively, if a particular anti-poverty purpose cannot be efficiently managed via federal guidelines to state and local governments, should that purpose be abandoned to the vagaries of general and special revenue sharing? These are not easy questions. The Nixon Administration has proposed to virtually federalize public assistance and at the same time to de-federalize manpower training.

Perhaps we should regard these issues not as signs of failure of the poverty program, but as indications of the problems of success. The goal of reducing poverty has been established, substantial resources have been committed (and more are likely to be); the problem now is how to rationalize and manage the use of these resources, by dealing with overlaps of programs and integrating programs for the poor with those for the non-poor.

Equity and economy

In addition to the program-by-program analysis of effectiveness and management efficiency referred to above, the evolution of the federal government's role against poverty has forced two other critical issues forward. Both are potentially explosive as equity issues and as "budget busters." One issue arises out of Congressional willingness to emphasize new in-kind benefits for the poor, to establish high standa ds for them, and then to *underfund* them so that few of those poten'ially eligible can in fact get such benefits. Consider what would happen if Congress managed tax laws in a similar manner! For example, child care standards are set at over $2,000 per year per child, which is more than most non-poor working mothers are willing to pay for such care; part-subsidy for child care may extend to families well above the poverty line, but the benefits are in fact distributed almost randomly. Currently, about $1.5 billion is allocated to day care, but many who are eligible cannot find places, and some who are poor consume more of the service than do most of those who are not poor. To straighten these equity issues out will require either a great deal of extra money—perhaps as much as $15 billion a year—or a sharp reduction in the cost of each child care place. Similar problems are to be found in housing—public low-rent housing may cost the government more than most near-poor families spend on housing and it is available for only a small fraction of all the poor. Rent assistance and rent supplements tied to specifically approved new construction are not much more equitable. About $2 billion now goes to these three programs. Again, to design a replacement that would produce an equitable result poses the choice between expanding the number of beneficiaries and cutting back on the level of maximum benefit per family. Problems akin to this are found in public job creation, medical care, food stamps, and college scholarships.

The second issue arising out of the achievement of anti-poverty goals as stated 10 years ago is: How many income-conditioned cash and in-kind benefits can we offer simultaneously? If Medicaid and child day care and housing and food stamps and college scholarships and cash public assistance are each made more equitable—that is, fully funded at a uniform national level—and if all eligible persons below some moderate cut-off income level (say, twice the poverty line) take advantage of all of them, then the current federal, state, and local outlays for income-conditioned benefits, which now total $25 billion, will rise by several times that amount. In such a situation, a family headed by a non-worker might have combined benefits of Medicaid with an insurance value of $1,000, a housing allowance worth $1,000, a food stamp bonus worth $1,300, a college scholarship for one youngster worth $1,400, and a cash income of $2,400 (to select the figure offered by Nixon's Family Assistance Plan). This means a combined guarantee of $7,100. But each of the benefits has a take-back rate or a rate at which the benefit falls to zero as earnings or other income rises. This is sometimes called an implicit tax rate. In Aid to Families with Dependent Children it amounts to 67 per cent; in the Basic Educational Opportunity Grant it is 20 per cent; in the food stamp program it is 30 per cent. These tax rates have a way of combining and building a "dependency trap." Hence, even if each of the revised and more equitable benefit programs were to have what is now thought of as a reasonable tax rate, a family might well lose 50 cents in cash benefits, 30 cents in food stamps, 25 cents in housing allowance, 25 cents in health insurance, and 20 cents in college scholarship for every extra dollar earned. In this hypothetical example, the combined tax rate is 150 per cent. This confiscatory rate of take-back of benefits means that a family would have to earn an amount substantially greater than $7,100 before it is really any better off than it would be without work, even if child care subsidies come into play. The fact that a number of benefits in our example are payable to people at twice the poverty line ($8,600 for a family of four) makes millions of non-poor families subject to high cumulative tax rates. If tax rates are lowered on each program, then additional families, who are subject to both payroll tax and income tax, are added to the benefit rolls.

There appear to be only a few ways out of this dilemma. One is to eliminate all but one or two of the enumerated programs and keep the combined guarantee and tax rates low. The other is to convert some of the income-conditioned benefits into non-income-conditioned ones. Thus, to combine these ways, we could trade off food stamps and housing allowances for a higher cash guarantee, and convert Medicaid into universal health insurance. But there seem to be powerful forces at work to expand rather than to contract income-conditioning of benefits, and the separate federal departments and separate Congressional committees tend to respond in an uncoordinated manner to these forces. A subcommittee of the Joint Economic Committee, chaired by Representative Martha Griffiths, is currently studying this problem and may come up with recommendations on how to improve legislative consideration of income-conditioning of benefits.

Participation by the poor

Thus far we have argued that the war on poverty is best interpreted as a logical extension of the liberal welfare state. It was based on a confidence that the poor—especially the well-educated young blacks among the poor—would benefit from a stronger economy. It was also grounded in the belief that the rapidly growing set of health, education, and income maintenance institutions could be extended and adapted to improve the well-being of the poor. Hence, income poverty and poverty in key goods and services could be reduced.

However, a third type of poverty was also recognized, namely, lack of participation, and the remedies for this were not so clear. Indeed, it was not spelled out what participation poverty is, any more than it was detailed what education poverty or health care poverty might be. Some seemed to assume that it was confined to those in income poverty and would be overcome as a by-product of the elimination of the latter. Some argued quite the other way around, that only with the participation of the poor in the planning and execution of anti-poverty programs would the other aspects of poverty be overcome. Like general revenue sharing, participation is advocated as both a preferred means and a desired end.

It was known, of course, that the poor voted less frequently than the non-poor. Voting rights legislation would help on that. Few among the poor were members of unions, cooperatives, or voluntary associations of any kind. Many of them felt they had little influence over what went on in their own neighborhood, to say nothing about policy determination at the national level. Numerous remedies for participation poverty and the feelings of powerlessness were offered. Voluntary organizations, including churches, the Boy Scouts, and community charities, should be encouraged to include the poor not only as "clients" but as full participants. Poor people should be helped to organize as workers, consumers, and clients. New types of unions, tenant associations, and "welfare rights" organizations were to be formed to help people "gain control of their own destinies." But the most unique invention to reduce the powerlessness of the poor was the "community action agency," which was to have a hand in administering some federally funded social welfare efforts at the neighborhood level. These agencies were to facilitate "maximum feasible participation" by members of target neighborhoods, not all of whom were necessarily in income poverty. They were, in effect, a fourth level of government, distinct from state and local units. They were encouraged by OEO to design their own anti-poverty strategies, to adapt standard programs to their own local situations, and to employ and otherwise to involve as many local individuals as they possibly could.

The community action or participation strand of the war on poverty may be evaluated on several levels. One has to do with the effectiveness or efficiency of specific social services delivered in the participatory framework. These differed widely from place to place and year to year. They included such diverse activities as family planning, pre-school education, legal services, recreation, vocational training, and ombudsman services. In some instances, the purposes were inspired by OEO officials who saw community action as a way to go around established federal, state, and local administrations and to try out various "non-bureaucratic" approaches to the delivery of services.

In a detached scientific vein, one must acknowledge that even a discovery of what fails to work against poverty is valuable. The flexibility of this variant of the revenue sharing technique makes it attractive, but the variability of projects defies a summary evalua- tion. Some critics allege that community action was counterproduc- tive in some instances because it promised more than it could deliver, thus setting up expectations that were later frustrated. Others, most notably Edward C. Banfield in his provocative book *The Unheavenly City*, fault community action along with other anti-poverty tech- niques for failing to change the life style of the chronic poor or to stop the anti-social behavior of urban youth who riot, as Banfield puts it, "for fun and profit."

Another question for evaluating community action is whether it improves participation levels for the poor and lessens feelings of powerlessness? There are examples to support any conclusion, but no good scales for measuring how these important variables may have changed over time. Local community action agencies did provide valuable work and leadership experience for many from impover- ished backgrounds. Such techniques as demonstrations, rent strikes, and class action lawsuits were used to protect the rights of some groups. On the other hand, some found that the troubles and risks of taking part in the "politics of the poor" outweighed the gains, and they became even more cynical than they were before about par- ticipation.

On a still different level, one can ask whether the community action approach attracted support from the general public for the major programs against poverty. It did dramatize in human terms what poverty was like in affluent America. It appealed to conservatives on the grounds that welfare services should be tailored to the specific situation and confined to the poor, rather than centralized and uni- versalized. (President Nixon found kind things to say about com- munity action in 1969 only to withdraw his support in 1973.) It offered ways for non-poor volunteers to follow their charitable impulses and to learn about poverty at the grass-roots level. At the same time, some community action leaders or their rivals may have undermined public support for anti-poverty programs by their radi- cal critiques of the "real" causes of poverty and the "crisis of a sick society" which it supposedly represented. Perhaps it was inevitable in such troubled times that anti-poverty action groups would serve as a forum for a heady brew of social criticism. The fact that community action seemed at times to be working at cross purposes with prevailing institutions and attitudes undoubtedly contributed to confusion and doubt in the minds of many voters.

"What does it do for the poor?"

The efforts of the last 10 years to achieve a society in which no one has to live below a poverty level, in which access to a minimum of certain key goods and services is assured, and in which government invites the political participation of all have been at best partly successful. We have noted, however, that even the successes have been called failures by reference to newer and higher goals which have tended to emerge almost before the ink is dry on the old ones. Eliminating income poverty is not enough; income inequality must be modified. Improving expenditures for goods and services going to the poor is not enough; they must be effective, efficiently managed, and equitable. Allowing the poor to participate in decisions about how to allocate a small part of the nation's anti-poverty budget is not enough; they must be assured full participation in all matters that affect them, and rivals for leadership of the poor must have a chance to be heard.

We have asserted that some of this escalation of goals is evidence not of failure but of the problems of success. But some part of this tendency may be put down to failure to make the goals more specific and limited at the outset. A target date for the elimination of income poverty could have been set. Definitions and measures of poverty with regard to key goods and services and participation could have been offered. Failure to count in-kind benefits in the measure of income poverty and lack of coordination of the target populations for the several programs may have contributed to a feeling of less accomplishment than would otherwise have been the case. In our pluralistic system, goals seldom hold as originally enunciated. The President may announce them only to see Congress modify them in one way, and state and local governments, administrators, courts, outside experts, and participating groups in yet other ways. Goals are likely to run on ahead not only of achievement, but of knowledge of how to achieve them. There is a tendency for planners at the Presidential level to set wide goals and to embrace a variety of sometimes contradictory methods in order to rally a wide spectrum of support. This tendency may explain why anti-poverty efforts have not been confined to a limited set of carefully targeted measures, and why they have not emerged at the expense of—but rather in addition to—other social welfare expenditures.

There is still much unfinished business on the anti-poverty agenda —particularly with regard to families with children. Thus it is still relevant to address new policy with the rude and restrictive challenge, "What does it do for the poor?" What started out under the

anti-poverty flag as an emphasis on social welfare expenditures for
the poor is now enmeshed in efficiency and equity issues involving
much of the population. That flag is not wide enough to symbolize,
for example, the new range of issues associated with Congressional
willingness to set high benefit levels in a series of separate in-kind
programs such as those having to do with food, housing, health care,
job creation, and college scholarships. It seems likely that these programs will pay out the greater part of their benefits to non-poor
people, but will not exclude the remaining poor. Knowledge gained
in the war on poverty should be applied to establishing new priorities
and constraints for the next stage in the development of the American
welfare state.

5

The
uses and limits
of
manpower policy

LLOYD ULMAN

OLICIES that had been billed in
the 1960's as specifics against inflation, unemployment, or poverty can
hardly expect many enthusiastic endorsements today. Certainly, criticism of the so-called manpower policies, which had been touted for
all three jobs at one time or another—and whose financial support
from the federal government had increased tenfold over the decade
—should come as no surprise. On the other hand, the criticism seems
to have come most strongly and with equal fervor from the opposite
ends of the political spectrum; and some readers may wonder whether any policy that has become the target of such wide-angle cross
fire can—like the man who hates children and dogs—be all bad.

Public manpower policies have come to embrace a wide range of
personnel activities, including (but by no means restricted to) counseling, training (in both educational institutions and on the job), the
provision of better and cheaper information to employers and job
seekers, and financial subvention of employers and trainees. Yet this
broad range of activities constitutes only a subset of what a group of
economists in the Swedish Confederation of Trade Unions (or LO),
led by Gösta Rehn and Rudolf Meidner in the early post-War period,
termed "active labor market policies." By the end of the 1940's,
Sweden, like other countries in Western Europe, began to experience

the unemployment-inflation dilemma, which was often posed most acutely during crises in the balance of payments. Since wage determination in Sweden has proceeded under a highly centralized system of collective bargaining, the LO responded to one such crisis by accepting a wage freeze, only to see its collective sacrifice nullified by extra wage increases (or "drift") at the local levels, and a subsequent "wage explosion." This sorry sequence of events—which, unfortunately, was to be replicated in other countries in subsequent years—left the Swedes disenchanted with wage and price controls as an instrument for containing inflation at high levels of employment.

Particularly disillusioned were the trade union leaders. As bargainers, they, like their counterparts in the Employers' Confederation, felt that collective bargaining could be effective only in the presence of employer resistance sufficient to preclude local wage drift. Yet they rejected completely the creation of excess capacity and unemployment as a means of generating such resistance and reducing the rate of inflation. Moreover, as egalitarian Social Democrats, they aimed at a policy of income redistribution through "wage solidarity," or the narrowing of wage differentials through centralized bargaining (among other policies); and such solidaristic bargaining would also be frustrated by local side deals that permitted occupational or industrial groups held back under the central negotiations to restore their traditional favorable differentials.

The Swedish approach

How, then, might what *The Economist* in the early 1950's called the "uneasy triangle" of full employment, price stability, and collective bargaining be made more tolerable? And how, at the same time, might the cause of greater economic equality be served and economic growth be promoted? A hopeful answer begins with the observation that the sum total of unemployment in a country at any point in time is not uniformly distributed among all industries, occupations, and regions, but tends to be concentrated more heavily in some labor markets than in others. Indeed, at levels of unemployment that, while relatively low, are still short of what the public and the policy makers would regard as "full" employment, some markets would even experience shortages (or bottlenecks).

A lower overall unemployment rate could be achieved by conventional measures that would increase aggregate demand through some combination of tax reductions, increased government spending, and easier money. But under such aggregate expansionary measures, demand for labor (and for capital as well) would be increased indiscriminately in bottleneck markets and slack markets alike. This would be undesirable on one and quite possibly two counts. In the first place, while excess supplies of labor would be reduced, the rate of absorption of labor in excess supply might be limited by bottlenecks in other types of labor (used with more plentiful varieties in the same processes of production). Indeed, excess demand would be increased by such blunderbuss measures, as existing bottlenecks grew larger and new ones emerged in markets that previously had been close to a balance between supply and demand. As a result, the rate of inflation would be increased while the economy remained short of its overall employment goal.

To be sure, bottlenecks tend to shrink and disappear as businessmen expand their training programs and seek ways to economize on the use of scarce labor, and also to the extent that consumers find substitutes for goods the prices of which have risen especially rapidly because their rates of production have been retarded by shortages. However, such corrective processes may be associated with (and, indeed, partly rely upon) exceptionally big wage increases for workers in short supply who, if skilled, tend to have relatively high wages to begin with. This would constitute a second reason why a union movement committed to a narrowing of wage differentials would oppose exclusive reliance on general reflationary measures. Such a union movement could, and in fact would, attempt to maintain pre-existing differentials by bringing up the wages of the groups still in plentiful supply, but this would merely accelerate the overall rate of wage and price inflation without redressing the imbalances in various labor markets.

An alternative approach consists of a variety of selective measures that the Swedes have subsumed under the rubric of "active labor market policy." Some active labor market policies would be aimed directly at concentrating a desired increase in demand on the labor-surplus markets—e.g., by financing investment in less developed regions and by the creation of jobs in the public sector and in sheltered workshops for people of relatively low employability. Other labor market policies would be aimed directly at specific areas of excess labor supply by increasing the mobility of labor through manpower policies, including training and relocation assistance. At least in principle, substitution of the laser beam for the blunderbuss would enable a given reduction in unemployment to be secured with a smaller increment in aggregate demand and, therefore, with a lower rate of inflation. At the same time, conditions would be less conducive to wage drift and hence more conducive to the reduction of wage differentials through central bargaining.

The Swedes believed that active labor market policy was superior to wage and price controls under the conditions of excess demand caused by the application of conventional "Keynesian" aggregate demand policy for two broad reasons. In the first place, they felt that employment could be expected to respond more promptly to policies that were aimed directly at the specific loci of unemployment than to general policies that depended more heavily on secondary multiplier or trickle-down effects (although this is not to suggest that large-scale application of selective policies would not also generate secondary effects). In the second place, they saw that wage and price controls under conditions of very high employment frequently fail because they have to work against market forces. Conversely, to the extent that they are able to keep the lid on, controls reduce economic efficiency and inhibit growth. Active labor market policies, on the other hand, should make the market work more effectively than it otherwise would. Left to itself, the wage structure may respond only sluggishly to changes in demand and supply; and workers whose mobility is often impaired by financial as well as other barriers to the acquisition of skills, job information, and geographic relocation tend to respond only sluggishly to changes in the wage structure.

The idea behind active labor market policy generally has been either to redirect market forces, as with some demand policies like regional assistance or public works programs for "the hard-to-employ," or (more frequently) to move the markets more efficiently in the directions indicated by existing concentrations of bottlenecks and unemployment. In all cases, however, the object is to make the market work in the direction desired by the policy maker rather than, as in the case of controls under full employment, to seek to frustrate the operation of a set of preexisting market forces which are left in place under the policy.

A good example might be found in the different means often employed by incomes policy (or direct restraint of money wage and price movements) and manpower policies in pursuing the objective of improving the relative position of low-paid groups. Incomes policy seeks to grant these groups exceptional treatment, or at least partial exemption from the general "norm" for wage increases, but it has often been frustrated when higher-paid groups demanded the same favored treatment for themselves to restore or maintain what they regarded as "equity." Manpower policy, in contrast, should increase the supply of the more highly trained workers relative to the supply of untrained workers. Thus manpower policy should tend to raise the wages of the unskilled by making them relatively scarcer at the same time that it inhibits the rise in wages of the more skilled groups by making them more abundant. To the extent that there has been unsatisfied demand for skilled labor, the policy increases total employment without adding to aggregate demand. (The same strategy was pursued in a related area: The great post-War expansion of college education in Sweden has been motivated in good part by the Social Democratic governments' desire to facilitate income redistribution by increasing the relative size of the highly educated sector of the population.)

The U.S. response to "creeping unemployment"

The United States introduced its modern manpower policies at a later point in time than Sweden, but also at what the Swedes and all Europeans would consider an earlier stage in economic evolution. The federal government began granting financial aid to the states for vocational education during the First World War (under the Smith-Hughes Act of 1917); it established what is now known as the Federal-State Employment Service and also an apprenticeship policy in the 1930's (under the Wagner-Peyser Act of 1933 and the Fitzgerald Act of 1937, respectively). However, it did not directly establish occupational training programs and subsidies until the early 1960's, with the passage of the Area Redevelopment Act in 1961, the Trade Expansion Act in 1962, and most important, the Manpower Development and Training Act (MDTA) that same year. Moreover, when the MDTA was passed, inflation was not a current concern, while unemployment was much more severe in the United States than it was and had been in post-War Europe. In 1961, the first year of recovery from a recession, unemployment averaged 6.7 per cent, and in 1962 it stood at 5.5 per cent, while price levels remained virtually stable.

Nevertheless, these levels of unemployment were diagnosed by some as "structural" in nature. Many people were impressed by the observation that, whereas unemployment in the peak (or final) year of the upswing of 1949-53 had fallen to 2.7 per cent, it went no lower than 4.2 per cent in the peak year of the 1954-57 upswing, and in the following cyclical rise of 1958-60, its downward progress was arrested at 5.1 per cent. Apprehension over "creeping inflation" in the early and middle 1950's had to make room for apprehension over the trend of "creeping unemployment" in the late 1950's and early 1960's.

Concern over creeping unemployment was shared by a fairly odd assortment of bedfellows. At one extreme were the economic conservatives, including those in the Federal Reserve Board and the Treasury, who opposed the tax cuts and other deficit-increasing measures advocated by the "new economists" in the Council of Economic Advisers and the academic community. The former argued that the unemployment was structural in nature and coexisted with job vacancies elsewhere in the economy; hence, expansion of aggregate demand would simply generate more inflation than employment.

At the other extreme were various groups, notably the Ad Hoc Committee on the Triple Revolution, that were mightily impressed by automation. They regarded automation as a radical departure from conventional technology which was causing a quantum jump in the rate of increase in productivity in the economy. Unemployment resulted from two properties of this phenomenon: (a) wide-

spread technological displacement of labor and (b) a growing satiety of demand, caused by the economy's capacity to satisfy existing
private consumer wants more rapidly than (employed) people were
able to develop new wants.

Under such dramatically changed circumstances, unemployment
could not be reduced by fiscal-monetary measures designed to increase the level of private employment because the level of private
employment could not be increased. Demand creation would have
to take the form of public spending, which could increase employment because, it was alleged, non-market communal needs were still
unsatisfied. For the most part, however, unemployment would have
to be reduced, not through the expansion of employment, but by providing the unemployed and the poor with enough income to induce
them to withdraw from (or not to enter) the labor force, i.e., to stop
looking for remunerative employment. A radical redistribution of
income would thus be required, because "the traditional link between jobs and incomes is being broken."

The middle ground of structural diagnosis was mainly occupied by
labor market economists in the Department of Labor, in the trade
union movement, and in the academic community. They were impressed with the decline in the proportions of non-skilled blue-collar
jobs in the economy, and they were deeply apprehensive over technological displacement. Unlike the conservatives, they were not particularly inhibited by the prospect of budget deficits. Nor did their
opposition to the proposed tax cuts—which, it should be noted, was
not shared by all in this group—dwell on the allegedly inflationary
effects of such measures. Rather, it was based on the opinion that
tax cuts could not reduce unemployment to the level of four per cent,
which the Council of Economic Advisers had proclaimed as an "interim target." Like the radical structuralists, the moderates did believe in the efficacy of job creation in the public sector. But they did
not particularly subscribe to the glut hypothesis, and they did believe in the unemployment-reducing potential of retraining programs.
They were the champions of the Manpower Development and Training Act.

The Council's position

It should be noted that the Council was not averse to manpower
policy, although it did reject the structuralists' interpretation of the
economic evidence. It subscribed to the view that the slowdown in
the rate of economic growth and the "creeping unemployment" during the Eisenhower years resulted from failure to maintain adequate
levels of demand in the economy rather than from any *increase* in
the degree of structural unemployment over the preceding decade,
which, it was claimed, did not occur. And the Council reasoned that

the injection of more money demand would be both necessary and sufficient to move the economy from 5.5 per cent unemployment to four per cent unemployment without sacrificing price stability. In essence, these economists claimed that the problem was a "Keynesian" problem and not a "post-Keynesian" problem—and, it might be added, they had their hands full teaching the Keynesian lesson about unbalanced budgets to parts of the Administration, to the Congress, and to the public at large. At the same time, they were far from oblivious to the trade-off problem. However, they addressed it through the advocacy of incomes policy (or wage and price "guideposts"). Hence they implicitly took issue with the Swedes who had regarded incomes policy as unnecessary when the economy is operating well below capacity, as well as an inferior competitor to active labor market policy under full capacity utilization.

Although the various structuralist arguments were presented with less than compelling rigor, they did call attention to certain phenomena and they did foreshadow some concepts which were later to assume considerable significance for the development of manpower policy in this country. (We shall return to this point.) Meanwhile, however, two events—or rather one non-event and one event— tended to cast some doubt on their analysis of the unemployment problem and on their policy prescription. The non-event was the failure of the manpower administrators to uncover significant numbers of skilled workers who had been displaced from their jobs by technological change and who, as a consequence, were suffering prolonged spells of unemployment. By 1963, according to Stanley Ruttenberg, then Economic Advisor to the Secretary of Labor, "it was already evident that we were working on the wrong woodpile."

The event which did occur was the enactment of major tax cuts and the development of an inflation-free upswing that lasted until 1965 when the interim target of four per cent unemployment was reached. This association sufficed to vindicate recourse to broad macroeconomic policy for the purpose at hand in the minds of the public and of most professionals, although dissenting interpretations also were advanced by "monetarists" and by some "structuralists." (The latter pointed to the role of increased Vietnam involvement in directly increasing public expenditure and in withdrawing young men from the civilian labor force.) But the less advertised part of the Council's analysis was also roughly confirmed by events, in that once the interim unemployment target was passed, price stability rapidly began to give way to inflation. In the mid-1960's, the high-employment, inflation-prone economy returned to the United States after a decade of relative price stability. This was the type of economy for which the Swedes had developed manpower policy, and it was also the type of economy which the American Keynesians believed called for structuralist measures (among others) to improve the trade-off between unemployment and inflation. It might also be added that their "monetarist" adversaries also believed that structural reforms were necessary, in order to reduce the "natural rate of unemployment" (i.e., the minimum unemployment rate sustainable without an accelerating rate of inflation), and that such measures include improved labor information services.

The new structuralism

The prospects for manpower policy seemed further improved by analysis which revealed the occurrence and significance of large-scale changes in the composition of the labor force and unemployment in the 1950's and 1960's. In particular, attention was drawn to the great increase in the proportion of women in the labor force and an associated rise in the unemployment rates of women relative to those of men in the same age groups. Concern was also voiced over the great increase in the teenage portion of the labor force and in teenage unemployment relative to adult unemployment. There was no evidence of increase in the occupational or geographic dispersion of unemployment; and this has been construed as inconsistent with the earlier structuralist position, which stressed technological displacement and related changes in the composition of demand.

Structural unemployment can be increased, however, by an increase in the supply of labor in a particular market as well as by a decline in demand for that sort of labor; and the number of vacancies can be increased by a reduction in supply as well as by an increase in demand. Of course, changes in relative labor supplies (e.g., in the age or sex composition of the labor force) do not necessarily result in more unemployment together with more shortages. This unhappy outcome can be produced, however, in one or more of the following circumstances: (1) when the labor that has become more plentiful is inferior in quality to the labor that has become less plentiful, in the opinion of employers of the latter variety; (2) when wage structures are sufficiently sticky so that wages of the groups which had grown more plentiful cannot be reduced relative to the others by enough to offset their lower efficiency; (3) when changes in the composition of demand for labor do not fortuitously match changes in the composition of supply, so that new arrivals might find employment in the same lines of work and at the same relative pay as their predecessors.

Unfortunately, all these conditions (including the last, negative one) seem actually to have prevailed in the post-War period. First, youthful and female labor has been regarded by employers as less productive than so-called prime-age male labor, the former because of lack of experience, and the latter due to less steady attachment to the work force. Second, institutions such as minimum wages and collective bargaining have made for wage rigidity; under collective bargaining, entry rates rose relative to the minimum wage, and, at least until the late 1960's, skill differentials generally failed to narrow (in some cases they widened) despite a relative surplus of unskilled labor. Both of these conditions tended to make the increased youth and female work forces rather imperfect substitutes for men between the ages of 25 and 64, whose unemployment rates fell sharply relative to the national average, and even absolutely, over the last two decades. Finally, occupational and industrial shifts in the demand for labor were not very congruent with demographic changes in the composition of the labor force. In the post-War period, the demand for unskilled blue-collar labor in the high-productivity, manufacturing sector no longer exerted a "pull" on the low-productivity, agricultural sector (as it has in such rapidly industrializing countries as Japan, Germany, Italy, and France). Agriculture, however, under the stimulus of very rapid technical change, supplied a powerful "push." Farm employment fell from 9.9 million in 1950 to 4.5 million in 1970; and the shrinkage of this sector, a heavy employer of teenagers, was superimposed on a bumper crop of youths. Yet there was a gap to be bridged between technological displacement and unemployment; and it must be remembered that the disproportionate decline in the demand for production labor in manufacturing was accompanied by dramatic increases in employment in the service sector and in white-collar occupations. Moreover, if the demand for inexperienced workers in manufacturing had grown apace with the supply, the demand for more experienced labor would have expanded even more rapidly than it did.

The American rationale

To the extent that limited substitutability of youthful and female labor for experienced male labor has accounted for the widening of unemployment differentials among demographic groups, it has tended to make the American economy more inflation-prone. Economists have established that the greater the dispersion of unemployment rates among the various "compartmentalized" or "segmented" labor markets in an economy, the greater the rate of inflation that is generated at any given rate of overall unemployment; and econometric studies have suggested that the increased spread of unemployment rates among age and sex groups has indeed tended to worsen the inflation-unemployment trade-off in the United States. Presumably, therefore, any policies that are designed to reduce the watertight integrity of various compartments—in the case of manpower policies by increasing the efficiency of less productive labor and by improving the flow of information about job openings—can potentially improve this trade-off and thus appeal to policy makers and others concerned with overall demand management. This might be regarded as an American version of the rationale for manpower policies originally provided by the Swedes.

Moreover, it must be noted that benefits can result from improving the occupational or geographic mobility of labor in *any* compartmentalized markets and not simply in markets where supply has been increasing relative to demand. Mobility-improving policies could potentially be productive when applied in markets where unemployment rates are relatively *high* whether or not they have been relatively *rising*. This is of particular significance in the case of the non-white groups whose unemployment rates might actually have improved relative to the national average toward the end of the last decade. (However, this improvement might have been more apparent than real since the proportions of black men reported as actively seeking work also declined during the same period, which might indicate growing frustration and despair.) But even if non-white unemployment has not been growing faster than the over-all rate, it has certainly been relatively high—over twice as high for non-white men as for white men.

Support for manpower policy might be provided by post-War innovations in the economics of education, as well as by the structuralist refinement of the aggregate trade-off analysis referred to above. The economics of "human capital" regards the acquisition of information as an investment, since it involves incurring present costs (both direct and indirect in the form of earnings foregone during the learning period) in exchange for future returns (in the form of increased earnings for the individual and greater productivity and output for the community). Such investments are made by the student or trainee himself (or by his family), by the employer, and by the general public.

The provision of public support for education has been defended on the grounds that poor people are less able to incur the costs of education than others since, even if they sought to borrow for that purpose, their own human capital could not be held as collateral by the banks. Moreover, because they are poor, each dollar of income diverted from present consumption represents a greater sacrifice for them than it does for others; hence the poor may be less willing to invest in education. The same could be said of all expenditure made by poor people, but the public is presumed to have a special interest in the spread of education. Thus, in the absence of public support, the community's total investment in education would be too low, and its productive capacity would be correspondingly reduced. Public provision or support of training might be defended on similar grounds, given that the formal education provided to the poor—especially the non-white poor (and particularly those in the rural South)—is lower in quantity or quality than the community average, and given that on-the-job training can be viewed as a sort of postgraduate extension of institutional education, building on the latter. Employers are willing to incur training costs to the extent made profitable by their employees' expected quit rates (which in turn vary inversely with the wages paid), but they can economize on their training outlays by hiring better educated—hence better "prepared"—workers. Therefore, public support or subsidization of training for the educationally disadvantaged could compensate for their lower trainability on the job.

The results should be greater equality of opportunity and of unemployment rates, more training provided, and a less inflation-prone and more productive economy. Moreover, this line of argument can possibly lend support to the existence, and conceivably the extension, of public employment exchanges. Like education and training, the acquisition of information about jobs, workers, and terms of employment can also be regarded as an act of investment; and outlays on "search" should be increased as long as they are exceeded by increased flows of income resulting from increased mobility of labor (and capital).

Thus, manpower policy in the United States could find some intellectual support both in the new structuralist approach to inflation and unemployment and in the human capital approach to information and work. This, however, does not imply that the development of manpower policy in the 1960's was in sole and direct response to these economic analyses. In the next section, we shall find that other influences were predominant. Nor is it suggested that all those who erected the theoretical constructs were strong advocates of manpower policy, let alone that the policy has gone without serious challenge. We shall consider some of the main lines of criticism in the two sections following the next one.

Manpower policy meets the war on poverty

Having discovered that they were "working on the wrong woodpile" in 1962, the Manpower Administration did not require much analytic guidance to find the right one; in 1963, resources were switched from unemployed family heads with work experience to programs designed to reduce youth unemployment. Then came the Johnson Administration's war on poverty, with the passage of the Economic Opportunity Act in 1964 and subsequent amendments in the three following years, passage of the Civil Rights Act in 1964 and the Elementary and Secondary Education Act of 1965, and the amendment of the Social Security Act in 1967. Broadly speaking, these legislative developments, together with a torrent of administrative initiatives, might be regarded as having impinged on manpower policy in two ways.

In the first place, manpower programs were regarded by the anti-poverty warriors as part and parcel of a wider complex of approaches and activities directed to such areas as education (including pre-school and remedial education), legal aid, social services, anti-discrimination and affirmative action, welfare reform and income maintenance, and community action. (The latter came to be regarded as both a form of group therapy for the demoralized and a way to create pockets of political power for minority groups whose only source of leverage on the white middle-class electoral majorities seemed, at the time, to be a disposition to lay waste their own neighborhoods.)

In the second place, the inclusion of manpower programs in the anti-poverty complex resulted in a broadening and redirection of manpower policy itself. To attempt a catalogue of such modifications fortunately is unnecessary for the purpose at hand, since such a task lies beyond my own capability. But even superficial observation supports certain summary observations.

First, the clientele of manpower training was broadened to include not only the young, but individuals from the most disadvantaged groups in the community, including welfare recipients (notably under the Work Incentive Program) and the handicapped. This required an attempt to redirect two older state-controlled activities, vocational education and the provision of labor market information. The share of funds allocated to institutional training, which was carried out by the vocational education system under the MDTA, was greatly reduced in the second half of the decade in favor of the subsidized On-the-Job Training (OJT) program; and the Secretary of Labor was empowered to select both the occupations for which training would be offered and who the trainees would be. The Employment Service was instructed to redirect its efforts to serve disadvantaged groups. It was supposed to change over from "screening out" to "screening in," since two thirds of the training slots were reserved for the disadvantaged.

Second, accommodation of the disadvantaged meant that relatively more resources had to be devoted to subsistence allowances and to other subsidies to the trainees as well as to private employers (as in the On-the-Job program under MDTA and in Job Opportunities in the Business Sector). Sometimes it was difficult to ascertain whether the main thrust of the activity was training or subsidy. (The summer program of the Neighborhood Youth Corps was charged with being primarily a device to buy civic peace in the ghettos rather than seriously fulfilling its stated objective of providing teenagers with work experience and earnings that would induce them to remain in school.)

Third, the establishment of community action agencies was supposed to result in a sharing of the authority to design and administer programs with representatives of the communities from which the trainees or clients were drawn.

Although the war on poverty clearly helped to redirect the manpower programs, the multiplicity of legislative and administrative authorities, coupled with the absence of a clear notion of what everybody was supposed to be doing, helped to produce a bewildering variety of programs. Many of these trod on one another's jurisdictional toes; many died young, only to be reincarnated in some different form. Some of the administrative disputes involved differing objectives and concepts, as evidenced by the bruising triangular struggle between the state-based Employment Services, an old-line bureaucracy with an undistinguished reputation for effectiveness, the Manpower Administration in the Department of Labor, which sought to divert funds to training the newer client groups, and the Office of Economic Opportunity, which represented the local Community Action Agencies. Disputes such as these, involving federal agencies, state governors, mayors, and neighborhood organizations, led to the establishment of still more administrative structures designed to coordinate fragmented activities. These were generally unsuccessful. As a result, few programs were able to operate as efficiently as one might otherwise have expected; this was especially true where there were competing programs in the same locality, with each being run on a small and inefficient scale.

The sympathetic critics

Although the war on poverty broadened, redirected, and complicated the administration of manpower policy, it left intact, and indeed strengthened, its emphasis on unemployment and the unemployed. This emphasis was further reinforced at the end of the decade by legislation of a "trigger clause," whereby additional funds would be released once unemployment had reached and remained for three months running at (or above) a level slightly exceeding 5.5 per cent. But in neither its modified nor its pre-war on poverty form has the policy escaped criticism. And the criticism has emanated from sympathetic as well as skeptical quarters.

The sympathetic critics themselves are in two camps, one housing those who believe in a grand policy aimed primarily at the macroeconomic targets originally specified by the Swedes, and the other characterized by the belief that the policy should be directed and restricted to such high-unemployment groups as non-white minorities, women, young people in their late teens, and the aged unemployed. Both groups agree on the desirability of improving administration and efficiency through some "decategorization" and "decentralization"—i.e., reducing the number and halting the proliferation of specifically legislated and separately administered programs, and granting local authorities more discretion in determining the mix of the manpower programs in their respective communities. Both groups call for at least a partial return to "creaming," or selecting the more promising or better qualified applicants for training. This practice was largely abandoned during the war on poverty in favor of concentrating on the most disadvantaged individuals in the disadvantaged groups. But the latter practice tended to produce more trainee dropouts and, even in cases where the training was completed, to result in the displacement in dead-end jobs of the unskilled people who did not go through the public manpower programs by those who did.

However, the trade-off-oriented critics want the policy directed to job bottlenecks as well as to disadvantaged people; they would extend "creaming" to cover admission of employed people as well as the unemployed, so that, as the more advantaged trainees move up the ladder to the unoccupied rungs, their places at the bottom could be filled by more marginal workers. By the same token, they would have the policy devote more resources to subsidizing private employers to provide training for their own skill requirements. On the other hand, less ambitious critics—including observers with greater familiarity with the actual operation of the American programs—feel that subsidy funds have already supported training that would have been provided by employers in the absence of such support.

Finally, the big-policy buffs believe that the American policy is carried out on too small a scale to be effective, and that substantial enlargement would yield significant results. They are undeterred by the record of growth—with training enrollments rising from 34,000 in 1963 to 1.4 million in 1971, as federal obligations climbed from $56 million to $1.5 billion for training, and from under $300 million in 1961 to $4.8 billion in 1972 on the whole array of programs. They would place this in perspective by pointing out that the tax cut of 1964 released some $14 billion, or noting that manpower programs cost only about a third of one per cent of GNP in the United States compared to 1.5 per cent in Sweden. The more cautious critics point out that the Manpower Development and Training Program's efforts in the past to train for skill shortages have not been very successful. Moreover, they fear that a magnification of such efforts under a large-scale, demand-oriented policy would more likely than not result in the planners' nightmare, i.e., the attempt to forecast trends and changes in occupational demand.

The skeptics

To the skeptics, the growth of manpower policy means simply that an ugly duckling has been turning into an ugly duck. Their skepticism about even the potential effectiveness of manpower policy derives primarily from their views of the nature of post-War unemployment and poverty, although not all who share these views in fact reject all labor market policies. Their analyses lead them to reject the structuralist diagnosis, at least to the extent to which active labor market policy is indicated as a prescription. On the other hand, these analyses differ among themselves in various important respects, so that different skeptics find different reasons for their skepticism. We might distinguish at the outset two main sources of skepticism. The first is the view that much of the unemployment at which manpower policies are aimed has been voluntary and socially useful in nature. The second is the view that such unemployment is socially undesirable and is caused by various barriers to mobility, but that the barriers in question will not yield to the application of manpower policy.

The argument that much contemporary unemployment is voluntary, and that it might be socially useful, is related to the inability of the manpower administrators in the early 1960's to find long-time unemployed married men in large numbers. Instead, unemployment was found to be concentrated increasingly among women, the young, and the non-white, and to be predominantly characterized by short duration and high (and for some groups, increasing) incidence, including high quit rates. (Indeed, the high levels of unemployment that have prevailed in the United States, relative to other industrialized countries such as the United Kingdom and Sweden, have been traced to relatively high quit and layoff rates, which have helped to make the trade-off between inflation and unemployment more adverse on this side of the Atlantic.) There are two main reasons for holding that such unemployment is voluntary in nature and that it does not constitute as serious a social problem as unemployment of middle-aged family men. In the first place, it is pointed out that married women and teenagers may become unemployed more readily than married men because they have more useful alternatives to paid work, either at home or in educational institutions. As the representation of such secondary groups in the labor force increases, the proportion of total unemployment motivated by such relatively productive alternatives likewise rises.

In the second place, it is maintained that, as individual and family incomes and assets increase, individuals find it profitable to spend more and more time in job search activity, taking more time between jobs (or before accepting a first job) and possibly quitting one's job more readily in order to get a better one. Training programs are inappropriate solutions under such conditions. Lack of skill is not the problem, for there really is no problem at all. In fact, to the extent that such programs lure employed or voluntarily unemployed people out of the labor force into the programs (either as trainees or as instructors), they might even be a counterproductive source of inflationary bottlenecks. But it will be recalled that a case might be made for improving the quality of information about the labor markets; this would reduce the costs of search to employers and employees and hence would presumably lower the duration of both unemployment and job vacancies. Actually, efforts are being made to improve the Employment Service by establishing "job banks" and by planning for their conversion into a computerized system of job-matching. But such efforts also could be counterproductive, since they could induce workers to quit their jobs and look around more frequently. What is gained on the swings (lower duration) is lost on the roundabout (higher incidence).

The second body of skeptical opinion emanates from an analysis that posits the same characteristics of unemployment as the first: short duration and rapid turnover. It differs from the first, however, in maintaining that such unemployment is essentially structural rather than frictional in nature, resulting not from the purposeful pursuit of superior opportunity but rather from frustration and apathy induced by the existence of barriers to opportunity. But manpower policies are rejected as a corrective device since, it is maintained, the barriers are not caused by lack of education or information. One cause of immobility is discrimination based on color and sex, which has the effect of reducing the economic value of education to those discriminated against. Thus individuals with identical educational attainment can earn significantly different incomes. Lower rates of return on education in turn might well discourage investment in education by individuals in the groups concerned, who thus might indeed suffer from an educational deficiency. But compensatory training could not improve the situation substantially as long as discrimination remains to depress the return on training.

Discrimination, however, is not always regarded as a sufficiently powerful influence to create important or lasting barriers to mobility and opportunity all by itself. According to the neo-classical economists, the least bigoted employers in the dominant groups would be willing to hire discriminated-against labor at lower rates of pay, and thus enjoy and exploit a competitive advantage over their more bigoted rivals and drive them out of business. Hence discrimination is usually regarded as working in concert with other barriers to mobility. The latter, according to the "dual labor market" theory, have the effect of dividing the work force into two groups, one employed in sheltered markets—characterized by systems of internal training and promotion, great job security, and high wages—and the other crowded into "secondary" markets with low-wage, dead-end, short-term jobs. Since the number of entry-level jobs in the preferred sector is small relative to the supply of potential applicants from the secondary sector, employers might resort to racial or sex discrimination as a cheap means of screening some applicants out (just as they might use educational credentials as a cheap way of screening others in).

The theory is rather vague in its attempt to specify factors which make for "primary" internal markets in some industries and not in others, but technological considerations are supposed to play an important role. In this sense, this market segmentation approach is in the tradition of the early structuralists. But the newest structuralists part company with the oldest in at least one important respect. They regard unemployment as a quit-and-layoff phenomenon in secondary markets rather than as a displacement phenomenon; to them the main problem is not lack of job openings but low wages and dead-end jobs which induce frequent quitting as a symptom of poor morale. Training would not yield a satisfactory answer to a problem characterized by lack of motivation. Instead they have emphasized affirmative action measures to compel "primary" employers to abandon screening by color or sex; and they have advocated the negative income tax or similar transfer policies that would have the effect of supplementing the depressed incomes earned in the secondary sectors. On the other hand, advocacy of income redistribution in this context might be regarded as in the tradition of the Triple Revolutionaries who first insisted that income be divorced from work.

The question of efficiency

In the light of the administrative misadventures of manpower policy and of the strong *a priori* criticism reviewed above, one might have been led to predict a dismal performance on the part of the manpower programs. It certainly is true that the developments which inspired the policy persisted long after the policy's introduction and expansion had occurred. Manpower policies did not reverse the rise in unemployment among women and youth, nor did they prevent the nation's inflation-unemployment dilemma from deepening. Big-policy advocates, as we have noted, would object that active labor market measures have not been deployed on a sufficiently large scale to affect large-scale economic developments. However, in Sweden, where the policy has been developed on a scale that is quite large by United States standards, it has not been able to prevent adverse movements in the Swedish Phillips Curve.

In an attempt to determine whether some of the programs actually introduced in this country have been effective and hold promise for the future, numerous benefit-cost studies have been made. With benefits measured as some type of post-training differential in incomes, most of the studies of MDTA programs indicated very high rates of return. There is some indication that on-the-job-training programs, which cost less than institutional training, have yielded higher rates of return than the latter. It was also found that training exerted a greater impact on the most disadvantaged individuals—those with the lowest levels of education or of pre-training earnings or with the worst records of unemployment. For the Neighborhood Youth Corps programs, which offered more subsidy than training, results were rather mixed and did not unequivocally indicate a record of overall effectiveness either in increasing the earnings of enrollees or in reducing high-school dropout rates. Studies of the effectiveness of the Job Corps (an expensive residential training and rehabilitation program for underprivileged school dropouts with bad work experience) yielded mixed results. A rather rough study of JOBS (or Job Opportunities in the Business Sector, under which training programs were carried on by private employers, with or without subsidy) indicated large apparent increases in earnings between 1966 and 1968. The Work Incentive Program, designed to provide training and placement in public employment to welfare recipients, was misnamed, because the welfare system's eligibility requirements have constituted a notorious disincentive for recipients to strive for gainful employment. Predictably, its record of completions and placements was very poor.

Critics of labor market policy have included critics of the research on policy effectiveness. Since some of them are proponents of human capital analysis, which relies heavily on empirical benefit-cost research, it might appear that they were gently hoist with their own petard. They claim, however, that these studies did not yield accurate assessments of benefits. Perhaps the criticism most strongly advanced is that most of the studies were characterized by the absence of adequate reference or "control" groups (or of any at all). This is an important consideration; however, the difficulty in obtaining a control group which is the identical twin of the target group in every relevant respect save that of completion of the program in question is so great as to raise a serious question of operationality. Even among people alike in respect to education, age, sex, and color, there are motivational and other differences between those who sought admission to the program and those who did not, between those admitted and those who were not, between those who completed the course and those who dropped out. Another criticism of most studies is that they assumed that the income differentials observed a short time after completion of the course (the benefits involved) would persist over a 10-year period. In at least some instances, however, it is more reasonable to believe that the magnitude of such benefits would dwindle over time, since the higher earnings of the trainees reflect more aggressive placement efforts on their behalf as well as the acquisition of skills. A third line of criticism is that some programs train and place people in high-turnover, unskilled occupations, raising the possibility that the trainees might merely be displacing previous job applicants. Related to this is the observation that, even where earnings were significantly raised by the programs, they remained below poverty levels, so that manpower training cannot be regarded as a substitute for direct income redistribution. Finally, some of the studies were made when the administrators were still "creaming" the pool of applicants for the most able and qualified individuals; moreover, the instructors themselves might have been the cream of their own crop. Hence attempts to expand the programs could run into diminishing returns.

Proponents of manpower policy have also criticized the evaluations. They object to inclusion of support payments to trainees, which are transfer payments, among costs properly chargeable to manpower programs. This implies agreement with the assertion that manpower development cannot be regarded as a substitute for direct income supplementation. However, the proponents of course believe that manpower development is worthy in its own right. This view is implicit in another caveat—that it might be desirable to retain a program which yields significant benefits in the form of increased earning power even if its costs, which are borne by the public, exceed those benefits which accrue to the disadvantaged groups. By the same reasoning, they would reject the position that direct income transfers are preferable to manpower development programs because the cost of the latter is greater; they would hold that such cost differentials are overwhelmed by the extra social benefit derived from improving the employability of people. Also, as a counterpoint to the diminishing returns argument, it might be maintained that costs in the early period covered by the studies reflected the administrative growing pains referred to above, and that costly duplication and overlapping could be reduced as the manpower programs develop in the future.

A place for manpower policy

Although favorable (as well as unfavorable) results yielded by benefit-cost studies must be interpreted with great caution, they might also justify reexamination of the analyses which imply that all manpower policies would be largely ineffective. In fact, some interesting current research challenges the hypothesis that much of the unemployment, especially around cyclical peaks and among disadvantaged groups at such times, is either voluntary or frictional in nature. While awaiting publication and evaluation of this new work, we might give some thought to an old finding. In 1955, when unemployment averaged 4.4 per cent, 55.5 per cent of those who changed jobs (or 4.6 out of 8.2 million people) experienced no unemployment at all. (Another survey of the labor force, in 1961, revealed that 60 per cent of the people who made only one job change that year had experienced no unemployment, that 80 per cent of those who changed jobs once in order to improve their status did so without incurring unemployment, and that among male job changers 40 per cent of those without unemployment landed a high-er-paying job, as compared with only 26 per cent of those who experienced some unemployment between jobs. In 1961, however, the unemployment rate average was 6.7 per cent.) This casts some doubt on the assumption that job search is carried on most efficiently when the individual is not working and hence on the conclusion that unemployment is mainly voluntary. If unemployment is indeed involuntary, it does not follow that diversion of unemployed (and under-employed) individuals from the labor force into training programs would generate inflationary pressure on wages.

Nor does it follow that training programs need be ineffective in situations where barriers to mobility are thrown up by discrimination or even by a shortage of good jobs. Recourse to educational credentials as a cheap screening device (provided at public expense) by high-wage employers in protected labor markets suggests that at least some of the qualified applicants may be educated beyond pure-ly economic requirements. If so, even relatively short compensatory training courses might bring those with educational deficiencies up to entry levels. Moreover, the social pressure on employers to hire duly certified graduates of public training programs could consti-tute a salutary dose of compensatory credentialing. Certainly, the criticism that benefit-cost studies are likely to overstate the payoff to training per se, because they do not take into account the effective-ness of aggressive placement efforts, is wide of the mark.

It is true, of course, that merely lengthening a queue of qualified job seekers does not increase the number of jobs which they are qual-ified to hold. However, the number of good jobs annually available is greater than suggested by the dual market theory. The latter sug-gests, as a stereotype, two compartmentalized sectors; in the high-wage internal labor markets, all are protected by non-academic ten-ure, and turnover is negligible; in the unprotected, low-wage sector, quits and firings are the order of the day. In fact, all the theory really requires is that turnover in the good-job sector be significantly lower than in the bad-job sector; and in this respect it can claim anticipa-tory confirmation in long-standing findings that high-wage industries tend to have lower quit rates than low-wage industries (even after allowance for differences in skill levels).

However, the *absolute* levels of separations—including layoffs, discharges, and retirements, as well as quits—are quite high even in industries whose relative quit rates are low, and whose wages are relatively high. Thus in 1967 petroleum and coal products ranked first among 29 industrial categories in average hourly earnings, and last in separations of production workers, but the latter still averaged 2.2 per cent a month. This means that in a year of high employment (unemployment was 3.8 per cent in 1967) this industry had to hire about 125 persons to keep an average of 100 on the job. Figuring this way, the eight highest-paying industries in 1967 (the lowest wage was six per cent above the average for all manufacturing) turned over about three million production employees (out of a combined work force of about six million). Of course, if the ranks of qualified and credentialed job applicants were swelled by an expanded manpower development system, quit rates could be expected to fall. And if the overall unemployment rate were allowed to rise, fewer vacancies would be created on a replacement basis.

Nevertheless, the order of magnitude suggests that some potentialities for upward mobility exist, even within protected sectors. Some elbow room exists for labor market policies. It would permit the latter to contribute to a reduction in the spread of unemployment between the disadvantaged groups and the rest, and to a reduction in the concentration of employment of the disadvantaged in the secondary sectors, although the major problems in lowering the barriers to mobility would remain.

Although spreading the misery more evenly would serve the cause of distributive equity, that cause could better be served if there was happiness to spread around instead of misery. This could occur if the major barriers to mobility are greatly reduced *and* if, as they are being reduced, the total number of good jobs grows rapidly enough to absorb the unemployed and the underemployed. Experience has taught that the economy has tended to produce such a happy outcome when operating close to capacity or approaching that neighborhood. At such times, the maintenance of high and rising levels of demand acts like a giant suction pump as the relatively great growth in employment in the high-wage sectors forces wages up more rapidly elsewhere and results in a reduction of unemployment, both recorded and "hidden," which is especially great in the high-unemployment groups. Thus more jobs are created in the protected sectors, while more jobs elsewhere have their wages raised.

The trouble with this story, however, is that it does not end at this point. The process is invariably accompanied by inflation, which tends to perpetuate itself, and even accelerate, as unions in the protected sectors seek to make up ground lost while their employers have been raising prices to lift profit margins from pre-expansion levels. To counter these inflationary pressures, demand is then deflated, the suction is turned off, and wage and unemployment differentials widen again. This is the unhappy sequel which manpower policy was originally designed to prevent; and if it could reduce inflationary tendencies at high levels of employment, it could also indirectly reduce barriers to economic opportunity and equality—including barriers which might not have originated in lack of skill or information at all.

Moderate expectations

Few believe that manpower policy could satisfactorily perform either of these tasks unaided, even if it were scaled up to Swedish proportions. It is highly doubtful whether it alone could increase mobility and otherwise improve the trade-off sufficiently to induce employers to resist cost push, and to prevent them from "administering" price increases when they are still operating well below capacity. It is highly doubtful whether it alone could level barriers to mobility sufficiently to effect a satisfactory redistribution of employment, unemployment, and income, or to significantly reduce poverty levels. That is why most observers, proponents of the policy as well as critics, now agree that manpower policy cannot be regarded as an alternative to direct wage and price restraint, to efficient enforcement of anti-discrimination legislation, and to direct income transfers to the poor. The proponents would agree that these other policies would be necessary as a complement to manpower policy.

But they might also maintain that manpower policy complements the other policies, too. It could increase the efficiency of wage-price restraint (which certainly could use all the help it can get) by removing inflationary bottlenecks, which often fuel union demands for more widespread wage increases in order to maintain or restore traditional relationships. It could help anti-discrimination policy by compensating for deficiencies in worker training and education that might have resulted from past discrimination. However, with respect to anti-discrimination policy, and even more with respect to direct income redistribution, political complementarity is of greater importance than technical complementarity. The day may come when the egalitarian spirit of the American public might drive it to embrace policies that would divorce income from work as a general principle. But as the Presidential election of 1972 made plain, that day is not at hand. (Nor is the era of consumer satiety, on which the divorce was originally predicated, about to dawn.) The so-called work ethic still dominates, and it is held strongly not only by the white tax-paying middle classes but by the underprivileged and the poor themselves, who want intensely to enhance their sense of worth along with their incomes. Policies designed to help the individual achieve these two objectives range from counseling-training-placement through public employment to wage subsidies or supplements. The exact mix will vary in response to changing needs and the relative efficiency of the different approaches. But some programs to improve and equalize work opportunity must be offered, if only as a condition for the provision of separate income supplementation for those among the poor for whom income must truly be divorced from work.

If the existence of a battery of manpower development policies is essential to the development of more thoroughgoing and effective policies of income supplementation, the latter are also conducive to the efficiency of the former. In the first place, a more effective division of labor between the two types of policy would be feasible, so that the training and information programs could concentrate more exclusively on their more narrowly defined functions. In the second place, the training programs, even if concentrated on the groups with the greatest problems of unemployment and deprivation, would be able to select the more promising individuals in those groups for training or placement. This would minimize the "displacement" problem. Such "creaming" of the more trainable individuals, in turn, would permit training—even when conducted in educational institutions—to be geared more closely to ladder-job openings, whether in the private sector or in public service.

Manpower policies with these attributes could avoid much of the administrative inefficiency which has been experienced to date, including the wasteful overlapping and duplication of activities. "Decategorization" and decentralization through revenue sharing have been officially proposed as a means to the same ends. A concluding note of caution, however, should be clearly sounded. Revenue sharing is unavoidably susceptible to the diversion of federally-generated resources away from activities designed to increase the economic potential of the disadvantaged, and in the direction of more well-to-do groups with superior economic and political power in the local community—whether through public works, lower taxes, or negotiated wage increases. From the viewpoint of manpower policy, revenue sharing is not an efficient instrument. Efforts to promote local autonomy and flexibility cannot dispense with federal guidance and direction to the degree required to secure an acceptable level of efficiency in policies designated to further the agreed-upon objectives of manpower policy. For it is at levels of government farther removed from local grass roots that such worthy interests of economically weak minorities can be more decently and efficiently promoted.

6

Major
public initiatives
in
health care

HERBERT E. KLARMAN

To set the stage for discussing certain major public initiatives in the 1960's, a few selected figures are presented. Table 1 shows the amounts spent on health care in this country, the continuing increase in the ratio of health care expenditures to the Gross National Product, and the fraction of the total met by public funds, which had remained steady at one quarter for 15 years but increased in recent years, to three eighths.

Perhaps more striking is Table 2, which shows a sharp acceleration in the annual rate of change in expenditures after 1966. However, the rate of increase of eight per cent in the preceding intervals was not small.

Official figures for fiscal year 1973, ending June 30, are not yet available. Scattered evidence indicates that the amount spent will have exceeded $90 billion, despite the fact that the Economic Stablilization Program of the Nixon Administration singled out the health services industry for special attention.

It is fair to caution the reader that public programs in health are usually programs in health services, and that this should be kept in mind when reviewing the data. Excluded from the official scope of health care expenditures are such items as medical education outside the hospital, water supply, water pollution control, and solid waste disposal. When expenditures for these items were estimated for fiscal year 1964, they amounted to 20 per cent of total health care expenditures.

The most notable public initiatives in health in the 1960's were undertaken in financing. Following the 1964 election, Congress moved quickly to pass Medicare for the aged and Medicaid for the sick poor. Although Medicare comprises several sets of benefits and Medicaid is a state administered program with varying dates of inception, many elements of both became operative on July 1, 1966, and were promptly reflected in the financial data for fiscal year 1967.

In the reports of the Congressional committees and the language of the laws, the intention is expressed that programs in financing must not impinge on the practice of medicine. They were intended to buy care from the private sector without interfering with it. To the historical role of the federal government as provider of care in the Public Health Service hospitals and the Veterans Administration hospitals were added a small number of neighborhood health centers financed and sponsored by the Office of Economic Opportunity (OEO). Although the latter would render health services to some residents of poverty areas, they were meant primarily to afford a demonstration in the delivery of comprehensive health services to designated populations.

Whatever major influence government sought to exert on the system for delivering health services as a whole was to be promoted

TABLE 1.   *Expenditures for Health Care in the United States, 1950-72*[1]

YEAR	AMOUNT (IN BILLIONS)	PER CENT OF GNP	PER CENT BY PUBLIC FUNDS
1950	$12.0	4.6	25.5
1960	25.9	5.2	24.7
1966	42.1	5.9	25.7
1972	83.4	7.6	39.4

[1] Source: Social Security Administration

TABLE 2.   *Annual Rate of Change in Expenditures for Health Care in the United States, 1950-72*[1]

INTERVAL	ANNUAL RATE OF INCREASE
1950-60	8.0%
1960-66	8.4
1966-72	12.1
1966-70	12.8
1970-72	10.8

[1] Source: Calculated from Table 1

indirectly through strengthening health planning. The 89th Congress enacted two new programs: one authorizing Regional Medical Programs (RMP's), and the other, Comprehensive Health Planning

(CHP) agencies on both a state and local basis. Initially, RMP prospered, while CHP kept busy with organizational arrangements. But by the spring of 1973, RMP was slated for dismantling, and the fate of CHP remained uncertain.

At the official level the major reason for disenchantment with the new planning mechanisms is that they failed to curb the rise in health expenditures; a second reason is that they did not bring about a more equal distribution of health resources geographically. By 1970 the Nixon Administration joined the traditional critics of the American health services system and proclaimed a crisis in American medicine. Although much of the evidence adduced, such as international comparisons in life expectancy, represented a continuation of long-term trends, the major emphasis was put on stemming the post-1966 rise in health expenditures, with the additional point that the larger expenditures had not yielded corresponding improvements in health status. The Administration turned to a newly named vehicle, the Health Maintenance Organization (HMO)—a title which some observers did not take literally—to introduce competition into the health services system. Discussion of the HMO continues, with almost everybody in favor of it. In the effort to launch 1,000 HMO's in this country, some of the underlying assumptions and original justifications of the HMO concept are frequently forgotten.

This introduction serves also as an outline of this article, which undertakes to review some major public initiatives undertaken in health in the 1960's. Certain important initiatives, such as the community health centers and funds for health manpower training, are omitted. In subsequent sections the article discusses what was expected of a program, what happened in the course of its implementation, how major departures from what was expected are being explained, and what some implications are for public policy of the actual results, expected or unexpected.

Public financing, private care

In 1965, after Lyndon Johnson's landslide election victory, Congress added two titles to the Social Security Act. Title 18 is known as Medicare and provides health insurance under Social Security to persons 65 years and over. One part of Medicare deals with care by institutions, mostly hospitals, and is mandatory. Another part deals with professional services, mostly the physician's, and is voluntary, with enrollment subsidized by a federal contribution to the individual's premium of 50 per cent. Title 19 is known as Medicaid and offers health benefits to persons on public assistance and to other persons unable to pay for medical care who fall into certain legal categories. Medicaid is a federally assisted state program, and allows each state to make its own determinations regarding eligibility of beneficiaries, scope of benefits, and payments to providers (within federal guidelines).

When the Truman Administration's proposals for national health insurance were rejected in the late 1940's, some supporters retrenched and proceeded to concentrate on national health insurance for the aged. Such insurance, which usually envisaged hospitalization for a limited interval (30 or 60 days), came to be known as Medicare. It was believed that any attempt to incorporate physicians' services in health insurance for the aged would arouse opposition from the politically powerful American Medical Association (AMA) and endanger the hospitalization benefits that were acceptable to the American Hospital Association. It was Congressman Wilbur Mills, chairman of the House Ways and Means Committee, in search of a face-saving compromise after the 1964 election, who engineered the merger of the longstanding Democratic proposal for mandatory hospitalization benefits with a very new Republican proposal for voluntary insurance against physician expenses.

The proposal for hospitalization benefits had received thorough professional examination and public discussion. By 1965 some experts envisioned a possible 300 to 400 per cent increase in the use of hospital care by the aged. In this forecast they were mistaken, since the actual increase fell within the actuarial projection of 25 to 40 per cent. It is remarkable, however, that the contemporary literature shows no discussion of the probable effects of such insurance on the unit cost or price of hospital care. It turned out that the trend in patient-day cost veered sharply upward after 1966, rising at an annual rate of 13 to 14 per cent in the late 1960's, compared with a rate of six per cent in the early 1960's. Thus, outside observers missed the mark on both elements of the projection of hospital expenditures under Medicare, the element that they had studied and the one that they had neglected.

It is not known why the experts were so far off on hospital utilization. My own guess is that the conditions governing hospital utilization may not have changed all that much between 1965 and 1967. More than one half of the aged did have hospital insurance before Medicare, and many large cities and some of the states provided free hospital care to the sick poor, including the aged. It is likely, too, that prevailing patterns of medical practice governing hospital use are slow to change except as the supply of hospital beds changes.

By contrast, the rise in hospital cost has been studied. The conclusions reached vary, so that no consensus can be said to have emerged regarding the causes of the marked and persistent rise in hospital cost after 1965.

Some explanations, I believe, can be discarded, since they focus on certain features that have long characterized hospital care in this country. Included are the non-profit ownership of most hospitals, the hospital-physician relationship under which the doctor has the authority to allocate resources to his patients, and the educational role of hospitals.

Another set of explanations that are associated with changes in the mid-1960's, such as unionization and extension of the federal minimum wage law to non-profit hospitals, does not withstand close analysis. Although wages rose appreciably, the non-payroll component of hospital expenditures rose even more. The proportion of payroll to total expenses has declined steadily from 61 per cent in fiscal year 1966 to 58.3 per cent in 1970 and to 56.5 per cent in 1973.

Rising costs and prices

Two explanations continue to receive major support. One focuses on the demand side. Medicare increased the flow of funds to hospitals. Along with other forms of health insurance or prepayment, Medicare also perpetuates a dual set of prices—a gross price received by the provider and a much lower net price paid by the consumer out-of-pocket at the time of illness. The dual price distorts reality for the consumer and encourages the provider to enhance and elaborate the quality of care, even at a higher cost.

The other explanation, which I tend to stress, focuses on cost reimbursement, which was widely adopted under Medicare (and Medicaid). Under this method of payment a hospital is paid a daily rate related to its own cost of operation. The hospital administrator can no longer deny requests for higher wages or more supplies on the ground that money is lacking; to get money, he need only spend more.

From general experience it is known that cost-plus contracts are not likely to promote efficient operation. However, in 1965 the Social Security Administration faced a record of experience in the hospital field that could not be gainsaid. First espoused as a desirable method for paying hospitals in the early 1950's, cost reimbursement was established by 1965 as the vehicle for financing the care of two thirds of all Blue Cross subscribers. The expressed intention of Congress not to interfere with existing arrangements and the aim of the Social Security Administration's representatives not to antagonize anybody needlessly should also be considered. It was therefore determined to reimburse participating hospitals in relation to their own cost, with two adjustments. One, hopefully on the downward side, took account of the relatively lower use of ancillary services by aged patients. The second was a two per cent allowance, representing any possible cost omissions. This plus factor was later dropped when the body of the formula was liberalized.

What was not anticipated in 1965 was the possible change in a hospital administrator's behavior associated with a shift in the proportion of total patient days paid for at cost from 20 to 30 per cent to 75 to 90 per cent. This change was described by administrators from the outset and received confirmation from the high rate of increase in non-payroll expenses.

Although the importance attached here to cost reimbursement is not supported by research findings, it is fair to state that no study has yet analyzed individual hospital data showing both the proportion of total patient days reimbursed at cost and the proportion of total patient days financed through prepayment. It is conceivable that if such data were collected, they might display too little variation to enable multivariate statistical techniques to reveal the actual effects. Yet the steady decline in the rate of occupancy of hospitals since 1969 is more consistent with the cost reimbursement hypothesis than with the prepayment hypothesis.

To emphasize cost reimbursement is not to deny the importance of prepayment, which makes reimbursement by a wholesale purchaser necessary. The reason for stressing the distinction is that it may be possible to alter reimbursement mechanisms that do not work well with less harm than would be inflicted if the health insurance benefit package were changed. Already steps have been taken in parts of the country to switch cost reimbursement from a retrospective rate to a prospective one. A twofold problem remains. An automatic formula will always require adjustments after a year or two, which must be negotiated; and the three major sources of prepayment funds—Blue Cross, Medicaid, and Medicare—continue to apply different formulas to the same hospital.

My own judgment is that no procedure short of budgetary review will prove to be effective. Although the several provinces of Canada are now trying out diverse approaches to hospital payment, including budgetary review, little is known about them in this country.

The provision of Medicare dealing with professional services did not attract discussion prior to passage because prospects of enactment were considered to be poor. With respect to use it has turned out that the aged continue to have more physician visits per capita than the rest of the population. However, the number of visits per capita has declined for the aged since 1964, as it has for the population as a whole. There has been a tendency toward more equal use by income class, particularly among adults under 65. At a given time, classification of families by current income serves to understate the difference in use as income increases, because current income is depressed by illness of the breadwinner.

The possibility of an occasional decline in physician use was not foreseen. What seems to have happened is that as the price of physicians' services rose, it became reasonable for some physicians to trade additional income for leisure. The phenomenon of a manpower supply curve that displays a negative response to an increase in fees is not commonly associated with a developed economy like that of the United States.

The other component of expenditures is price. Officially the physician component of the Consumer Price Index rose at an annual rate of less than three per cent between 1960 and 1965 and at almost seven per cent during the period 1966 to 1970. However, these figures probably understate the actual price increases, especially in the later period when physicians increasingly tended to fractionate fees.

It is not known why the rate of increase in physician fees rose so sharply after 1966. I venture to offer at least a partial explanation, based on the physician reimbursement formula promulgated under Medicare. Unlike the cost formula for paying hospitals, the usual and customary fee formula for physicians had no basis in tested experience. It calls for paying a physician who accepts assignment of the patient's bill 80 per cent of his customary fee (which for several years he was permitted to change at will), subject to two limits. One is the prevailing fee in the area in which the physician practices, or the cut-off point for the frequency distribution of fees for a given service. The cut-off point has varied a good deal; but the important fact is that the physician who does not know his place in the area's frequency distribution of fees is constantly tempted to move as close as possible to the cut-off point. The other limit is the usual fee charged to other patients who are considered to have similar ability to pay. This means that if a physician wants to charge more to his aged patients, he must raise fees to all patients.

The formula just described is bound to lead to increases in physician fees; indeed, it is not evident why the increases have not been higher. Perhaps it is one of the advantages of alternative methods of physician payment, such as capitation or salary, that they avoid the problem of how to set physician's fees for individual services. However, fee-for-service payment is likely to continue for some time, and methods of dealing with this problem must be devised.

Medicaid

Like Medicare, Medicaid passed through Congress quickly, and its provisions received little discussion. In general, of course, this nation favors the idea that lack of ability to pay should not serve as a barrier to the receipt of needed medical care. A review of the literature by this writer in 1950 showed that this position was widely shared among experts and politicans, liberal and conservative. Responsibility for access to medical care by the poor was discharged in part by the private sector, with individual physicians applying a sliding scale of fees by charging a higher fee for the same service to well-to-do patients than to the poor. Philanthropy played a role in the hospital, helping to defray the cost of care to the poor, while semi-private patients were charged at cost and private patients above cost. Some large cities and states operated general hospitals for the poor, with criteria of eligibility depending on the number of beds in the public hospital system. In the 1940's and 1950's the tendency grew to place less reliance on voluntary action for two reasons. The cost of care was rising, so that a given amount of philanthropic support could buy less. At the same time, and perhaps not coincidentally, voluntary health insurance was experiencing an unprecedented growth. Not only did prepayment and employer contributions to health and welfare funds (untaxed to the employee) reduce the need for free care; but if possession of health insurance were to serve as an indicator of ability to pay for care, as it sometimes did, the buying power of insurance was eroded and the sliding scale of fees became untenable.

As cost rose and medicine was able to do more for patients, it came to be recognized that only the wealthy could be certain of escaping medical indigence. For large numbers health insurance replaced income as the measure of ability to pay medical bills. Even so, there remained discernible groups of persons not on cash public assistance who were able to meet most of their day-to-day expenses, but unable to pay for unexpected medical care. Since the aged had long been singled out for attention, they were obvious candidates to become the first beneficiaries of federal-state programs providing health services to low-income persons not on public assistance. For various reasons, mostly political, the Kerr-Mills program of Medical Assistance for the Aged was not forcefully implemented in most states. When the aged received Medicare coverage in 1965, certain younger population groups were given an expanded version of Kerr-Mills in the new Medicaid program.

With little prior public discussion and scarcely any actuarial experience to draw upon, it is not surprising that budgetary projections and actual expenditures under Medicaid did not coincide. Some experts thought that Medicaid might become an even larger and more influential program than Medicare. In successive years expenditures under Medicaid, which like cash public assistance grants are open-ended in the federal budget, exceeded budgetary estimates. Moreover, a large fraction of total expenditures was incurred in four large states (New York, California, Massachusetts, and Michigan) with a liberal tradition of free health services. That the concern was over excessive total expenditures, rather than over any single factor that may have raised expenditures, is demonstrated by the fact that the states varied considerably in scope of benefits, fee structure, and the criteria governing eligibility. Congressional committees conducted hearings and staff studies, which often concentrated on alleged abuses by providers.

To this day, however, we lack nationwide data to show the

sources of the short-fall in budgetary projections. A low initial estimate of expenditures may have possessed some political appeal, but surely such appeal would diminish over time. It is fair to say that with proper record-keeping the contribution of fee changes in unit cost or price to the increase in expenditures could have been documented. Total utilization of services remains to be accounted for, broken down into per capita use of services and the number of participating persons. Per capita use requires an eligible population and that is almost unpredictable, because participation in a subsidy program depends not only on the formal demographic and socioeconomic criteria governing eligibility but also on shifts in public attitudes toward the acceptance of benefits not based on prior entitlement and on changes in administrative practices. Trends in public assistance rolls throughout the 1960's indicate how changeable some of the underlying factors may be. Finally, Medicaid has played an increasing role in financing nursing home care for the aged, as Medicare has successively curtailed the benefits provided in extended-care facilities. Unexpectedly, Medicaid furnished a cushion when Medicare denied widely anticipated long-term care benefits to the aged.

Examining the available data

Suitable data on changes in population, use of services, unit cost, and program expenditures have been published for California.[1] My own reanalysis of the data shows the following percentage distribution among the sources of increase in expenditures between 1964-65 and 1969:

Increase in eligible population 42%
Rise in unit cost or price 32%
Increase in per capita use 13%
Shift from free to paid physician services 13%

When Congress and the state legislatures acted to curtail rising Medicaid expenditures, they took a variety of steps. In some states the range of benefits was narrowed; elsewhere limits were put on the amount of hospital or physician benefits per episode of illness or period; in other states fees paid to providers were reduced or co-payment by the medically indigent was introduced; finally, criteria of eligibility for Medicaid were restricted everywhere. The result was that in states or cities with a history of liberality toward the medically indigent, certain segments of the population were worse off after a few years of Medicaid than previously. Not only had they lost access to free or part-free care, but along with the rest of the

---

[1] Foline E. Gartside, "Causes of Increase in Medicaid Costs in California," *Health Services Reports*, Vol. 88, No. 3 (March 1973), pp. 225-35.

population they were confronted with much higher price levels for medical services.

In my judgment it was a combined reaction to the loss of eligibility for free care by some and to the high prices facing all that led to a revival of interest in national health insurance in the late 1960's. It was not so much the attraction of the remedy, which took varied forms and was sometimes nebulous, but rather a growing feeling that government had an obligation to try to undo what government had helped bring about—high prices.

I noted previously the tendency in the late 1960's toward equality of use of health services by income class. Use data are not the same as information on access, which is more akin to the opportunity to use services and comprises several dimensions, such as distance, waiting time, comfort and convenience, and so on. Conceptualization and measurement of access have been unduly neglected. Moreover, as use is equalized, the tendency is to proclaim equal health status as the goal, implying inequality in the use of health services to offset need. Equality in health status by income class does not strike me as a realistic goal for the health services industry, since medical care is not always the key to improved health.

Programs for health care planning

The two new programs in health planning—RMP and CHP—had no connection with urban planning in general or with the two new programs in financing, Medicare and Medicaid. Nor did they relate to the single ongoing health planning activity in this country that had emerged from the 1940's. Under the Hill-Burton Act passed in 1946, federal grants to the states for hospital construction were conditioned upon the preparation of an annual inventory of facilities and a state plan indicating priorities for the coming year. Federal support for hospital planning was expanded in the early 1960's when direct federal grants became available to areawide planning agencies within the states. Mostly these took the form of hospital councils under voluntary non-profit auspices operating without official mandate but with support from philanthropic capital fund raising agencies and from corporate donors. Sometimes sanctions were brought to bear by the refusal of large purchasers of care, such as the local Blue Cross plan, to pay for care provided in facilities not approved by the planning council.

The impetus for the new planning programs came from two disparate sources in the health field. The progenitor of RMP was the medical education and research community, which through the intercession of Mary Lasker persuaded President Johnson to establish the President's Commission on Heart Disease, Cancer, and Stroke, with Dr. Michael De Bakey as chairman. The point of departure was the belief that technological devices and procedures had come into existence that were not being widely applied outside the great university medical centers. As Dr. De Bakey put it, by having funded medical research, the federal government had built up an equity in having the fruits of medical research applied. The De Bakey Commission recommended the establishment of regional centers of excellence throughout the country, but neither the Administration nor Congress was prepared to finance or otherwise undertake such a venture. What Congress passed in October 1965 was a program to encourage regional cooperative arrangements in the diagnosis and treatment of heart disease, cancer, stroke, and related diseases. It was left to each region, with boundaries defined locally, to plan for developing an RMP organization and then to propose specific operating programs for support by the federal agency. There was no national agenda, no set of nationwide priorities—other than to encourage cooperative arrangements at the regional level.

The impetus for CHP was an unusual conjuncture of preferences and opportunities. State health officials had wanted for a long time to do away with the numerous categorical public health grants-in-aid to the states. Congressional leaders in health were opposed to a consolidation of grants on the ground that federal monies should be spent in accordance with priorities set at the national level. However, the same leaders were somewhat interested in promoting health planning at the official level. A compromise was struck, with some of the categorical grants merged into a general public health grant to the states in return for the creation of a health planning mechanism in the states. The amount of money involved was of the order of $84 million in 1965, but on this modest base a new era of "Partnership in Health" was proclaimed between the federal government and the states and between official agencies and voluntary organizations. An elaborate structure was designed to plan for the optimum provision of comprehensive health services, consisting of "A" agencies to plan statewide, "B" agencies to plan locally or areawide, and "C" agencies (universities) to train staff for the A and B agencies. Provision was made for majority participation by consumers.

CHP was enacted in November 1966. Since their sponsorships and constituencies differed and their mandates were far from concrete, the two programs were not linked in implementation except fortuitously. They were, of course, connected in the labor market, as the two new programs created a boom demand for top-level health planning staff, of whom there was a scanty supply.

The two programs were adopted independently of one another, and each developed in its own way. The federal administrators of RMP thought that the absence of nationwide goals was an advantage. Let each geographic area organize to mobilize its resources and then let each agency propose what it wishes to do, in light of its capabilities, priorities, and opportunities. Money for RMP was adequate relative to the proposals made. With the medical school in a region typically playing a central role in organizing the cooperative arrangements, the most common program was provision of postgraduate medical education for physicians.

Divergence of interests

It has taken CHP much longer to get organized and functioning. In some parts of the country problems of substance still await consideration. The notion of comprehensiveness, which ultimately came to encompass environmental health as well as personal health, has led to a scattering of effort. Agencies that had gained experience in hospital planning in the 1950's and early 1960's were either submerged or discarded when the earmarking of Hill-Burton funds for areawide hospital planning ceased. Where planning agencies have passed from the organizational phase and begun to deal with substantive matters, they are often immersed in reviewing individual proposals for construction. Little time is left for dealing with the conceptual, technical, and public policy aspects of health planning.

A vital omission is the failure to consider the essential nature of a desirable community health plan and thus the very basis for health planning. Most often the view adopted by hospital planning agencies in this country is that a sound community plan is the sum of the best possible plans developed by individual institutions. That would of course hold true if the interests of the individual institutions and of the community always coincided. In that case, the planning agency could furnish information on socio-economic developments in the area and on the future outlook that would help improve the planning performance by individual institutions.

There are good reasons to believe, however, that a divergence of interests frequently exists between an individual institution and the public at large. One example of such divergence is the desire on the part of the individual hospital to attract the best possible medical staff, while the community continues to receive care from physicians without a hospital staff appointment as well as from physicians with one or more appointments. Lack of a hospital appointment bars a physician from the most ready and likely source of continuing education in medicine.

A second source of divergence of interests is the inability of the physician to care for patients in a hospital in which he does not hold a staff appointment. This means that if a special facility for the care of a disease with infrequent occurrence were confined to Hospital A, physicians in Hospital B would lose out. It would be an act of self-denial for the latter to support such a proposal. The problem of regional coordination of health services in a metropolitan area cannot be resolved in the absence of appropriate policies on the extent and types of multiple staff appointments for physicians.

A third example of divergence of interests, which has arisen since World War II in connection with the growth of prepayment, is conveyed by the proposition generally associated with Milton Roemer. Roemer's Law says that under conditions of prepayment, hospital beds, if built, will be used. In the early 1960's a good deal of controversy surrounded this proposition, but in the late 1960's it gained increasing support from scholars and almost unanimous support from active hospital planning consultants. The case of England, where there had been no hospital construction for 25 years and longer, was conclusive evidence that geographic areas did differ in the ratio of beds to population but were fairly uniform in rate of occupancy. It is worth spelling out the serious policy implications of Roemer's Law. A high rate of occupancy is taken as a sign of full use of resources. It is beneficial to the community, as well as to the hospital to which it assures more revenue, as long as a low rate of occupancy denies revenue and threatens the financial survival of a hospital. However, if prepayment assures a high rate of occupancy to a hospital, and the bed-to-population ratio in the area makes no difference, any deterrent to continuing expansion by individual hospitals has been removed. It then becomes incumbent upon the community to decide how many hospital beds it wishes to support. So far, within the range of bed-to-population ratios observed, there is no reason to base that decision on the effects that a change in the number of beds presumably exerts on the health status of a population.

If potential divergence of interests lays the substantive basis for health planning, it should constitute the core. The aim to reduce the supply of beds entails mandatory controls, exercised by seizing the opportunities that present themselves, such as proposals for rebuilding and relocating individual institutions. The other examples of divergence of interests entail the operation of more subtle factors, such as the gamut of physician-hospital relationships, and may call for complex actions which are best left to voluntary arrangements until they are better understood.

The information problem

An important contribution of planning agencies in the past has been their service as repositories of information. The question persists: What types of data are useful and necessary for health planning? The first answer is that planning in accordance with so-called health need is fruitless, since people always use more or fewer services than indicated by purely biological and technological factors. To collect a good deal of information to measure the need for services is bound to be an idle exercise. Beyond that, however, it is helpful to recognize that the most voluminous information routinely collected is unlikely to illuminate every problem that arises. It is best to rely on a combination of a modest, routinely collected data base and an organization capable of collecting special purpose data with competence and speed.

Data pertain to the past, and all best efforts do not guarantee an accurate description of the future. Uncertainty is greater for small areas than for large ones; yet for the most part the market for health services is local. Let us therefore acknowledge the following: It is a statistical property of small numbers to display greater variation or instability than large numbers; many projections for small areas are bound to be in error; the best protection against erroneous forecasts lies not in technical improvements in forecasting but in flexible operation; provision for flexibility costs something extra; and therefore it may well be the principal business of planning organizations to develop and disseminate devices that promote flexibility.

Three other changes seem necessary. First, in order to be effective, a planning agency must focus its efforts. To try to plan everything is to accomplish nothing. It is useful to ask not only what the most important problems are, but which of them are most susceptible to solution at present. Second, the preoccupation in health planning with structure and process has been excessive and may reflect in part the new requirement of consumer participation, which is sometimes translated into attempts to secure local control. The sources of decision making in a society are diverse and subtle, and it is difficult to articulate precisely what makes for legitimacy of authority. Continuous preoccupation with the decision making structure is unsettling and unlikely to yield action on substantive matters. A third requirement for progress in health planning is a reversal of the tendency to dam the flow of information. Without access to systematic information, we lack knowledge of the dimensions of most of our problems and of trends.

Certain organizations, governmental and other, are collecting more and better information than ever before. However, they are holding on to it for internal processing and analysis, while other agencies are barred from collecting similar data. In this instance the quest for efficiency in information gathering has created data monopolies. A monopoly over information exercised for an extended period does not serve the public interest, because some problems go unexplored. The work done by insiders escapes criticism, and outside scholars work in areas where information is more readily available.

New organizations

The increased flow of public funds into health in the mid-1960's led to the purchase of additional services from the private sector at large. Production by government facilities did not increase and there was only a modest expansion of facilities aimed exclusively at government beneficiaries.

The latter facilities were the neighborhood health centers, most of which were launched by the Office of Economic Opportunity (OEO) and later supplemented with centers funded by the Department of Health, Education, and Welfare. Neighborhood health centers were meant to exert a direct influence on the way in which medical care was provided to persons in low-income areas. They were to provide comprehensive, or a broad range of, services, including out-reach services by indigenous workers and legal services that do not usually fall within the purview of a health facility; their services were to be continuous, in contrast to the fragmentation and discontinuity that characterizes services in hospital out-patient departments. Accordingly, they could assume a measure of responsibility for the health care of the registered population.

The results achieved by neighborhood health centers have varied, and the conclusions drawn from the findings depend to some extent on the priority assigned to the several goals. The extent of comprehensiveness depends on the size of the budget. Continuity, in the sense of seeing the same physician in successive visits, is difficult to achieve, so continuity is often sought through the patient's chart. The idea of serving a designated population is similar to a bounded catchment area, which is easier to implement in rural areas than in a large city. But even apart from feasibility, it is necessary to spell out the circumstances under which it serves the interests of a group to limit their options.

Published figures show that the neighborhood health center compares favorably in cost with other methods of delivering personal health services. I have reservations concerning these findings. Allocations of overhead can make a big difference in allowing for services that some programs provide and others do not. More important is the fact that a "registered" population is not the same as a population enrolled in a health insurance plan, in that members of the former lack the financial incentive of the latter to obtain care within a particular program and not outside. The concept of a "registered" population associated with a neighborhood health center serves to overstate the denominator in any per capita computation and thus understates per capita cost. These technical reservations seem to receive some support from the reluctance exhibited by neighborhood health centers to change from lump-sum funding to financing through the sale of services to patients under the usual financing programs, such as Medicaid and Medicare. It is now recognized that this method of delivering health services is unlikely to be extended to large numbers of people for reasons of cost and because of recurring doubts about the desirability of maintaining separate health services systems for the poor. What reason is there to believe that a separate system for the poor will provide health services equal to those received by the rest of the population?

To many people the concept of the Health Maintenance Organization continues to pose a mystery. Depending on the context, it seems to change in form. At times the HMO seems to be prepaid group practice dressed in a respectable legislative cloak. Sometimes the HMO is either prepaid group practice or the medical foundation, which is an association of solo practitioners. To those who formulated the concept, the HMO is prepaid group practice *or* the medical foundation *or* any other organization that meets the requirements of a basic definition: Subscribers will receive contractual assurance of access to a specified, fairly broad set of health care benefits in return for a stated premium. The form of HMO ownership, non-profit or otherwise, is left open, as is the method of paying providers of service.

The HMO concept is most closely associated with Dr. Paul Ellwood, who has developed, modified, and promoted it in the course of serving as consultant to both the Nixon Administration and a Senate subcommittee chaired by Senator Edward Kennedy. Disenchanted with the course of events in the late 1960's, particularly the continuing rise in expenditures and cost without a sign of improvement in the geographic distribution of health resources, Dr. Ellwood placed the blame on the ineffectiveness of government regulation and planning, and sought relief through competition in the market place. The aim in promoting the HMO and fostering its growth is to obtain diversity; HMO's would compete with one another, as well as with the more traditional health services system. The inherent incentives of the HMO were toward efficiency; any tendencies toward underserving the consumer could be mitigated by feeding him information on the quality of care.

It is worth acknowledging the political ingenuity displayed by Ellwood in bringing under the HMO umbrella both prepaid group practice and the medical foundation, arch-rivals in California. While prepaid group practice has long enjoyed support from liberals, a medical foundation is the creature of the local medical society. Extending the HMO even further, without restriction as to form of ownership, serves to attract support also from other health insurance plans and business corporations.

Bringing costs under control

The main interest of the Nixon Administration was to do something to bring health expenditures under control, and prepaid group practice has a record showing lower per capita expenditures than other forms of health financing and delivery. The major source of savings in prepaid group practice is in hospital use, and the most widely quoted figure on the magnitude of the savings is 20 per cent, popularized by Donald Straus, consultant to the Rockefeller Panel Reports. It is noteworthy that by 1960 it was no longer taken for granted that more hospital care for a population is necessarily better.

Given the desirability of savings in hospital use, three questions arise concerning the reports on prepaid group practice. First, prepaid group practice is usually associated with a tight bed supply, as in California, or with difficulty in access to a hospital, as in New York City. Is the effect attributed to prepaid group practice confounded with these other control mechanisms? Second, how are the savings attributed to prepaid group practice to be explained? Thus, why is the length of stay the same in prepaid group practice as in other insurance plans? If the admission rates are equal, a longer average duration of stay is to be expected for the population with a more selective hospital admissions policy. Furthermore, the 20 per cent savings figure in New York is over a matched insured population and in California, over the population at large. Should it not be higher in California, where physicians in prepaid group practice share in hospital economies? Third, prepaid group practice in this country has been limited to five million persons and to a few thousand physicians. It has been out of the mainstream of medicine, attracting doctors and clientele with a special taste for this form of medical organization. Is it proper to extrapolate past experience to much larger numbers, such as the 60 million subscribers projected by the Committee for National Health Insurance?

Proponents of the HMO have also claimed possible savings due to economies of size in the medical firm; at present there is no evidence for this. It is also argued that solo-practice fee-for-service medicine is inherently inefficient, so that methods of organization and payment that differ from it in basic respects may be presumed to be more efficient. Yet the HMO proposal takes a neutral position with respect to the manner in which the provider is paid.

The HMO is intended to secure the benefits of competition. In any meaningful sense competition depends on the presence of large numbers of buyers and sellers. Constraints on the number of sellers can stem from low density of population, establishment of a legal monopoly—as through a medical foundation organized by a local medical society—or even implementation of the concept of the catchment area, under which local resources serve only the residents who are excluded from prepaid benefits elsewhere.

What concerns me most about the HMO is the tendency to overlook Ellwood's original premise and promise to provide consumers with useful measures of quality of care within a couple of years. When such measures are lacking and consumers remain unable to judge the quality of medical care they get, it is no longer tenable to posit an identity of interests between the consumers and the HMO that they join. To introduce a new institution, such as a for-profit HMO, is to attempt to replicate through the market the traditional relationship of trust that is believed to characterize the physician-patient relationship at its best. It is not evident that this is an acceptable risk to impose on the consumer.

Most of the complex, apparently irrational arrangements in the health services stem from certain unique and peculiar characteristics of medical care, particularly the inability of the consumer to determine how good it is and how much to get. If our capability for identifying and measuring the quality of care were improved, the risks posed by new organizational arrangements would diminish greatly. But so would the warrant for many existing arrangements, such as licensure of personnel and paying doctors and hospitals at their individual rates. If consumers had adequate knowledge about health care, the service could be priced in the market.

The point I wish to emphasize is that our present inability to measure the quality of care and to disseminate such information among consumers is not a mere detail to be noted and passed over. Rather, it is a central consideration in any effort to grapple with the fundamental problems of health policy. To wish that we had such knowledge is not the same as to have it. To acknowledge that such knowledge is now lacking is to recognize that substantial risks may inhere in departing from existing arrangements between consumers and providers, particularly doctors.

The HMO prototype in prepaid group practice represents a marked deviation from mainstream arrangements, as would the establishment of for-profit HMO's. Yet many planners, scholars, and politicians seem to prefer the risks of a sharp break from the present to the potentially large savings that could be derived from intensive concentration on more modest changes, such as a reduction in the supply of hospital beds or abandonment of cost reimbursement. In view of the fact that the more modest proposals are also reversible at will, I do not understand why.

7

The
successes and failures
of
federal housing policy

ANTHONY DOWNS

To ASSESS the effectiveness of federal housing-related policies in the 1960's and early 1970's, it is necessary to make some arbitrary distinctions, heroic assumptions, and controversial judgments. The first arbitrary distinction is to divide all federal housing-related policies into the following four categories:

1) *Indirect influences:* Actions influencing *housing production* through monetary, fiscal, and credit policies aimed primarily at maintaining prosperity or fighting inflation.

2) *Direct financial influences:* Actions aimed at affecting the *total supply* of housing through credit and institutional arrangements rather than direct financial aid. An example is the creation of the Federal Home Loan Mortgage Corporation to help establish an effective secondary market in mortgages.

3) *Direct housing subsidies:* Actions aimed at increasing the supply of housing directly available to low-income households. Examples are the Section 235 and 236 programs.

4) *Community-related programs:* Actions that affect the structure of urban areas and therefore impact housing markets and the neighborhood conditions incorporated in the everyday meaning of the term "housing." Examples are the Interstate Highway Program, urban renewal, and the Model Cities Program.

The second arbitrary distinction consists of dividing the time under consideration into three periods: 1. low-priority period (1960 through 1965); 2. reassessment period (1966 through 1968); 3. high-production period (1968 through 1972, and perhaps longer).

Evaluating policies requires comparing their results with the objectives they were intended to achieve. Congress adopted in 1949 a national housing goal of "providing a decent home and a suitable living environment for every American family," and in 1968 Congress linked that goal to a production target of 26 million additional housing units from 1968 through 1978, six million for occupancy by low-income and moderate-income households. Since that basic goal conceals many ambiguities, I will make the heroic assumption—derived from Congressional legislation, Administration statements, and my observation of federal behavior—that federal housing-related policies were designed to achieve the following major objectives: 1) *High-level housing production*—Encouraging private construction of enough new housing units to serve needs created by rising total population, rising incomes, demolition, and migration. 2) *Adequate housing finance*—Providing a sufficient flow of mortgage and other funds to finance the production described above. 3) *Reduced housing costs*—Reducing the cost of housing occupancy (including costs of construction, land, financing, and operation) so that more households can afford decent units. 4) *Overall economic stabilization*—Causing countercyclical changes in total housing production to help stabilize the overall economy. 5) *Stabilization of housing production*—Insulating the home-building industry from large-scale fluctuations associated with the general business cycle. (This objective is diametrically opposed to the preceding one.) 6) *Attraction of private capital*—Designing incentives to encourage private capital to finance most housing production, including that for low-income and moderate-income households. 7) *Housing assistance to low-income and moderate-income households*—Enabling such households living in substandard quality units to occupy decent units, and financially aiding such households who now pay inordinately high fractions of their incomes to occupy decent units. 8) *Increased home ownership.* 9) *Improved inner-city conditions*—Helping large cities to upgrade deteriorating older neighborhoods and to prevent further decay in aging "gray areas." 10) *Creation of good new neighborhoods*—Helping private developers and local governments create desirable new neighborhoods in subdivisions and new communities.

Many other secondary objectives were also served by housing-related policies, but I have limited this enumeration to only the primary ones. The objectives listed above are not entirely consistent with each other. Overall economic stabilization, in particular, often conflicts with almost all the others, since it requires sharp reductions in housing production during upswings in the rest of the economy.

The "trickle-down" process

To evaluate housing-related policies, it is necessary to understand the "trickle-down" or "filtering" process that dominates American urban development. All newly-built U.S. urban housing (except mobile homes, which are not allowed in most parts of metropolitan areas) must meet the relatively high standards of size and quality set in local building codes and zoning regulations. The cost of meeting those standards is quite high. Consequently, less than half of all U.S. households can afford to occupy newly-built housing without either receiving a direct subsidy or spending over 25 per cent of their incomes on housing. Hence, only households in the upper half of the income distribution normally live in brand-new housing.

This pervasive exclusion of low-income and moderate-income households from brand-new units has profound impacts upon our housing markets—and upon American society in general. Throughout the world, new urban housing is mainly constructed on vacant land around the edges of already built-up neighborhoods. Therefore, all urban areas normally expand outwards. Most of the newest housing is always on the outer edge; most of the oldest housing is in the center; and moderately-aged housing lies in between.

Outside the U.S., households of all income levels may be found at any given distance from the center of urbanization. Both poor and rich live in older housing near the center—the poor in deteriorated units, the rich in units they have maintained or rehabilitated. Similarly, both poor and rich live in brand-new housing on the urban periphery—the poor in low-quality shacks they have built themselves, and the rich in new units constructed to high-quality standards. Middle-income groups concentrate in the rings between the center and the outer edge, occupying "used" housing that is still of good quality.

In the United States, it is illegal both to build brand-new low-quality housing units and to allow older units to deteriorate into low-quality status. But the laws against these two types of substandard housing are not enforced to the same degree. Laws against *new* low-quality units are rigorously enforced in all urban areas. Therefore, only households in the upper half of the income distribution can afford to live in much of the urban periphery where new growth is concentrated. But laws against *older* low-quality housing are only moderately enforced in most older neighborhoods. They are almost totally ignored in areas where the most deteriorated units are found. This is not an evil conspiracy between local officials and landlords. Rather, it is a necessary recognition of the inability of many very poor households to pay for high-quality housing. No such recognition, however, is extended to the poor in newly-built areas. There, local officials zealously exclude the poor by enforcing high-quality housing standards to the letter.

This process creates a major spatial separation of households by income group in U.S. urban areas. The most affluent urban households reside mainly around the suburban periphery; the poorest urban households are concentrated in the oldest inventory near the center (sometimes in older suburbs too); and middle-income groups live in between. Moreover, each neighborhood goes through a typical life cycle. When it is first built, the brand-new housing units there are occupied by relatively affluent households. Then, as these housing units age slightly, the most affluent households move on to still newer areas farther out. Other households move in who are somewhat lower in the *relative* income distribution, but still have good incomes. This "trickle-down" process continues as these housing units age. But they still provide excellent shelter as long as their occupants maintain them well.

Eventually, however, the income groups who move in are too poor to maintain these units—especially since maintenance costs have by then risen, and lending institutions are reluctant to risk funds in improving them. Then the housing deteriorates markedly and the neighborhood becomes a "slum." This life cycle normally takes from 40 to 60 years. (Some older neighborhoods never experience it because they are so well located that wealthy households remain and maintain the property in good condition.)

For the predominant majority of households in U.S. metropolitan areas, this "trickle-down" process works very well. It furnishes good-quality housing in neighborhoods free from the vexing problems of extreme poverty, since nearly all very poor people (except some elderly residents) are excluded. But for the poorest urban households, especially poor minority-group members, this process is a social disaster. It compels thousands of the poorest households to concentrate together in the worst-quality housing located in older neighborhoods near the urban center. This causes a "critical mass" effect that multiplies the impact of many problems associated with poverty. Such neighborhoods become dominated by high crime rates, vandalism, unemployment, drug addiction, broken homes, gang warfare, and other conditions almost universally regarded by Americans as undesirable. Most households with high enough incomes to have a choice of living somewhere else move out. So do many employers and retailers anxious to escape such conditions. This withdrawal of those with economic and other resources further weakens the neighborhood and removes many possible checks to the negative forces described above. Only a minority of the people living in these areas of concentrated poverty engage in destructive behavior; so the real victims are the non-destructive majority of poor residents there. They are prevented from moving out by the exclusionary barriers erected in most middle-income and upper-income neighborhoods. Thus, they must bear the social costs of providing the fine-quality neighborhoods enjoyed by the upper two thirds of the income distribution.

Yet prosperous households have strong arguments against opening up their neighborhoods to unrestricted entry by low-income households. They have observed the destructive environments in concentrated poverty areas, and they do not want such conditions where they live. They have no way of screening low-income households entering their areas to keep out destructive ones while admitting the non-destructive majority; so they prefer to keep *all* poor households out. This attitude is reinforced by their experience that nearly all non-poor households stop moving into a neighborhood whenever many poor people enter. As normal housing turnover proceeds, the area inevitably becomes mainly poor, because only other poor households are willing to move in. This causes a temporary decline in property values that threatens the major investment residents have made in their homes. Thus, many powerful forces pressure middle-income and upper-income households to persist in exclusionary behavior—in spite of its unjust consequences for the non-destructive majority of low-income households "trapped" in concentrated poverty areas.

This explanation may seem far removed from evaluating federal housing-related policies, but understanding the "trickle-down" process is crucial for comprehending how those policies actually worked. In fact, the failure of federal officials to develop such an understanding caused them to be surprised by the many unexpected consequences of their actions, as will be explained below.

Other key background factors

Before examining federal housing-related policies and actions, it is necessary to describe several additional background factors. First, there was an acute housing shortage during and right after World War II. But from 1950 onwards, the number of housing units built each year exceeded the number of new households formed, gradually easing the shortage. (Table 1 shows housing starts from 1950 through 1972.) *An approximate balance was attained between total supply and total demand in most urban housing markets by 1960.* True, several million urban households were still in substandard or overcrowded units. But most urban households that could afford decent housing were living in such housing by 1960, except in racially segregated areas.

Second, until the late 1960's, *housing production had a natural tendency to move in a countercyclical pattern in relation to general economic activity.* Most buyers of new or existing homes borrow large fractions of the total cost and finance it over long time periods. Hence the amount they must pay each month is strongly affected by the interest rate. When interest rates rise, therefore, many households who could formerly afford to buy new housing can no longer do so. Conversely, when rates fall, many more households can afford to buy homes. Developers of rental apartments also borrow heavily and are therefore similarly affected. But short-term borrowers of money for other purposes—such as consumer loans or business investment in plants and equipment—are less sensitive to changes in interest rates. When the economy moves from a recession into general prosperity, there is rising competition for funds, and interest rates of all

TABLE 1. *Annual Housing Starts by Type, 1950-1972*[1]

YEAR	CONVENTIONALLY-CONSTRUCTED HOUSING STARTS[2]	MOBILE HOMES	TOTAL HOUSING STARTS
1950	1,951,648	63,100	2,014,748
1951	1,491,207	67,300	1,558,507
1952	1,504,520	83,000	1,587,520
1953	1,438,372	76,900	1,515,272
1954	1,550,445	76,000	1,626,445
1955	1,645,715	111,900	1,757,615
1956	1,345,739	104,800	1,450,539
1957	1,221,647	107,600	1,329,247
1958	1,375,588	100,400	1,475,988
1959	1,528,836	120,500	1,649,336
1960	1,272,137	103,700	1,375,837
1961	1,365,000	90,200	1,455,200
1962	1,492,400	118,000	1,610,400
1963	1,642,000	150,840	1,792,840
1964	1,561,000	191,320	1,752,320
1965	1,509,600	216,000	1,725,600
1966	1,195,900	217,000	1,412,900
1967	1,321,817	240,000	1,561,817
1968	1,545,500	318,000	1,863,500
1969	1,499,920	413,000	1,912,920
1970	1,466,759	401,000	1,867,759
1971	2,084,500	496,570	2,581,070
1972	2,378,500	575,900	2,954,400

[1] Source: U.S. Department of Housing and Urban Development, Division of Research and Statistics; and Mobile Home Manufacturers Association.
[2] Conventionally *constructed* housing starts can be financed with either VA- and FHA-insured mortgages or *conventional mortgages*.

types go up. Because a slight rise in mortgage interest rates cuts down the number of borrowers sharply, lenders shift their funds into non-housing channels where they can get higher rates without losing volume. Housing starts therefore decline because of inability to finance mortgage loans. When a general recession occurs, other demands for funds slack off, and more money becomes available for mortgage loans. Mortgage rates drop and terms (length of loan and amount of down-payment required) improve, so housing production rises.

Third, *the single most dynamic force in the housing markets of most large metropolitan areas in the 1960's was the rapid growth of the black and Spanish-speaking populations in central cities.* The resulting "massive" transition of whole neighborhoods from mainly white to mainly non-white occupancy did not reduce housing segregation, but it greatly improved the amount and quality of housing available to minority-group members. Moreover, it generated large-scale movement of white households into outlying suburbs.

The low-priority period: 1960-1965

In the early 1960's, housing was not regarded as a high-priority item of domestic concern by Congress or the executive branch. The general goal of providing "a decent home and a suitable living environment for every American family" had been stated in 1949, but no specific production targets had been adopted by Congress. Federal housing policy was vested in the Housing and Home Finance Agency (HHFA), which did not enjoy departmental status. Major housing-related policies and actions in this period can be summarized under five principal headings.

1) *Total housing production was still viewed by federal economic policy makers as a countercyclical force useful in stabilizing the economy as a whole.* Hence, the monetary and fiscal conditions dominating housing production were oriented toward non-housing objectives, with their impact upon housing treated as a residual rather than a controlling or central factor.

2) *The preferential tax and mortgage insurance treatment provided to home owners continued to stimulate ownership as a preferred form of tenure during this period, although apartment construction began rising toward the middle of the decade.* Home owners who occupy their own dwellings can deduct their mortgage interest and local property taxes from their federally-taxable incomes. This tax saving provides a hidden housing subsidy that accrues mainly to households in the upper half of the income distribution. Even in the early 1960's, this hidden subsidy to the relatively affluent was far larger than all direct subsidies to poorer households combined. Moreover, mortgage insurance provided by the Federal Housing Administration made home ownership possible for more and more Americans. By 1960, 61.9 per cent of all occupied housing units were owner-occupied, as compared to 55.0 per cent in 1950, and 43.6 per cent in 1940. Home ownership held its own in the 1960's but did not expand much. This resulted from the rise in multi-family units (mainly rental units) to around 33 per cent of total starts in the mid-1960's and 40 per cent in the early 1970's.

3) *Federally-financed highway construction and urban renewal programs were designed in part to bolster central-city economies, but they actually stimulated rapid population growth and job expansion in the suburbs.* Urban expressways were supposed to help downtown centers maintain dominance over their surrounding areas. Urban

renewal was intended to remove blight and to promote economically self-sustaining redevelopment. These programs succeeded in aiding many downtowns—as evidenced by the surge of major downtown investments in private office buildings and public facilities in the late 1960's. But such programs also produced the following unforeseen "side effects" that heavily counteracted their positive achievements:

• Thousands of small industries and retail businesses displaced by highways and urban renewal simply went out of business, and even more displaced industries and retail operations moved to newer, larger, and more efficient suburban sites.

• Hundreds of thousands of low-income households displaced by urban renewal and highway clearance shifted into older housing in nearby once-stable neighborhoods. Hence, blight was often just moved rather than eliminated.

• Radial and circumferential expressways made outlying locations more convenient than congested near-in locations; so many warehouse and distribution facilities moved away from central-city sites.

• Commuting between relatively distant suburban homes and downtown or other in-city jobs became much easier; so millions of households shifted from central-city housing into growing suburban subdivisions.

• Since the worst urban blight was in concentrated poverty areas, urban renewal efforts focused upon removing blight-created vacant sites in such areas. But most firms and households with enough money to support self-sustaining redevelopment would not locate there, because those sites were still surrounded by concentrated poverty.

• Highway routes and urban renewal projects were often deliberately located in poor, minority-group neighborhoods to force relocation of groups regarded as undesirable by the local power structure. This tactic created unfair hardships for those displaced, and merely shifted minority-group occupancy to other nearby neighborhoods.

Why did the private interests, federal officials, and Congressmen who designed these programs fail to anticipate such consequences? First, very few of them understood the nature of urban areas or the dynamics of the "trickle-down" process. Second, each major federally funded policy was initiated for rather narrowly conceived reasons by a specialized group with no responsibility for coping with its broader consequences. For example, highway engineers and the automobile industry promoted giant urban expressways in order to move traffic and increase road capacity, but they had little comprehension of, or concern for, the likely impacts upon the local tax base or the fabric of urban life. Third, there was no effective way to coordinate all these specialized programs at the local level, since no one local government had overall responsibility for an entire metropolitan area. These three factors resulted in a complete inability to "orchestrate" specialized federal programs into a unified theme—or even to achieve minimal coordination among them.

4) *Production of directly-subsidized housing for low-income and moderate-income households was kept at very low levels during this period by small-scale Congressional appropriations and local resistance to such housing.* From 1960 through 1965, only 283,610 directly-subsidized housing units for low-income and moderate-income households were started. That was 3.2 per cent of all conventionally-constructed housing built during this low-priority period. Rising black occupancy of large high-rise public housing projects in big cities was generating increased local resistance to construction of any public housing except that occupied by the elderly. After the 221(d)(3) program was passed, some subsidized units for moderate-income households were created. However, federal officials responsible for promoting subsidized housing tended to measure their performance against past low levels of such output, rather than against any quantified concept of "national needs."

5) *In spite of low production of subsidized units directly available to the poor, housing conditions in most urban areas improved for all income groups because total production, less demolitions, exceeded net household formation.* Hence, the "trickle-down" process had some positive effects. From 1960 to 1965, the number of U.S. households rose by 4.452 million, according to Census Bureau estimates. But total housing starts (including mobile homes) equalled 8.161 million units. Subtraction of 600,000 demolitions per year yields a net increase of 5.161 million units—or 709,000 more than the increase in households during that period. This "surplus" should be reduced somewhat to allow for needs generated by migration. Nevertheless, subsequent data have shown that housing quality was improving in most urban areas from 1960 through 1965.

The reassessment period: 1966-1968

A number of dramatic events from 1965 to 1968 caused a nation-wide reassessment of the low priority the federal government had been placing upon meeting housing needs. Most striking were the civil disorders that occurred in over 150 cities from 1965 through early 1968. In the summer of 1967, President Lyndon Johnson appointed a National Advisory Commission on Civil Disorders to investigate the causes of and possible remedies for these disturbances. By March 1968, the Commission had produced a report setting forth its major findings. It recommended massive expansion of the production of directly-subsidized units for low-income and moderate-income households to 600,000 units in the next year, and six million units in the next five years.

A second crucial event was the severe "credit crunch" in housing mortgage markets in 1966. In 1965, just as the economy was recovering from its slight slump in 1963, rapid escalation of the Vietnam conflict required large federal outlays. Combined with ongoing prosperity, as well as spending on the space program and Great Society programs, this caused an extraordinary expansion in overall economic activity. By 1966, the Federal Reserve Board decided to sharply curtail the growth of the money supply to reduce inflationary pressures. This produced a sudden jump in interest rates, which in turn resulted in a startling reduction in available mortgage funds. Non-subsidized conventional housing starts dropped 22.3 per cent from 1.446 million in 1965 to 1.124 million in 1966—the lowest level since before 1950. In Southern California, the nation's largest housing market, total starts plunged to one third of the all-time record level attained in 1963, and the local building industry was decimated. Leaders in both home building and savings and loan associations began lobbying to insulate mortgage credit more completely from cyclical changes in general credit availability. This led to the creation of non-budgetary agencies capable of borrowing funds in the nation's bond markets to support mortgages when cyclically-tied sources of funds dried up. Moreover, a new form of security backed by mortgages was developed, but in a form more attractive to pension funds and other large-scale investors. Consequently, mortgage markets became considerably more insulated from the general business cycle than they had been in the past—though by no means fully insulated.

A further stimulus to the reassessment of housing priorities came from two reports by federally appointed commissions. The National Commission on Urban Problems, headed by former Senator Paul H. Douglas, was appointed by President Johnson in 1967 in response to a 1965 Congressional directive. The Commission held public hearings in many cities, commissioned dozens of fact finding studies, and presented a final report entitled *Building the American City* in late 1968. This report urged the federal government to measure its housing programs against some estimate of "national housing needs," rather than against past levels of performance. The Commission also recommended that 2.0 to 2.25 million housing starts be undertaken every year, including at least 500,000 units for low-income and moderate-income households other than the elderly. The second commission was the President's Committee on Urban Housing, a group of prestigious citizens headed by industrialist Edgar F. Kaiser. Appointed by President Johnson in June 1967, it focused on methods of making housing available to American households at lower cost than in the past. The Committee's final report, *A Decent Home*, recommended that Congress adopt a 10-year production goal of 26 million additional housing units, including at least six million for lower-income families. Still another major event contributing to the reassessment of housing priorities was the elevation of the former Housing and Home Finance Agency to Cabinet status in 1965 as the new Department of Housing and Urban Development.

The culmination of all these events was passage of the Housing and Urban Development Act of 1968. This landmark bill set an official housing production target of 26 million additional new and rehabilitated units to be built from 1968 through 1978, including six million units available to low-income and moderate-income households. Toward this end, it created two new, generously funded housing-subsidy programs for moderate-income households that combined an interest subsidy, depreciation tax shelter, and some features of a housing allowance. These were the Section 236 program for rental housing, and the Section 235 program for ownership housing. Also included among the Act's provisions were the creation of secondary mortgage market instruments to help insulate mortgage credit from the business cycle; liberalization of credit terms on market-rate mortgage loan insurance for households in high-risk areas, or with relatively poor credit, or making very small down-payments; expanded funding for public housing, and an emphasis on creating scattered-site, low-rise units to avoid excessive poverty concentration; guaranteeing of privately-issued bonds to finance new communities; and changes in the urban renewal program emphasizing shorter-range, more comprehensive actions and requiring more housing for low-income and moderate-income households on renewal sites.

This bill, plus the major appropriations for it passed by Congress, signalled a dramatic rise in the status of housing and housing-related problems on the nation's priority list. Combined with the Model Cities Act passed earlier, the Housing and Urban Development Act of 1968 created a whole arsenal of housing and community development tools that—in theory—were capable of responding effectively to many of the physical and social problems plaguing urban areas.

The high-production period: 1968-1973

Before the Democratic Administration responsible for the Housing and Urban Development Act of 1968 could carry it out, it was replaced by a new Republican Administration in 1969. As a result, there was an almost total turnover of top-level personnel in HUD, the Bureau of the Budget, and the White House. But even if the Democrats had stayed in power, a major turnover would probably have occurred in accordance with the "Law of Inescapable Discontinuity": *High-level federal personnel change so fast that almost no major federal program is ever initially conceived of, drafted into legislation, shepherded through Congress, and then carried out by the same offi-*

cials. Therefore, no program is ever perceived in the same way by those who put it into effect as by those who invented it.

Another important determinant of the behavior of federal officials is the "Law of Compulsive Innovation": *Newly-installed administrators have a strong desire to reject what their predecessors have started, and to emphasize programs they create themselves so they can claim full credit for whatever success results.* Consequently, they tend to ignore the lessons their predecessors have learned from experience. It was difficult, however, for the incoming Republicans to start over completely, since the massive Housing and Urban Development Act of 1968 had just been passed and funded. So HUD's new managers expressed their originality by emphasizing housing production and technology as the keys to urban problems, and de-emphasizing other facets of urban development. Unfortunately, as Secretary Romney soon discovered, this partial approach to solving urban problems ignored the perplexing social difficulties that had become visible in the reassessment period.

A corollary of the "Law of Compulsive Innovation" had an even more drastic impact upon HUD's behavior: *Whenever one party replaces the other in the executive branch, the newcomers have a compulsive desire to reorganize nearly every agency.* Since all human organizations are imperfect, and large bureaucracies are especially subject to inertia and malfunction, it is always easy to justify reorganization as "required" to improve performance. HUD and FHA were subjected to several overlapping reorganizations that involved both reshuffling functions in Washington and creating a whole new decentralized layer of regional offices. The internal confusion generated by these reorganizations had a devastating impact upon HUD's capabilities.

The new team at HUD charged off in pursuit of technical improvements in housing production by launching Operation Breakthrough. This was to be a three-phased movement encouraging more mass-production of housing in factories to meet large aggregated markets, thereby achieving economies of scale that would reduce housing costs. The first phase was to design new ways to build housing industrially; the second phase was to demonstrate those new methods by constructing such housing on a number of prototype sites; and the third phase was to serve large-scale markets with those systems that appeared most successful.

Meanwhile, however, a series of other developments stimulated the most massive housing production in American history. The Nixon Administration's response to inflation in 1968 and 1969 was to induce a nationwide recession through flattened federal spending and tight monetary policy. Hence builders had difficulty obtaining adequate mortgage credit in 1970 for conventionally-financed units. But Section 235 and Section 236 financing was available, so thousands of builders shifted to the new direct-subsidy programs. Non-directly-subsidized housing starts fell from 1.382 million in 1968 to 1.036 million in 1970— the lowest total since before 1950. But subsidized starts shot upward from 163,360 in 1968 (the record high before the new programs were available) to over 430,000 in both 1970 and 1971. Thus in 1971 the number of directly-subsidized housing units started was *nine times* as great as the annual average in the low-priority period.

At the same time, the number of non-child-oriented households was rising rapidly in the late 1960's, and many wanted to find relatively inexpensive housing even if it did not meet the high-quality standards required of conventionally-built new units. Therefore, consumer acceptance of mobile homes escalated dramatically. From 1955 through 1961, around 100,000 mobile home units were shipped annually. But from 1962 onwards, annual shipments rose steadily, reaching over 500,000 units by 1972. In fact, since 1969, one out of every five new housing units created in the United States each year has been a mobile home.

Moreover, in 1971 there occurred the usual huge movement of financial resources into housing right after the low point in a general recession as savings flows into savings and loan associations reached all-time highs. This traditional surge of mortgage credit was augmented by the flight of investment funds from the stock market. Although the stock market recovered sharply from its 1969-70 downslide during 1971 and 1972, by 1973 it was well below its 1965 and 1966 levels. In the past, major controllers of many investment funds had always avoided real estate as too risky and specialized. But now they compared this long-term stagnation in stock values with the steady and seemingly endless rise in land values and real property prices during the same period, and consequently, pension funds, bank trust departments, and large corporations began to put billions into real estate from 1970 through 1973. Moreover, dozens of real estate investment trusts (REIT's) issued stock in equity markets and used the billions so raised to invest in real estate. The result was a flood of credit into real estate markets unprecedented in both size and duration. This flood was responsible for the sudden escalation of non-subsidized conventionally-built housing starts from the post-War low of 1.035 million units in 1970 to 2.028 million in 1972—almost a doubling in two years. Millions of 95-per cent loans greatly expanded the market for housing ownership, helping to support these enormous production levels without any great rise in vacancies. By 1972, rising prosperity offered another such support as the economy moved into a traditional upswing. But real estate credit did not soon decline as in past upswings.

The consequence of these various developments was a rise in total housing starts to a plateau of about 1.9 million units annually from 1968 through 1970—a total exceeding any previous annual production

level except the 2.0 million units in 1950. Then, in 1971 and 1972, housing starts shot up to 2.6 million and 3.0 million units respectively.

The dark side of high production

The massive levels of housing production generated a number of
major consequences wholly unexpected by the federal government,
and quite disruptive to its housing policies:

1) The ability of the supposedly obsolete housing industry to
produce 3.0 million units in a single year—including 2.4 million
"stick-built" units (i.e., not factory-built like mobile homes)—proved
that industrialized housing was not necessary to reach the nation's
housing goals, as Operation Breakthrough had supposed. Operation
Breakthrough did persuade many states to adopt statewide building
codes for industrialized housing, but it failed to produce housing
units at lower cost than traditional methods or to aggregate markets
that were large enough to absorb truly mass-produced factory
housing.

2) HUD and the Congress had assumed the nation had a housing
shortage when they established the 10-year goal of 26 million additional units in 1968. They failed to recognize that many of the worst-
quality units to be replaced were in rural areas—but most new housing
production was in urban areas. Hence, the total number of housing
units available in many large metropolitan areas shot up well above
the number of households there. This accelerated the entire "trickle-
down" process. Millions of white households moved out of central
cities to new suburban units, and black and Spanish-speaking households moved out of the worst housing into the units thus made available. *The stunning success of HUD's efforts to increase total housing
production—actually produced largely by factors beyond HUD's
control—thus generated the unexpected and undesirable result of
rising abandonment and vacancy in the concentrated poverty
"ghettos" of many large cities.*

3) The new direct-subsidy programs shifted the initiative in creating housing for low-income and moderate-income households to
private builders rather than government bureaucrats. These programs
also funded large numbers of such units and created strong tax-shelter
incentives for private investment in them. As a result, HUD's new
area offices were swamped with applications to create and purchase
new and rehabilitated subsidized units, and high-level officials
pressured the area offices to speed up processing. This occurred in
the midst of the personnel disruptions caused by HUD's reorganizations, and thus led to a breakdown in HUD's administrative controls
in many areas. Thousands of poor households were bilked by un-
scrupulous speculators. A few outright corrupt practices by FHA
officials were uncovered in some cities, and the resulting scandals

shocked Secretary Romney and FHA leaders into denouncing their own programs.

4) HUD began experiencing the high costs of emphasizing housing production without paying much attention to neighborhood conditions. Many poor families bought housing units at full market interest rates under programs that allowed tiny down-payments or accepted poor credit risks. The majority of such purchases successfully enabled low-income households to benefit from home ownership for the first time, but a significant number resulted in defaults and HUD repossessions. These defaults were concentrated in big-city poverty areas at the bottom of the "trickle-down" process. The number of units across the nation repossessed by FHA rose from its normal level of about 50,000 at any one time to over 200,000 by 1973. HUD officials regarded this not as a costly if unavoidable result of rapid escalation of housing aid to the poor, but as a "disaster."

5) The high annual cost of directly subsidizing large numbers of new housing units over the lifetimes of their mortgages began to dawn on HUD officials (although it had always been readily calculable). This cost might escalate to $7.5 billion per year by 1978 if all six million subsidized units are built by that time. True, $5.7 billion per year was already being spent in 1971 on *indirect* subsidies through home owner deductions of mortgage interest and property taxes. But those subsidies mainly to the affluent did not appear in the federal budget, so Administration officials ignored them in calculating costs.

6) Other difficulties began appearing in the direct-subsidy programs. Where many subsidized new units were clustered together—as in many public housing projects—the "flooding" of the neighborhood with low-income and moderate-income households often led to general deterioration in the surrounding area. Some subsidized units were of poor-quality construction; many were occupied by households who were not "truly poor," such as young married graduate students with temporarily low incomes. Furthermore, the rising number of directly-subsidized units placed in middle-income suburbs began to alarm the Administration's political constituents. Finally, many middle-income households began complaining when they saw poorer households living nearby in better units than they enjoyed themselves, thanks to subsidies they were helping to pay for.

These developments led the Administration to declare a moratorium on further approvals of directly-subsidized units after January 1973—both to cut costs and to reassess alternative subsidy policies. HUD also stopped all federal community development programs (urban renewal, sewer and water facility construction, open space support, Model Cities, and public facility construction) for one year. It proposed that Congress shift future funding for them into a special revenue sharing fund to be distributed directly to cities and states in accordance with a fixed formula. This proposal amounted to abdication of any specific responsibility for these activities by the federal government. Apparently, the Administration thought that categorical aid programs had failed to improve urban conditions, or it wanted to pass the political "hot potato" of making decisions concerning these touchy matters to someone else, or both.

Evaluating federal housing-related policies: 1960-1972

Because both federal housing-related policies and their objectives are so complex, there is no simple way to evaluate those policies. As a means of assessing them, I have prepared the *evaluation matrix* which appears directly below. It presents my evaluations of the

Evaluation Matrix: Types of Federal Housing-Related Policies

Objec-tives	I INDIRECT INFLU-ENCES[1]	II COM-MUNITY RELATED PROGRAMS[1]	III DIRECT FINANCIAL INFLUENCES[2]	IV DIRECT HOUSING SUB-SIDIES[2]	V ALL TYPES CON-SIDERED TOGETHER
1) High-Level Housing Production	++	NR	++	+	++
2) Adequate Housing Finance	++	NR	++	+	++
3) Reduced Housing Costs	— —	NR	— —	— —	— —
4) Overall Economic Stabilization	++	NR	—	—	+
5) Stabilization of Housing Production	—	NR	++	—	—
6) Attraction of Private Capital	++	+	++	++	++
7) Housing Assistance to Low- and Moderate-Income Households	— —	— —	—	+	+
8) Encouraging Home Ownership	+	—	++	+	+
9) Improved Inner-City Conditions	— —	—	—	—	— —
10) Creation of Good New Neighbor-hoods	++	+	++	+	++

[1] Assessed for period 1960-1972
[2] Assessed only for period 1968-1972

relative effectiveness of all four types of housing-related policies (shown in the first four columns of the matrix) in achieving all 10 primary objectives (shown in the rows). The matrix also contains a fifth column that shows my opinion concerning the *overall effectiveness* of *all* federal policies in achieving each objective. In each of the 50 cells of this matrix, policy effectiveness is "scored" on a five-position scale: very effective ($+\,+$), moderately effective ($+$), moderately ineffective ($-$), very ineffective ($-\,-$), and not relevant (NR). These ratings represent my subjective judgments, based upon the points set forth throughout this paper.

I have assessed the performance of both *Indirect Influences* and *Community-Related Programs* (columns I and II) over all three time periods (that is, from 1960 through 1972). I believe these policies were applied throughout all three periods to about the same degree of intensity in relation to their maximum potential. In contrast, I have assessed the performance of both *Direct Financial Influences* and *Direct Housing Subsidies* (columns III and IV) only during the high-production period—that is, from 1968 through 1972. I believe these policies were not applied with sufficient intensity during the two earlier periods to provide a fair test of their effectiveness. A second qualification is that the entire evaluation matrix applies only to the effectiveness of these policies in metropolitan areas. Most federal housing-related policies have not been aimed at rural areas and small cities; hence, they have been very ineffective in those places. This summary evaluation indicates that, in my opinion, federal *urban* housing-related policies of all types considered together were:

● *Very Effective* in generating high-level housing production, providing adequate housing finance, attracting private capital into housing, and creating good-quality new neighborhoods.
● *Moderately Effective* in promoting overall economic stabilization, providing housing assistance for low-income and moderate-income households, and encouraging home ownership.
● *Moderately Ineffective* in stabilizing housing production.
● *Very Ineffective* in reducing housing costs and improving conditions in deteriorating inner-city neighborhoods.

Additional conclusions

Some additional conclusions can be drawn from this analysis, and from other data not included here. First, neither the executive branch nor Congress has developed any clear, accurate, widely accepted conceptual "model" of how housing markets and the dynamics of urban development really work. This lack has resulted in the adoption of federal policies that generated theoretically foreseeable—but in fact unforeseen—adverse consequences. I believe the description of the "trickle-down" process presented in this article provides a basis for such a model.

Second, the level of total housing production crucially affects nearly all aspects of federal housing-related policy. When really high-level production is attained (as from 1968 through 1972), metropolitan area housing markets "loosen" as net additions to supply exceed the additional demand generated by population increases and rising incomes. Most of the newly-built units are located in suburban areas, and their availability tends to draw middle-income and upper-income households out of older and less desirable central-city and near-in suburban neighborhoods. This allows all income groups—including the poorest—to improve their housing, because it increases the housing choices available to them. But it may also result in abandonment of the worst-quality units, a spreading of concentrated poverty into adjacent neighborhoods, and falling property values in older areas. Hence it can be fiscally and socially damaging to central-city governments. Conversely, when total housing production remains moderately low, as it did in the early 1960's, metropolitan area housing markets tend to "tighten"; and when total production falls drastically—as it did in the 1940's—acute housing shortages may develop. Such conditions generate rising rents and home values (unless they are constrained by rent and price controls). These conditions aid central-city governments fiscally, but reduce the housing choices available to all income groups, especially the poorest.

Third, although high-level housing production aids low-income households through the "trickle-down" process, their housing conditions are improved to a much greater extent when large numbers of good-quality units (either new or existing) are made available to them through direct housing subsidies—as was done from 1968 through 1972. Consequently, providing adequate housing aid to such households requires a high level of direct federal housing subsidies, as well as high-level total housing production.

Fourth, housing production in the United States is much more strongly affected by indirect financial influences—especially federal monetary policies—than by federal policies aimed specifically at housing. Hence the federal government's key housing policies are still determined more by its attempts to influence the general level of prosperity than by its attempts to affect housing in particular. Moreover, improving housing conditions clearly has a lower national priority than maintaining general prosperity. The "natural" countercyclical forces in housing markets make the deliberate varying of housing production levels a relatively easy and effective way to help maintain general prosperity. Since (1) the vast majority of Americans are already well-housed, (2) the poor as a group receive much greater benefits from high-level prosperity than from federal attempts to improve their housing, and (3) the housing industry exhibits amazing flexibility of output (though with some serious internal costs), at least some subordination of housing improvement to the maintenance of general prosperity seems reasonable.

Fifth, the most serious urban housing problems involve many factors other than physical dwelling units, including income poverty that prevents millions of households from being able to pay for decent housing; high-quality local housing standards that exclude the poor from living in more prosperous areas; destructive personal behavior patterns exhibited by a small percentage of the residents in concentrated poverty areas that make their neighborhoods undesirable places in which to live; and middle-class withdrawal that takes place in and near concentrated poverty areas. Experience proves that attempts to combat the most serious urban housing problems are certain to fail unless they respond effectively to these factors, as well as to needs for physical dwelling units.

However, governments at all levels (federal, state, and local) almost never adopt policies that adequately respond to *all* the relevant factors. Instead, they tend to make partial, selective policy responses focused mainly upon physical production or construction, rather than social factors, because the former are both more visible and much easier to control than the latter. Governments are not likely to take actions that would upset the basic institutional structures supporting the entire "trickle-down" process, or the established behavior patterns involved in that process. The "trickle-down" process depends institutionally upon fragmented local government jurisdictions, plus spatial separation of lower-income households (especially those containing minority-group members) from middle- and upper-income households. Hence federal policies rarely challenge these established arrangements—at least not intentionally. Another class of policies that governments usually avoid are those requiring considerable time between inputs (which cost money) and outputs (which generate political support); the timing of recurrent elections gives most political leaders short-run perspectives. These biases make federal policies far less effective in dealing with the needs of low-income households in areas of concentrated poverty than in dealing with the needs of middle-income and upper-income households on the urban periphery.

Finally, despite the intractability of urban "housing problems," a major change in federal housing-related policies in the mid-1960's greatly increased their effectiveness in dealing with those problems. Instead of continuing to measure the performance of federal housing-related policies solely in relation to what they had achieved in the past, the federal government reassessed its priorities and began measuring that performance against a quantified conception of "national needs." Moreover, that conception was based upon the almost utopian goal of completely eradicating substandard housing in the United States in a single decade. This radical shift of perspective was

accompanied by a sharp escalation in the resources devoted to housing production, and outputs of both total housing units and directly-
subsidized units shot up so high that many unexpected adverse consequences began to appear. This led to the current pause in direct
federal subsidies (and probably a slowdown in total production),
which may be accompanied by another reassessment and a new
perspective.

Looking toward the future

As was noted earlier, housing problems are closely interrelated
with poverty, business cycles, the nation's financial structure, inner-
city decay and crime, and many other social issues. Therefore, it is
almost impossible to answer the question of what future federal
housing-related policies should be without going into the nation's
entire range of social and economic policies. The best I can do here
is discuss what I believe federal policy ought to be toward certain
key housing variables.

Total housing production. To meet the needs of future population
growth plus replacement of deteriorated dwellings, annual total production of new units over the next decade ought to average much
more than in the 1960's—say, about 2.6 million units including mobile
homes. (It is inescapable and probably desirable, however, that
housing production fluctuate countercyclically to at least some degree; thus this high average level would not be attained in every
year.) Because most new units will be built in the suburbs, such
high-level production could run into two serious problems. First, it
will stimulate continued withdrawal of middle-class households from
central cities. This will cause spreading abandonment and neighborhood decay unless we devise new methods of managing older neighborhoods and fund significant urban renewal efforts there. Second,
rapid extension of suburban development is already generating tremendous resistance in the form of a burgeoning "anti-growth movement" all across the nation. Activists in this movement range from
ecologists rightly worried about environmental damage to selfish
suburbanites trying to evade their share of metropolitan costs and to
exclude the poor. Because of their combined efforts, future urban
growth will be accompanied by stricter public controls and regulations aimed at upgrading the quality of urban development. This is
clearly desirable, but it will probably raise development costs and
may make sustaining high-level production difficult.

Community development and land use planning. Instead of waste-
fully "throwing federal money" at tough domestic problems like
these, the Nixon Administration proposes to throw federal money at
state and local governments and let them worry about such problems.
This "hot potato" policy involves minimum federal guidelines and

therefore only a small chance of achieving any national objectives across the country. It will, however, probably result in special state-wide or regional regulation of proposed land development with large-area impacts—big shopping centers, airports, power plants, express-ways, and environmentally fragile sites like beaches or wetlands. It would be desirable for the federal government at least to sponsor the formation of some model standards for setting ground rules with-in which private developers must operate and passing judgment on their proposed projects. But to achieve any national goals like form-ing well-planned, economically integrated "new cities," it will also be necessary either to maintain federal categorical subsidy programs, or to sneak tougher federal guidelines back into revenue sharing.

Providing housing for low-income and moderate-income house-holds. The Nixon Administration has proposed permanently cutting back the annual level of newly-constructed subsidized units for low-income and moderate-income households. Instead, it would eventu-ally assist such households through a nationwide housing allowance. Undoubtedly, we need to supplement the incomes of the poor through improved income maintenance and job creation programs even more than we need to improve their housing. Since a housing allowance is mainly a form of general income maintenance, it is sensible to adopt one as long as Congress will not adequately fund direct income maintenance. Moreover, providing aid to such households on the demand side (by *either* direct income maintenance or a housing allowance) would stimulate their greater use of the existing inventory of older housing, which is more efficient than building new units for them. Yet we also need to construct significant numbers of new units for such households. This would (a) expand the supply available to them and thereby avoid the inflationary effects of just increasing demand (as happened with Medicare); (b) allow some economic integration in new-growth areas where 50 million more Americans will reside in the next 25 years, but where there is no existing inven-tory; and (c) create certain types of units not provided by private builders (such as large ones for big families). Thus, *both* demand-side and supply-side subsidies—funded at significant levels—are re-quired to meet the housing needs of low-income and moderate-income households.

Combatting inner-city decay. The greatest *urban* housing deficien-cies are in the decaying environments of inner-city "crisis ghettos" and nearby areas. Paradoxically, I believe the intractable social problems of these areas cannot be resolved without creating many subsidized housing opportunities for poorer households in suburban and other non-poverty neighborhoods. In the long run, reducing the poverty concentrations produced by the "trickle-down" process is essential to either upgrading existing inner-city populations or redeveloping their neighborhoods with "balanced mixtures" of households from all income groups. And such reduced concentration of the poor can occur only through their voluntary dispersal into housing scattered outside inner-city areas. Middle-class resistance to such a dispersal strategy is so powerful, however, that few politicians dare to confront it. In the absence of any significant start toward dispersal (which had begun on a small scale through the Section 235 and 236 programs stopped by the moratorium), the best federal policies toward such areas would include: improved income maintenance and job opportunities, rather than direct physical investment in housing; reform of the criminal justice system to produce at least a minimal degree of security in these areas; experimental testing of new methods of centrally managing entire inner-city neighborhoods to combat abandonment and decay; and requiring that a certain fraction of special revenue sharing funds be used to cope with inner-city problems.

Financing future housing. Two big factors in financing the recent high level of housing production have been the big shift of institutional investors into real estate from the stagnant stock market, and the requirement that savings and loan associations must invest most of their assets in mortgages. If the recent dual devaluation of the dollar stimulates a boom in U.S. manufacturing and agriculture, and thereby creates a rising stock market, institutional funds may not flow into housing so strongly. Also, if some financial reformers have their way, savings and loan associations will be freed from ties to mortgages in return for giving up rate ceilings on the interest they and banks can pay to depositors. These developments could prevent a return of the easy mortgage money conditions that stimulated record housing production from 1971 up to the tight-money period in late 1973. In that case, either future consumers would have to pay higher fractions of their incomes for housing, or production totals would remain at 1960's levels, causing possible market shortage conditions in many areas. Ironically, the best way to insure good financing for housing is to keep the U.S. economy in a near-recession condition—or at least to keep the stock market from rising. What federal policy should be in this thorny matter is hard to discern, since every alternative produces serious negative results. But in any case, considering these potential financing difficulties, the rising costs to builders of wages, material, and land, and the increasing environmentalist resistance to suburban growth, the chances are great that in the future housing will absorb a higher percentage of the average consumer's income than it does today.

Clearly, diagnosing the past is easier than prescribing for the future with confidence. Yet housing is not a pressing concern for most Americans because they are better housed than ever before. Hence it is not likely that future federal policies will place a very high priority on removing the ever-diminishing—but still large—complex of social conditions erroneously known as America's "housing problem."

8

Economic developments in the black community

ANDREW F. BRIMMER

ONLY a few of the economic and social programs launched during the 1960's were focused primarily on blacks. The most visible effort in this category, the "black capitalism" program of the Nixon Administration, came very late in the decade. However, blacks were prominent among the target populations aimed at by many of the New Frontier and Great Society programs.

The most fundamental economic goal of the early 1960's, of course, was the stimulation of an economy that had remained sluggish for nearly a decade. Consequently, any appraisal of economic changes among blacks during the period must begin with an assessment of the benefits they received from economic expansion. These benefits can be traced in the growth of black employment and the reduction in joblessness, as well as in rising black income, especially among the better educated. Unfortunately, however, this progress must be viewed against the background of a deepening schism in the black community between those enjoying expanding prosperity and those caught in a widening web of poverty.

The economic history of blacks in the United States during the last decade mirrors that of the country at large. However, blacks as a group did slightly better in the 1960's—and considerably worse in the last few years—than the nation as a whole. The principal changes in employment and income among blacks can be traced in Table 1. From 1961 through 1969, the black labor force rose in line with the total civilian labor force; however, the participation rate (i.e., total labor force as a percentage of the non-institutionalized population) of blacks declined noticeably.

Blacks got a moderately larger share of the increase in employment during the 1960's than they had at the beginning of the decade. Within the black group, adult females got a relatively larger share of the expanded jobs than was true of black men. This general pattern paralleled that evident among whites, except that black men did slightly better than their white counterparts. On the other hand, black youths made virtually no progress toward improving their relative employment position during the decade. This was in sharp contrast to the situation among white youths, who expanded their share of the total.

Between 1960 and 1969, the total number of workers without jobs dropped by 1,021,000. Unemployment rose appreciably during the

TABLE 1. *Trends in Employment and Income in the Black Community*[1]

	1960	1965	1969	1972
Employment (thousands)	65,778	71,088	77,902	81,702
Negro and other races[2]	6,927	7,643	8,384	8,628
White	58,850	63,445	69,518	73,074
Per cent of total				
Negro and other races	10.5	10.8	10.8	10.7
Unemployment (thousands)	3,852	3,366	2,831	4,840
Negro and other races	787	676	570	956
White	3,063	2,691	2,261	3,884
Per cent of total				
Negroes and other races	20.4	20.1	20.1	19.8
Unemployment rate (per cent)				
Total	5.5	4.5	3.5	5.6
Negro and other races	10.2	8.1	6.4	10.0
White	4.9	4.1	3.1	5.0
Ratio: black to white	2.1	2.0	2.1	2.0
Median family income (current dollars)				
Total	$5,620	$6,957	$9,433	$11,116
Negro and other races	3,233	3,994	6,191	7,106
Black	n.a.	3,886	5,999	6,864
White	5,835	7,251	9,794	11,549
Income gap				
White/Negro & other races	2,602	3,257	3,603	4,443
White/Black	n.a.	3,365	3,795	4,685
Ratio: Negro and other races				
to white	.55	.55	.63	.62
black to white	n.a.	.54	.61	.59

[1] Sources: Labor force, employment and unemployment: U.S. Department of Labor, Bureau of Labor Statistics. Income: U.S. Department of Commerce, Bureau of the Census.
[2] About 90 per cent of the persons in this category are black.

1960-61 recession, but the subsequent growth of the economy during the decade was large enough to absorb an 11 million increase in the labor force and to take more than one million workers off the unemployment roles. Over the same years, the black labor force rose by 1.2 million, but unemployment among blacks still declined by 217,000. This reduction was about in line with the decrease in joblessness in the economy generally. On the other hand, the distribution of unemployment within the black community changed significantly. Among black adult males and black females, the level of unemployment decreased over the decade, as did unemployment among all components of the white group. But among black youths, the level of unemployment was 55,000 higher in 1969 than it was in 1960. The inability of the economy to meet the job needs of black youth was one of the main shortfalls in national economic policy during the last decade.

The 1969-70 recession had a disproportionately adverse impact on blacks, and the subsequent recovery brought them a relatively small proportion of benefits. In fact, after two and one-half years of substantial economic expansion, blacks as a group ended up with a smaller proportion of the nation's jobs than they had at the time of the recession. The relative decline in their job shares was especially noticeable in lower-skilled occupations.

Income trends among blacks

The extent to which blacks benefited from the long period of economic expansion during the 1960's can also be traced in income trends. In 1959, blacks' money income amounted to $19.7 billion, representing 6.2 per cent of the total for the nation as a whole. By 1969, the amount for blacks had just about doubled (to $38.7 billion) —compared with a gain of 89 per cent for whites—and their share had edged up to 6.4 per cent. Although blacks did not participate in the recent recovery as fully as did whites, by 1972 their total income had climbed to $51.8 billion—or 6.7 per cent of the total of $773 billion.

Over the decade of the 1960's, the median family income of blacks just about doubled. The figure for these families in 1969 was $5,999, compared with $9,794 for whites. In 1959, median income was $3,047 for blacks and $5,893 for whites. The ratio of black to white median income rose from .52 in 1959 to .61 in 1969. In absolute terms, however, black families in 1969 received an average of $3,795 less than their white counterparts, whereas they had received $2,846 less in 1959. By 1972, the median income of black families had climbed to $6,864 compared to $11,549 for white families, but the black/white income ratio declined to .60 in 1971 and to .59 in 1972—the level at which it had been in 1967. So the 1969-70 recession—like the recession in 1960-61—resulted in a widening of the white/black income gap, which in absolute terms amounted to $4,685 in 1972. The explanation of these shortfalls in black income is widely known: A legacy of racial discrimination and deprivation has limited blacks' ability to acquire marketable skills and barred them from better-paying jobs.

One of the dominant features of the black experience in the United States during the 1960's was the continued net migration of blacks from the South to the North and West. The explanation of this movement remains controversial. Some observers attribute it primarily to the relative attractiveness of the public welfare system in urban areas outside the South, but I attribute it principally to the pull of better employment opportunities and higher incomes in the rest of the country.

Between 1960 and 1970, the South expanded faster than any other major region in all principal types of economic activity, and blacks living in the South shared in the benefits yielded by this faster pace of economic growth. In 1960, the South had 61 per cent of the nation's black population, but this had declined to 53 per cent by 1970, mainly because of out-migration to the North and West. The net result was that blacks living in the South accounted for 6.04 per cent of the nation's total population in 1970 vs. 6.23 per cent in 1960. At the same time, their share of the country's total money income rose from 2.21 per cent in 1959 to 2.74 per cent in 1969. So some improvement occurred during the 1960's in per capita as well as in total income of blacks in the South.

Escape from poverty

One of the central aims of national economic policy during the 1960's was the reduction of poverty. It was generally assumed that accelerated economic growth would provide the main bridge over which the poor would escape into a better life. But numerous specialized programs were also launched, among which manpower and community action schemes were particularly important. Since blacks are heavily represented among the poorest of the nation's poor, they are especially affected by the success or failure of anti-poverty efforts.

According to the federal government's poverty index, a non-farm family of four was classed as poor in 1959 if its annual income was below $2,973. By 1968, the poverty threshold was $3,553. Measured against these criteria, there were 38.7 million poor people in the United States in 1959. Of this number, 9.9 million were black, 28.3 million were white, and the remaining .5 million were other races (mainly American Indians). By 1968, the total number of poor persons had declined to 25.4 million, of whom about 7.6 million were black, 17.4 million were white, and .4 million were other races. A closer look at these figures suggests, however, that the rate at which blacks were able to escape from poverty during the 1960's fell considerably short of that experienced by whites. The total number of persons classified as poor dropped by one third; for whites the decline was two fifths, but for blacks the decrease was less than one quarter.

The much more rapid exodus from poverty by whites during this period is partly explained by the fact that in 1959 the average poor white family was not caught nearly so deeply in poverty as the average poor black family. But a more important explanation of the differential success of the two races in escaping poverty lies in the changing structure of families within the two groups. During the 1960's, male-headed families were more likely to be successful in raising their income than were families headed by females. Between 1959 and 1968, the rate of decline in poverty among individuals in male-headed families for both blacks and whites was roughly equal and also rather rapid, but for female-headed families the pattern was quite different: For the white population, the number of poor individuals in female-headed households declined by one sixth, but the number of poor in families headed by black females *rose* by one quarter, and the number of children in these families increased by over one third. The 1969-70 recession checked the rate of escape from poverty by both blacks and whites. Yet by 1972, the number of poor whites had declined to 16.2 million, while among blacks the number of poor persons climbed fairly sharply and in 1972 amounted to 7.7 million.

Broken black families are among the main contributors to the expanding system of public welfare in the United States. This is especially true of the federally supported program of Aid to Families with Dependent Children (AFDC). In 1961, for example, black families constituted about two fifths of all AFDC families, and the proportion rose to about one half by 1970. The representation of blacks in other segments of the welfare system is far less marked than it is in AFDC. In 1971, about 25 per cent of all black families received some form of public assistance, compared to five per cent of white families. However, those black families receiving public assistance had a substantially lower median income than their white counterparts ($3,353 vs. $4,117 in 1971).

Because of the persistence of poverty and the expanding public welfare rolls—particularly the growing dependence of families on AFDC—I was a strong supporter of the Family Assistance Program (FAP) proposed by the Nixon Administration in August 1969. Even in its most restrictive form (which would have provided a basic allowance of $1,600 per year for a family of four), the FAP would have made a sizable contribution toward easing the burdens of poor families on AFDC. More important, the FAP contained the basic elements of a nationwide income maintenance program. Benefits would have been available to poor families generally—whether they worked or not. The representation of blacks would have remained substantial, but by no means as prominent as under AFDC. The FAP failed to win Congressional approval for a variety of reasons—including bipartisan opposition, lack of support by the Administration, and persistent suspicion and hostility on the part of civil rights groups. The ultimate losers were the nation's poor. The revival of FAP (or some other version of an income maintenance arrangement) remains high on the nation's agenda of unfinished business.

Education and prosperity

If the discussion stopped here, we would leave an unbalanced picture of the black economic experience in the 1960's, and an underlying trend holding significant implications for the 1970's would be missed—the role of education and its contribution to blacks' advancement. Between 1960 and 1972, the proportion of the black population 20 to 29 years old who had completed high school rose from 38 per cent to 64 per cent for males and from 43 per cent to 66 per cent for black females. For white males in the same age group, the rise was from 64 per cent to 84 per cent; for white females the rise was from 66 per cent to 83 per cent. Moreover, within the last few years the proportion of young blacks completing high school accelerated noticeably. An even sharper acceleration occurred in the case of college education. In 1960, 4.1 per cent of all blacks in the 25-34 age range had completed four years or more of college, compared with 11.9 per cent for all whites in the same age group. By 1972, about 7.9 per cent of all blacks in the 25-34 age bracket had completed four years or more of college; among whites, the figure was 18.8 per cent.

An even more crucial trend is the rising propensity for young black people to attend college. In 1972, 540,000 blacks 18 to 24 years old were enrolled in college, compared to 297,000 in 1967. The 1972 figure represented 18 per cent of all blacks in that age range (vs. 13 per cent in 1967). For young whites, the enrollment was 4,710,000 in 1967 and 5,624,000 in 1972—27 per cent and 26 per cent, respectively. By 1967, blacks represented 4.9 per cent of total college enrollment, and this had climbed further to 8.8 per cent in 1972.

These advances in educational attainment made a substantial difference in the degree of economic progress made by blacks during the 1960's. Just how much difference is indicated by the figures in Tables 2 and 3. Table 2 shows median income in 1959 and 1969 and years of school completed by males 25 to 54 years old. The median income at each educational level is expressed as a ratio to the median for all men in the age range: $6,408 in 1959 (in 1969 dollars) and $8,465 in 1969. In Table 3, median income and education in 1969 are shown for both men and women for age groups 25-34 and 35-54. In this case, the base is the median income ($9,651) for white men, aged 35-54, who had completed four years of high school.

TABLE 2. *Median Income in 1959 and 1969 by Years of School Completed, Males 25 to 54 Years Old*[1]

	1959 (IN 1969 DOLLARS)			1969		
	TOTAL	BLACK	WHITE	TOTAL	BLACK	WHITE
Median Income	$6,408	$3,570	$6,637	$8,465	$5,222	$8,795
Ratio to Median	1.00	.56	1.04	1.00	.62	1.04
Education						
Elem: Total	.75	.47	.82	.70	.49	.75
Less than 8 years	.63	.44	.71	.61	.46	.65
8 years	.87	.58	.90	.80	.53	.83
High school: Total	1.03	.66	1.05	.98	.69	1.01
1-3 years	.98	.64	1.01	.88	.63	.92
4 years	1.06	.70	1.08	1.02	.73	1.04
College: Total	1.32	.82	1.35	1.28	.94	1.30
1-3 years	1.19	.78	1.22	1.14	.88	1.16
4 years	1.48	.88	1.50	1.44	1.02	1.46

[1] Median income at each educational level is expressed as a ratio to the median for all men in the age range 25-54 years. Source: U.S. Department of Commerce, Bureau of the Census, "Social and Economic Characteristics of the Population in Metropolitan and Nonmetropolitan Areas: 1970 and 1960," Current Population Reports, Series P-23, No. 37, June 24, 1971, Table 12, p. 54.

TABLE 3. *Median Earnings and Educational Attainment of Year-round Workers, 25 to 34 and 35 to 54 Years Old (1969)*[1]

	BLACK				WHITE			
	MALE		FEMALE		MALE		FEMALE	
	25-34	35-54	25-34	35-54	25-34	35-54	25-34	35-54
Median Income	$6,346	$6,403	$4,403	$3,901	$8,839	$9,736	$5,175	$4,966
Ratio to Median	.66	.66	.46	.40	.92	1.01	.54	.51
($9,651)								
Elem: 8 years or less	.49	.54	.30	.27	.69	.77	.41	.42
High School								
1-3 years	.60	.67	.38	.37	.82	.91	.44	.46
4 years	.70	.77	.48	.47	.89	1.00	.52	.53
College								
1-3 years	.80	.85	.57	.59	.95	1.19	.59	.60
4 years	.90	.97	.72	.76	1.16	1.51	.75	.76
5 years or more	1.03	1.27	.82	.94	1.22	1.74	.84	.96

[1] Median income at each educational level is expressed as a ratio to the median income ($9,651) for white men, aged 35-54, who had completed four years of high school. Source: Bureau of the Census, "The Social and Economic Status of the Black Population in the United States, 1972," July 1973, Tables 15 and 16, pp. 25, 26.

Several features stand out in these tables. As one would expect, for both races and for both men and women median income increased progressively with both age and education. However, education clearly had the greater influence. This general pattern also held for blacks, except that the extra income yielded by extra education was slightly smaller. In 1969, the grade school/high school and high school/college differentials were about the same as in 1959 for all men in the 25-54 age group. Among black men, the grade school/high school gap was also unchanged over the decade. But the earnings for black college graduates had climbed to two and one-quarter times those of grade school drop-outs, and the margin of college over high school graduates had widened appreciably.

In recent years, young black men with better educations have advanced their incomes relative to whites much more rapidly than older blacks have. For instance, in 1969, at both the elementary and high school level, black/white earnings ratios were approximately the same for men 25 to 34 years old and men 35 to 54 years old. In contrast, education past the high school level generally raised the ratio of black to white earnings for young black men more than it did for older black men. (The earnings of black female workers with education beyond the high school level roughly equalled the earnings of their white counterparts in both age groups.) Despite these improvements, however, the absolute income gaps between blacks and whites —at all educational levels—remain substantial.

As shown in Table 3, the average black man with a high school education was still earning in 1969 about the same amount as a white man who only went to grade school. Among black women, the situation was only slightly better. Black men with a college degree had earnings about equal to or somewhat below those of a white high school graduate. But taken as a whole, the evidence presented here supports an encouraging conclusion: Younger blacks are making substantial progress in achieving secondary and higher education, and this increased education is yielding higher incomes both absolutely and relative to whites.

Blacks and federal manpower programs

Black workers were among the chief target groups of manpower programs fostered by the federal government during the middle and late 1960's. Beginning with the passage of the Economic Opportunity Act (EOA) of 1964, manpower programs were reoriented to place much greater emphasis on the job problems of the "disadvantaged," a category comprising mainly young people and the undereducated and unskilled members of minority groups. Black enrollment in these programs as a proportion of all trainees (about 45 per cent) has been well above the black proportion of the labor force, but it parallels to some extent the black fraction of the low-income population. The various manpower programs are briefly described below:

● Manpower Development and Training Act (MDTA): general skill development efforts, offering both institutional and on-the-job training. (Black participation: one quarter to one third.)

● Job Opportunities in the Business Sector (JOBS): joint public-private efforts to find employment for hard-core disadvantaged workers in major corporations. (Black participation: roughly one half.)

● Neighborhood Youth Corps (NYC): youth programs, designed to provide earnings and work orientation (but little skill training), mainly for urban youths, and to encourage school attendance. (Black participation: one half.)

● Job Corps: originally a residential skills development program for the neediest youth, later revamped to stress occupational learning in non-resident training schools. (Black participation: three fifths.)

● Work Incentive Program (WIN): seeks to encourage recipients of public welfare—especially in families receiving aid to dependent children (AFDC)—to become self-supporting. (Black participation: two fifths.)

● Concentrated Employment Program (CEP): aimed at meeting rural area manpower needs. (Black participation: three fifths.)

● Operation Mainstream: seeks to provide work and augmented incomes for adults, many of whom are older rural residents. (Black participation: one fifth.)

● Public Employment Program (PEP): designed to create temporary jobs in public service to help offset rising unemployment following the 1969-70 recession. (Black participation: one fifth.)

Any attempt to assess the impact of the federal government's manpower programs on blacks must take several elements into account. In the first place, the success of any program depends heavily on the pace of national economic activity and the state of the labor market. It is also necessary to compare the experiences of enrollees in manpower programs with the experiences of a control group—i.e., a population group with similar characteristics that did not participate in the same training or other program activity. Unfortunately, only a few of the many program appraisals have satisfied this requirement. Moreover, virtually none of the evaluations has allowed for purely personal differences in motivation or work preferences that may distinguish enrollees from those who have not joined a training program. Finally, the choice of an appropriate measuring rod against which to judge the success of these programs is a difficult one. Most economists who have considered the matter have compared their costs (tax money) with their benefits (increased earnings of enrollees generated by expanded jobs and higher wages), but this cannot be done with much precision. Nevertheless, if we keep these cautionary comments in mind, we can turn to an assessment of the effects on blacks of four of the principal manpower programs: MDTA, NYC, Job Corps, and WIN.[1]

MDTA Programs: A central conclusion emerges from the numer-

---

[1] A comprehensive review and appraisal of the impact of different manpower programs can be found in *Studies in Public Welfare: The Effectiveness of Manpower Training Programs: A Review of Research on the Impact on the Poor*, a staff study prepared for the use of the Subcommittee on Fiscal Policy of the Joint Economic Committee, 72nd Congress, Second Session, 1972.

ous studies of MDTA enrollees: Disadvantaged persons as a group do derive measurable benefits from participation in the program. Trainees who suffer from drawbacks such as low educational attainment, long periods of unemployment, and low pre-training earnings obtain larger benefits from training than those who are less handicapped in the labor market. The evidence on the size of the benefits which accrue is somewhat mixed, but it is clear that the MDTA program has been worthwhile for the broad segment of the labor force that it was intended to serve.

It appears that the MDTA training programs have benefited blacks —but to a lesser extent than whites, regardless of sex. However, the benefits for all groups were well above the costs of making the investment. (Einar Hardin and Michael E. Borus, *Economic Benefits and Costs of Retraining*). These benefits are measured on the basis of increases in individual earnings before income taxes with no allowance for changes in income transfers (such as reductions in welfare payments). But allowing for these changes, it appears reasonably certain that the country at large gains more by spending public funds to train blacks than it does by making the same amount of investment in upgrading the skills of whites. The greater benefits to the country as a whole registered in the case of blacks arise mainly from a sizable reduction in welfare payments in the post-training period. Although the contribution of white trainees to net national product exceeded that made by blacks, blacks experienced relatively larger increments in income taxes paid as well as larger declines in welfare payments received.

NYC Program: In forming a judgment about the effectiveness of the NYC program, it is well to keep in mind the fact that it was *not* originally intended as a scheme for occupational training. In 1970, however, it was revamped, and more emphasis was given to supportive services, remedial education, and the acquisition of skills. If these revisions were successful, some of the old criticisms and evaluations may no longer be valid. But so far, the only three benefit-cost appraisals made of the NYC suggest that the original program, at least, was badly conceived.[2] It seems to have done little to solve the school drop-out problem—and, in fact, may have actually lessened the enrollee's prospect of graduating from high school.

But in terms of the effects of NYC on employment and earnings of trainees (compared with their peers not in the program), the

---

[2] Gerald G. Somers and Ernst W. Stromsdrofer, *A Cost-Effectiveness Study of the In-School and Summer Neighborhood Youth Corps,* Industrial Relations Research Institute, University of Wisconsin, Madison, July 1970; and Michael E. Borus, John P. Brennan, and Sidney Rosen, "A Benefit-Cost Analysis of the Neighborhood Youth Corps: the Out-of-School Program in Indiana," *The Journal of Human Resources,* Spring 1970, pp. 139-59.

benefits, at least in the short run, seem to be clearly positive. Trainees in the In-School program had higher labor force participation rates, lower unemployment rates, and a larger increase in earnings. Participants covered in a sample of trainees were enrolled in the NYC program for an average of 18.56 months; the gain in pre-tax earnings was about $831—or $45 per month. Among participants, males benefited more than females, mainly because the latter experienced greater unemployment and fewer hours of work per week when they did have jobs.

The operation of the Out-of-School program also seems to have yielded positive benefits. Expected annual benefits from 520 hours of training were approximately $173. However, only males had significantly larger gains in annual earnings resulting from NYC participation—$562 vs. $83 for women.

Enrollees in the Summer-Only NYC program showed no relative benefits from the exposure. This conclusion held independently of the measure of benefits and for all race-sex subgroupings. Consequently, this part of the NYC program can be justified only on grounds other than its effects on the enrollees' future earnings potential.

If we turn to the differential effects of the NYC program on blacks, it is clear that they benefited more from the In-School program than did whites. Blacks had significantly lower unemployment compared to their counterparts who were not enrolled in the program, while whites experienced no reduction in unemployment. Blacks also had larger increases in earnings ($130 per month vs. $51 for whites). The gains for black women were especially striking. White women trainees apparently did not benefit at all. In contrast, black women had shorter periods of unemployment (two months less) than non-trainees, and the increase in their earnings was quite large—about $90 per month of labor force participation. Black male trainees also did substantially better compared to non-trainees than did white men. For black men, after-tax earnings rose by $112 per month vs. $30 for white men. Here also there is no ready explanation of the more favorable effects of the program on blacks. It may be that counseling and job placement efforts on the part of NYC staff helped to overcome the obstacles to black employment normally thrown up by discrimination.

The assessments of the Out-of-School program suggest that blacks benefited from enrollment to the same extent as whites. However, the evidence also showed that high school drop-outs benefited relatively more than those who graduated. The relative gains were largest for those who dropped out after only one or two years of high school. In the population at large, black teenagers have a disproportionately high propensity to drop out of school, so the opportunities offered by NYC are especially important to them.

Job Corps: No studies have been made which would enable one to judge the differential impact of this program on blacks. In fact, the two benefit-cost analyses of the Job Corps based on a national sample have so many technical limitations that no reliable conclusions can be drawn from them.[3] Since these early assessments were made, however, the Job Corps experience seems to have improved considerably. Operating economies have reduced costs, and improved screening and counseling services seem to have sustained the reported educational and economic benefits (especially for those enrollees who went through all or most of the training schedule). Although no one has yet estimated a high economic rate of return on the Job Corps investment, the earlier studies may have overstated the costs of the operation. Those estimates did not allow for the savings from other income transfers (such as welfare payments) which most likely would have been made if these disadvantaged young people had not participated in the Job Corps. Moreover, it must be remembered that this program—unlike most other manpower efforts —has drawn enrollees entirely from the most needy and most disadvantaged segments of the population. So although the Job Corps may have provided its trainees the skimpiest of benefits, it may be the only form of assistance available to them.

WIN Program: Only one study of WIN enrollees has been made that used a control group. The authors of this inquiry concluded that participation in WIN did not significantly increase the employment or earnings of WIN trainees. (Ronald E. Fine, *et al.*, *Final Report, AFDC Employment and Referral Guides.*) The study was based on a sample of over 3,500 AFDC beneficiaries in nine counties in Florida, Michigan, and Minnesota whose cases were opened or reopened during 1969 and 1970.

The benefits under the program can be assessed from the perspective both of the welfare recipient and of the taxpayer. The average net benefit for *recipients* consists of earnings minus both the welfare grant reduction and any employment expenses paid by the client. Of the 268 cases on which this part of the study was based, none had a net benefit of more than $300, and only six had net benefits of more than $200. To put the findings in perspective, the net benefits were compared with the maximum amount a non-working welfare recipient could receive in each state. This proportion averaged 35 per cent in Michigan, 41 per cent in Minnesota, and 99 per cent in Florida (where welfare benefits were substantially lower than in the other

---

[3] Glen G. Cain, *Benefit/Cost Estimates for Job Corps,* Institute for Research on Poverty, University of Wisconsin, Madison, September 1968; and Harry R. Woltman and William W. Walton, *Evaluation of the War on Poverty: the Feasibility of Benefit-Cost Analysis of Manpower Programs,* Resource Management Corporation, prepared for the U.S. General Accounting Office, March 1968.

two states). The average net benefit to the *taxpayer* of WIN-asso-
ciated employment of welfare mothers was defined as the average
welfare grant reduction minus average publicly paid child care costs.
After allowing for both of these adjustments, the average net benefits to taxpayers were reduced to levels well below those accruing
to the welfare recipient alone: to seven per cent of the maximum
grant in Minnesota, 17 per cent in Michigan, and 28 per cent in
Florida. Thus, the authors concluded that—so far—neither welfare
clients nor taxpayers have benefited appreciably from the employment generated by the WIN program.

With respect to black participation in the program, the authors
found that black women had about the same employment and earnings experience as white women—except in Minnesota. There black
women had a lower probability of employment and lower expected
earnings than their white counterparts. In general, however, the
authors concluded that their own finding that race alone does not
usually account for differences in employment and earnings among
women is broadly consistent with evidence presented by other in-
vestigators.

The quest for equal opportunity

So far we have been discussing the benefits of general economic
expansion for blacks and the effects of manpower programs on them.
Federal program activities in two other areas, while not conducted
exclusively on behalf of blacks, focused on them as the principal
target population. These activities consisted of efforts to lessen racial
discrimination in employment and to afford blacks and members of
other minority groups greater opportunities to participate in business
ownership.

Title VII of the Civil Rights Act of 1964 created the Equal Employment Opportunity Commission (EEOC) to foster equal job
opportunity, and the Commission began operations on July 2, 1965.
It was, however, preceded by a generation of essentially voluntary
action at the federal, state, and local level, beginning with President
Roosevelt's Executive Order 8802, signed in June 1941 to avert a
"March on Washington" for better wartime jobs.

EEOC was not part of the original legislation proposed by President Kennedy in mid-1963 which was the basis of the Civil Rights
Act of 1964. Kennedy thought that the inclusion of such a controversial provision would further decrease the already unpromising
prospect of the bill's passage. Instead, he thought it best to expand
further—through executive action—the existing efforts to check job
discrimination. As the bill moved through the legislative process, the
EEOC provision was added at Congressional initiative and Lyndon
Johnson, who had by then succeeded to the Presidency, threw his
strong support behind the entire measure.

Nevertheless, EEOC started life with a number of handicaps. In the first place, the commencement of its operations was delayed for a full year after the bill was signed. Furthermore, its coverage was restricted for the most part to private companies in interstate commerce with 25 or more employees, and its actions had to depend on the filing of complaints by individual workers. This was an extension of the approach followed in World War II—despite evidence accumulated in the intervening years under state fair employment programs which demonstrated that the complaint mechanism had not been particularly successful. For the first seven years of its life, the Commission had no enforcement powers of its own. The Attorney General could bring suit when a "pattern or practice" of discrimination was discovered by EEOC, but for the most part the Commission was left to rely on education and persuasion—along with the provision of technical assistance—in its efforts to end job discrimination.

After nearly eight years of effort, the EEOC's authority was strengthened by the 1972 amendments to the Civil Rights Act. The most important of these gave the Commission enforcement powers of its own. When the new authority took effect in March 1973, EEOC could initiate civil actions in federal courts to enforce the provisions barring job discrimination and to remedy instances of their violation. Coverage of the statute was extended to employees of state and local governments and their instrumentalities, employees of educational institutions, and firms or labor organizations with 15 or more workers or members. Additional protection was also provided to federal government employees.

Armed with this new authority and an enlarged budget, EEOC in the last year has accelerated its drive against employment discrimination, concentrating on sex and language bias as well as on racial barriers. In fact, even before the new provisions were actually implemented, EEOC got considerable assistance from its prospective enforcement authority in achieving a landmark settlement of its suit against AT&T in January 1973. The compromise reflected in the consent decree required the company to pay $15 million to roughly 13,000 women and 2,000 minority-group men as compensation for past discrimination that restricted their occupational mobility. Moreover, it was anticipated that some 10,000 employees who might transfer to better-paying jobs would receive bonuses (ranging from $100 to $400 each) totaling $23 million. By September 1973, this latter estimate had risen to $35 million, reflecting a virtual flood of applications by lower-paid AT&T employees to move up to better jobs.

Occupational upgrading

Just how much official efforts to check racial discrimination contributed to the expansion of job opportunities for blacks during the

1960's cannot be precisely measured, but the fact that considerable occupational upgrading of blacks did occur is readily evident. This is particularly true of improvements in the highest-paying occupations. Between 1960 and 1971, the number of blacks in professional and technical positions increased by 128 per cent (to 756,000), while the increase in the total was only 49 per cent (to 11.1 million). Blacks had progressed to the point where they accounted for 6.8 per cent of the total employment in these top categories in the occupational structure in 1971, compared with 4.4 per cent in 1960. During this same period, the number of black managers, officials, and proprietors (the second highest-paying category) nearly doubled (to 342,000), compared to an expansion of 23 per cent (to 8.7 million) for all employees in this category. If blacks had not been handicapped by previous discrimination which limited their education and experience, they could have gotten an even larger share of the managerial positions which opened up during the decade.

In the 1960's, black workers left low-paying jobs in agriculture and household service at a rate one and one-half times faster than did white workers. The number of black farmers and farm workers dropped by two thirds (to 285,000), in contrast to a decline of about two fifths (to three million) for all persons in this category. Therefore, in 1971 blacks accounted for about 9.5 per cent of employment in agriculture, just over one-half their share in 1960. The exit of blacks from private household employment was even more striking. The number of black non-farm laborers also declined over the last decade, even though there occurred some increase in the total number of laborers.

Nevertheless, as already indicated, the accelerated movement of blacks out of the positions at the bottom of the occupational structure did not flow evenly through the entire occupational structure. For example, blacks in 1971 still held about 1.7 million (or one quarter) of the service jobs outside private households—most of which require only modest skills—about the same proportion as in 1960. Moreover, the number of blacks holding semi-skilled operative jobs (mainly in factories) rose by more than one quarter (29 per cent) to about 1.8 million during the decade, compared with an expansion of less than 10 per cent for all workers.

While blacks made substantial progress during the 1960's in obtaining clerical and sales jobs and also registered noticeable gains as craftsmen, their occupational center of gravity remained anchored in those positions requiring little skill and offering few opportunities for further advancement. At the same time, it is also clear from the above analysis that blacks who are well prepared to compete for the higher-paying positions in the upper reaches of the occupational structure have made measurable gains. Nevertheless, compared with their overall participation in the economy (11 per cent of total employment), the occupational deficit in white collar employment—averaging 40 per cent—remains large.

Data on occupational distribution of total employment by color for 1972 document the mixed job experience of blacks in the last two years. Black employment rose moderately, but blacks' share of the total jobs remained essentially unchanged. However, between 1971 and 1972, they raised their share of professional and technical jobs to 7.2 per cent.

From the foregoing discussion, the following points stand out: During the 1960's and continuing into the present decade, blacks made measurable strides in terms of occupational upgrading. Some of the advances were undoubtedly facilitated by federal government efforts to check racial discrimination. Yet on balance, it appears that the net impact of those efforts was not as decisive as it could have been. This failure was probably attributable more to the modest and halting character of government activities in this area than to any inherent deficiencies in the use of federal authority to combat racial barriers to employment. The recently enhanced authority and resources of the EEOC should permit much more concerted action to that end in the years ahead. The prospects would be even more promising if EEOC had authority to issue cease-and-desist orders to check discriminatory practices before taking cases to court.

"Black capitalism"

Perhaps no other federal effort of the 1960's promised so much to blacks as did "black capitalism." Sadly, however, this program has probably been the greatest failure of all. Promoted by Richard Nixon during his campaign for the Presidency in 1968, "black capitalism" called for a variety of government activities to aid black businessmen, and its focus was subsequently broadened to include members of other minority groups. Soon after taking office, President Nixon created by executive order the Office of Minority Business Enterprise (OMBE) in the Commerce Department to further the objective of giving blacks and other minority groups "a piece of the action."

In 1969, an OMBE-sponsored census counted 163,000 black-owned businesses. These enterprises represented about 1.4 per cent of all firms in the nation, and they had gross receipts of $4.5 billion, accounting for 0.24 per cent of the total. Both measures put into sharp focus the meager control by blacks in the field of business. A great deal of effort has been made by OMBE to lift that fraction. Its budget rose almost 15-fold over four years to $46 million in fiscal 1973, and for fiscal 1974 a sum of $91 million was in prospect; however, $17 million of this consisted of funds impounded during the last fiscal year, and $39 million was scheduled to come from the Office of Economic Opportunity (which was then thought to be destined for abolition). At the end of fiscal 1973, OMBE was operating from its headquarters in Washington and at 30 field offices. It was also co-operating with 140 local business development organizations in the provision of technical assistance and the processing of loan applications. Federal loans and guarantees (including those by the Small Business Administration) to minority-owned businesses amounted to about $400 million in fiscal 1973, compared with around $105 million in 1969. For fiscal 1974, the volume is projected to exceed $1 billion. Federal procurement from minority-owned firms amounted to about $400 million in fiscal 1973; four years earlier the figure was only $13 million. The target for fiscal 1974 is $600 million.

Financial institutions owned or controlled by blacks and other minority-group members have also enjoyed OMBE's support. Between 1969 and 1973, the number of such banks rose from 28 to 43, and their deposits increased from $397 million to roughly $875 million. Over the same four years, approximately 50 Minority Enterprise Small Business Investment Companies (MESBIC) were started. With total capital of nearly $25 million, they can borrow between $350 million and $450 million of commercial bank and federal funds for reinvestment in minority-owned businesses. Altogether, OMBE claims that almost 8,000 new minority-owned businesses were started under federal stimulus in the last four years.

While other evidence of OMBE's efforts could be catalogued, enough has already been presented to give the flavor of its activities. But now we must ask: What does it all mean? Unfortunately, one cannot say. No one has established performance goals for the program, and in the absence of quantifiable evidence showing results produced for the money spent, one cannot judge its overall impact. Yet the general impression one gets is that the program has fallen far short of whatever goals were projected for it. Moreover, given the plan to decentralize further OMBE's operations, the prospects for better performance in the future appear far from bright. The principal reason underlying this pessimistic expectation is the scarcity of expert talent to work on the kinds of specialized problems confronted by minority-group businessmen.

If we look ahead, the horizon for black-owned businesses appears rather cloudy. Despite the achievement of some growth and diversification, they are still heavily concentrated in the small-scale retail and service field. The already heavy burdens imposed on them by crime and other extraordinary risks of doing business predominantly in the urban ghetto are still rising. What is even more disturbing is that the fields in which black businessmen are concentrated are declining relative to the economy as a whole. Unless blacks can raise larger amounts of equity capital, acquire a higher level of managerial skills, and diversify into some of the high-growth industries, the road ahead is likely to be rocky indeed for black entrepreneurs.

In any case, the available evidence strongly suggests that the black capitalism approach has been a costly digression. It diverted national attention from the fundamental problems of poverty and deprivation which still plague the black community, and left blacks themselves in a state of confusion about the real problems they confront and the genuine opportunities open to them.

The economic future of blacks in the United States is bound up with that of the rest of the nation. Programs designed in the future to cope with the problems of the poor and the disadvantaged will also yield benefits to blacks. In contrast, any efforts to treat blacks separately from the rest of the nation are likely to lead to frustrations, heightened racial animosities, and a waste of the country's resources.

9

The
federal role
in
education

RALPH W. TYLER

URING the 1960's the federal government's financial aid to schools and colleges surged upward from less than $2 billion to more than $10 billion and continued at this level into the 1970's. A large part of this increase was in funds for elementary and secondary education. In 1960 federal grants to elementary and secondary schools amounted to about a half-billion dollars. By 1970 this had risen to about $3.5 billion. Although scores of educational programs were initiated by federal action in the 1960's, the most important ones can be grouped according to four major objectives: educating the disadvantaged, broadening the access to higher education, improving education for the world of work, and desegregating schools and colleges. Before describing these efforts in more detail, however, some background is necessary.

Although the Constitution does not specify education as a federal responsibility, the national government has long encouraged and often contributed to the support of schools and colleges. In 1785 the Congress of the Confederation adopted an ordinance for the disposal of public lands in the Western Territory that reserved one section of every township for the endowment of schools within that township. In the Northwest Ordinance of 1787 the Congress declared that "religion, morality and knowledge being necessary for good government and the happiness of mankind, schools and the means of education shall be forever encouraged." When Ohio became a state in 1802, the Congress began the practice of setting aside lands for school support at the time a state was admitted to the Union.

These early grants were for the aid of education in general without any stipulation as to its kind. But with the passage of the Morrill Act of 1862 (the so-called Land Grant College Act), the Congress began a policy of giving assistance to states for education in particular fields. The Morrill Act aimed to increase higher educational opportunities for youth from the "agricultural and mechanical classes" by providing instructions in "agriculture and the mechanic arts." With the passage of the Smith-Hughes Act of 1917, federal matching funds were made available to the states in support of vocational education in the public schools. This legislation was designed to expand educational opportunities at the high school level that might be attractive to youths from farm and working-class families.

Education and defense

Conflicting interests and the lack of Constitutional specification of federal responsibility for education resulted in only piecemeal legislation during the first part of this century. For example, the Vocational Rehabilitation Act of 1918 authorized rehabilitation for veterans unable to carry on a gainful occupation successfully. This legislation was justified as part of the federal responsibility for national defense. The Smith-Bankhead Act of 1920 extended the policy by providing assistance to the states in support of vocational rehabilitation for all disabled persons. During the Depression, using the general welfare clause of the Constitution as justification, several agencies were created to carry on educational activities as part of their relief program. The National Youth Administration was established to furnish work training for unemployed youths and part-time employment for needy students. The Civilian Conservation Corps (CCC) provided vocational training and work for unemployed youths. These new agencies, particularly the CCC, were attacked by organizations of school administrators on the grounds that these funds would be more effectively employed if used to support this training in the schools. However, a study of the educational effects of the CCC conducted by the non-governmental American Youth Commission indicated measurable benefits from these programs in terms of the development of work habits and skills.

During World War II, the federal government supported schools and colleges in a variety of programs designed to improve and increase the civilian contribution to the war effort. This effort was justified as a part of national defense, as was the Servicemen's Readjustment Act of 1944, commonly called the GI Bill of Rights. This

Act extended the scope of federal support for education far beyond that available to veterans of World War I. Each veteran who had 90 days or more of service between September 16, 1940, and July 26, 1947, was entitled to one year of training plus an amount equal to the time he spent in the military service up to a maximum of 48 months. The benefits included school costs up to $500 per year and subsistence allowances from $50 to $120 per month. A total of more than 7,800,000 World War II veterans participated in this program. Of this total, 2,230,000 went to colleges and universities, 3,480,000 were in institutions of less than college level, 1,400,000 were involved in on-the-job training, and 690,000 were enrolled in on-the-farm training.

Later, 2,391,000 Korean war veterans were covered by a similar program. The legislation was later amended to cover post-Korean war veterans, and so far almost 2,000,000 of them have enrolled. The total cost of these programs was: $14.5 billion for the World War II veterans, $4.5 billion for the Korean war veterans, and $1.1 billion for all post-Korean war veterans.

The GI Bill of Rights was the most important program of massive federal aid to education enacted prior to 1965. Most studies of the educational achievements of veterans enrolled in colleges and universities indicate that they have made somewhat higher grades and that fewer of them have dropped out of school than non-veterans of similar ability. These results have been commonly attributed to the higher motivation and more regular work habits of the veterans.

Using the justification of national defense, federal assistance to education was extended even further in the 1950's. On April 4, 1957, President Eisenhower said, "Our schools are strong points in our national defense. Our schools are more important than our Nike batteries, more necessary than our radar warning nets, and more powerful even than the energy of the atom."

The launching of Sputnik by the Russians on October 4, 1957, was interpreted by many Americans as proof of Russian superiority in education. One response to this cold war challenge was the passage of the National Defense Education Act of 1958, which authorized appropriations totaling more than a billion dollars for educational programs to be conducted largely within a period of four years. The policy embodied in this act is stated in its first title: "The Congress hereby finds and declares that the security of the nation requires the fullest development of the mental resources and technical skills of its young men and women. The present emergency demands that additional and more adequate opportunities be made available."

The Act authorized a federal contribution of 90 per cent of the capital of loan funds at institutions of higher education for low-interest loans to students, as well as federal grants to state educational agencies for strengthening science, mathematics, and modern foreign language instruction in public elementary and secondary schools and junior colleges, and for improving educational and vocational guidance. In its scope and amount of support, this Act was the most important educational legislation of the decade.

By 1960, the policy of the federal government regarding public education had developed around three major principles: (1) It recognized the responsibility of the states for the control and operation of public education. (2) It proclaimed federal responsibility when it identified a danger that the citizens were being insufficiently educated to maintain the nation's political and economic stability, and its defense. (3) It exercised its responsibility by contributing to the support of public educational activities, not by controlling them. There was no clear-cut policy with regard to the government's responsibility for education that would help to assure the civil rights of individuals. It was on this foundation that the educational programs of the 1960's were established and further federal educational policy developed.

Educating the disadvantaged

In the 1960's public attention in America was directed to a seeming paradox. The United States economy was operating at a high level and per capita income had reached a record high. Yet, at the same time, several million Americans were unemployed, and the incomes of one fifth of American families were below the level considered adequate to pay for the necessities of life. The numbers on welfare were high and increasing, and many were the children of earlier welfare recipients—that is, for two generations these families had depended on welfare for their subsistence. We were an affluent society, yet millions of Americans were in dire poverty, living in rural or city slums, without gainful employment. As these conditions became more widely known, explanations were sought and corrective action was demanded.

Several kinds of data suggested the significant role of education or lack of it in explaining this paradox. The average number of years of schooling of unemployed persons was quite low, and the figure for welfare recipients was even further below the national average. Of all persons aged 18-24, 20 per cent of those with an eighth grade education or less were unemployed. Unemployment of both youths and adults was much lower for those completing high school than for those who had not gone beyond the eighth grade. Similarly, the percentage of high school graduates on welfare was considerably less than the percentage of those who had not attended high school.

Studies of the backgrounds of children who were not making progress in school indicated that a large percentage came from homes where the parents had received very little education, where their incomes were below that necessary for a reasonable standard of living, and where the neighborhood or community furnished little or no assistance to home and school in stimulating and encouraging learning. It is estimated that at least 20 per cent of American children are disadvantaged in this way. They are found primarily in the inner cities and rural areas and include a disproportionate number of minority-group members.

Until recently, the American public was not conscious of the fact that a large number of children were not learning what the schools were teaching because in earlier days most children who were not succeeding in school dropped out as soon as legally possible and a considerable number in rural areas never enrolled in the first place. Most of them found jobs. Now, however, less than five per cent of the American labor force is employed in agriculture and there are fewer jobs for the unskilled. In the non-farm sector, less than five per cent of the work force is unskilled. In 1965, nearly 70 per cent of those with less than an eighth grade education were unemployed and most were on the welfare roles. When the public began to see this as a social and economic problem rather than as merely a personal tragedy, it demanded that greater efforts be made to educate the disadvantaged. The 1965 White House Conference on Education strongly recommended federal action on this problem.

However, it was not easy for the Congress to respond to these demands. Since the 1930's, educational organizations had pressed for federal aid to education, and in 1952 the late Senator Robert Taft, a conservative Republican leader, joined liberal congressmen from both parties in supporting legislation for federal aid. But in spite of these efforts, no general aid of significant magnitude was enacted. Efforts were blocked by coalitions of several different interests. Some opposed the aid out of fear that it would be an entering wedge for federal control of education. Some were against it because it was seen as a further widening of the gap between the resources available for parochial schools and for public schools. Some refused to support it because it would be an additional burden on an already strained federal budget. The success in eventually getting an act that provided public schools with substantial supplementary funds to be used in educating disadvantaged children was an impressive political achievement.

This legislation was the Elementary and Secondary Education Act of 1965. Title I of the Act stated "it to be the policy of the United States to provide financial assistance to local educational agencies serving areas with concentrations of children from low-income families." The amount appropriated in the first year was less than one billion dollars; in subsequent years it was increased to about $1.5 billion. This represents about four per cent of the total annual school expenditures. Assuming that 20 per cent of American school children are disadvantaged, the current appropriation, if divided equally among them, would provide a supplement of only $150 per year for each disadvantaged child. However, those who drafted this bill hoped that it would be followed by more adequate funds as the seriousness and difficulty of the problem were recognized.

In the first two years of operation of this program, it became apparent that most local schools had not analyzed the complex problems involved in improving the education of disadvantaged children. The plans of many schools in the first year or two were simple ones, such as adding teachers or teacher aides to the school staff, or using more audio-visual materials. Many schools also identified some of the more obvious problems of the children, such as inadequate nutrition, need for eye corrections, frequent illness. After the second year, more attention was given to the problems arising from the differences between the child's experience in school and in the home and neighborhood. For example, many disadvantaged children had had no experience with books at home. The vocabulary used at home was often different from that the child heard in school; sometimes it was in a different language (Spanish, for example) or a different dialect of English. In many neighborhoods, the attitude was negative toward the school, which was not considered helpful or even relevant to the matters of real concern to the children or their families. Mothers frequently viewed the school as a place where the children might get into trouble and pleaded with them to be quiet in school and not do anything bad.

Assessing Title I programs

As local school authorities began to identify the variety of difficulties faced by disadvantaged children, they recognized that their initial efforts were not adequate to compensate for the range of problems that were discerned. Gradually, more and more of the programs were designed to deal with the actual problems identified in the particular schools. By the end of the 1967-68 school year, sample studies indicated that approximately one fourth of the programs were producing measurable results in reading and arithmetic, and by 1970-71 about one third were reporting positive results. The Office of Education published descriptions of successful state programs that were evaluated in 1970-71. In May 1973, the New York State Education Department reported a study of a sample of 58,289 pupils in Title I programs who achieved "far more than expected." For example, more than 45,000 elementary school pupils who had previously made only six-month gains in reading for every 10 months of instruction, after entering the Title I program achieved 13-month gains in 10 months. For 3,000 secondary school students, the increase in reading and mathematics achievement was three times that of the previous year.

The Office of Education reports, the state reports, and the published reports of other investigations all point to the same conclusion. There has been a steady increase in the number of Title I programs that are producing measurable improvements in the educational achievements of disadvantaged children, although there are still many programs that appear to be ineffective. These reports also show that improvements in learning can be maintained and increased when the program provides for a sequence of three to four years rather than one-shot efforts to help. But to bring the learning gains of disadvantaged children up to the national average generally requires an expenditure per pupil that is 50 per cent higher than average.

These results may seem incredible to some who have gained a contrary impression from the reports of recent large-scale studies, particularly the Coleman report on *Equality of Educational Opportunity* and Christopher Jencks' book *Inequality*. However, there is no real contradiction. Neither of these two large-scale investigations dealt with the amount of school learning achieved by disadvantaged children in the period since the Elementary and Secondary Education Act of 1965 became operative. Both the Coleman and the Jencks studies examined differences in scores on standard tests among different groups of children. They did not ask what different groups of children had learned but rather what measured variables were related to differences in scores. The standard tests used were norm-referenced tests. In building these tests, questions that most children could answer correctly were eliminated, but questions which only about half the children could answer correctly were retained. This was done in order to spread the scores as widely as possible so that children could be arranged on a scale from highest to lowest. The purpose of norm-referenced tests is to sort students, not to assess what they have learned. It happens that many of the items that are effective in sharply sorting students are those that are not emphasized in a majority of schools.

As an illustration, by age 13 about 80 per cent of American children can read and comprehend a typical newspaper paragraph. Such an exercise is included in the National Assessment of Educational Progress because its purpose is to report what proportion of children have acquired this useful reading skill. The exercise is not included in standard tests for 13-year-old children because it does not sharply separate the very skillful reader from others. Standard tests will include items with unusual vocabulary and complex sentence structures or other reading tasks that are not emphasized by most schools and thus are not answered correctly by a large proportion of the age group. Coleman and Jencks were using these tests because they show the largest differences among groups. They found that family background factors were more related to these differences than school factors, but neither the test data nor the method of analysis of variance that they used could answer the question of what most children had learned in school.

Another matter that is sometimes overlooked in discussions of these reports is their use of historical rather than current data. The test results analyzed by both Coleman and Jencks were obtained before schools became greatly concerned with the problems of learning encountered by disadvantaged children. Since schools have identified the problem, more effort has been focused on it.

Head Start

The increased concern for the education of poor children in the early 1960's created unusual public interest in studies of child development and the recommendations of pediatricians, child psychologists, and specialists in early childhood. These studies and the recommendations agree on the critical importance of the early years in the development of children. According to various psychological measures, by the time most children of families with low incomes had reached the age of six, they were a year behind the average child of that age. As they progressed through school, the gap widened. It seemed a sound strategy to provide educational assistance to young disadvantaged children in the hope of closing the gap before it widened. This was a major purpose of the legislation authorizing Head Start programs. Other purposes were to promote better health through physical examinations, nutritious lunches, alternations of rest and exercise, and a safe environment.

The Head Start legislation authorized the use of federal funds to support programs conducted by various public and non-profit agencies. Civic organizations, churches, and community action groups were the most common sponsors. The chief opposition came from those who feared public intervention in child rearing and the home, and some organizations of professional educators expressed the fear that the non-professional character of many sponsors would result in programs of little worth or ones that would impede the child's development.

Because the only precedents were existing nursery schools that had been established for other purposes, the early programs of Head Start varied greatly from place to place, and many appeared to have no rationale to guide them. In an effort to identify successful programs and to discover major problems, the Westinghouse Learning Corporation and Ohio University were commissioned in 1968 to conduct an extensive evaluation of the impact of Head Start on children's cognitive and affective development. Among the findings of this study were: (1) Summer programs did not produce results that persisted into the early elementary years; (2) full-year programs had no significant impact on affective development, and marginal impact on cognitive development; (3) programs were more effective in Negro centers, central cities, and in the Southeast; (4) Head Start children remained below national norms on standard tests of language. This study was not designed to ascertain the effects of Head Start on the health of children nor on the education in child rearing gained by parents who participated. It did, however, identify four types of programs that seemed to have more impact, and these are now being studied and evaluated as promising approaches for general use. One of these involves parents in the training of their children; a second program uses immediate incentives and rewards to reinforce the children's learning of language and number exercises; a third focuses on perceptual training of the Montessori type; and the fourth engages the children in seeking answers to the questions they raise, thus emphasizing inquiry learning.

It seems clear that Head Start, like Title I programs, began with a variety of approaches, varying degrees of conscious planning, and great differences in the extent of systematic attempts to make continuing improvements in the light of experience. It also seems clear that successful programs can be designed and implemented. Federal expenditure for Head Start, however, was reduced from $652 million in 1968-69 to $369 million in 1971-72, and it is not likely to be expanded to provide adequate support for nationwide efforts to provide preschool education for a majority of disadvantaged children. If this task is to be successfully undertaken, it will require a determined effort covering 10 or 15 years.

The Job Corps

Another intensive effort to educate the disadvantaged was the Job Corps, which enrolled youths aged 16 to 21. Authorized in the Economic Opportunity Act of 1964, it established rural and urban residential centers where youths were to be given education, vocational training, and useful work experience. The Job Corps without doubt presented the most difficult problem of any of the programs for the disadvantaged. Those enrolled were adolescents, not children. They were not in school but rather already among the hard-core unemployed. The establishment of special residential centers removed the enrollees from many of the negative influences of their environment, but the young members of the camp comprised a peer group whose attitudes and habits were largely similar, so that the camp depended heavily on the adult staff's constructive examples for corpsmen to emulate.

Many of the educational efforts were initially ineffective, partly because they required the development of new programs. In addition, crises of discipline and of relations with nearby communities blunted training programs. Nevertheless, there were some manifest successes. Not only were a majority of the corpsmen placed in jobs for which their training was adequate, but some made spectacular gains in education and in employability. The Job Corps program demonstrated that many youths from the most impoverished of backgrounds can be helped to learn the knowledge, skills, and attitudes required for constructive work roles. But it also indicated that the task is much more difficult than was appreciated when the Job Corps was established. It is much harder and much more costly than compensatory education for young people; however, for the present generation some type of educational program for the most disadvantaged youths will be necessary if they are not to be left to the tragic life of continuing unemployment.

The experience with pre-school children, elementary school students, and adolescents has provided greater understanding of the long-term educational development problems of the disadvantaged. The educative process begins at birth, and the complex of home, neighborhood, and school factors is involved throughout childhood and youth. During this entire period, not just at a single stage, the disadvantaged child learns less of the things the schools teach than do other children. A number of studies estimate that the disadvantaged child is a year behind the average child when he enters school and three years behind when he is in high school.

The formerly widespread notion that once the disadvantaged child had caught up with the others he needs no further special assistance overlooked the complex of factors within and without the school that influence effective learning. For example, the content of much instruction uses illustrations familiar to middle-class children but not to the disadvantaged. The lock-step method of teaching so frequently followed allows too little time on a topic for disadvantaged children to master it. The method of grading continually discourages slow learners from attempting school assignments on which they receive only poor marks. At home, disadvantaged children often lack reading materials on which to practice their slowly developing reading skills, and their parents give them little encouragement because of their own lack of success in school. The experience with Head Start brought out the need for several years of assistance to enable disadvantaged children to gain an elementary education. Measurable gains in cognitive development during Head Start largely disappeared as the children continued in school, except when the school provided a continuing program of special service.

It is clear now that disadvantaged children can gain in education, but this requires changes in their total educational experiences from early childhood to adolescence. This necessitates large financial support and commitment to long term programs. The returns from these larger expenditures, however, should come not only from the contributions made to this generation of children and youth, but also to those who follow. Disadvantaged children who gain an education today are educated parents of the next generation. Their children will not suffer the same handicaps that they encountered. But without an adequate program for educating today's disadvantaged, there seems little likelihood that there will be fewer disadvantaged in the next generation. An adequate program reaching the 20 per cent of American children who are disadvantaged and are distributed among thousands of local schools requires a long-term commitment to furnish funds and to develop programs and the professional competence needed to guide them. An entire generation of children is involved, which means a 20-year effort. The experience of the 1960's suggests that the cost will be two or three times that of educating children of middle-class background. The development of programs and materials and the acquisition of professional competence to guide new programs is likely to take five to eight years. Americans are not accustomed to long-term commitments of this magnitude. It is a real challenge.

Broadening access to higher education

The 1948 post-War Commission on Higher Education appointed by President Truman called attention to the great difference in college enrollments of youths from families of different income levels. It recommended a federal scholarship program as well as government assistance in the expansion of higher educational institutions as a means for providing increased opportunities for American youth. These recommendations did not result in the necessary legislation at that time, although the National Science Foundation was then authorized to award scholarships and fellowships in the fields of science, mathematics, and engineering to increase the supply of persons trained in these fields. The Foundation established graduate fellowships and traineeships but did not support undergraduate scholarships. The GI Bill of Rights had furnished a successful example of a federal program that enabled 3,443,000 veterans of World War II and the Korean war to attend college, most of whom would not otherwise have been able to do so. It demonstrated that many youths from backgrounds of poverty could succeed in college when provided support for tuition and subsistence. But this example was not immediately followed by legislation to support non-veterans because the GI Bill was justified as part of the federal government's responsibility for the national defense.

Public interest in affording greater opportunities in higher education for low-income youths was aroused both by the post-Sputnik fear of wasting human talents and by the civil rights movement, which publicized the serious deprivation of college education among minority groups, particularly blacks, those with Spanish-speaking backgrounds, and American Indians. In response to mounting public concern, the federal government in the 1960's took several major steps to increase the access to colleges and universities of persons with low incomes and those from minority groups. Some of these efforts are continuing today.

The first of these was to assist in the expansion of the capacity of existing institutions and help support facilities for the many newly established ones, many of which were junior and community colleges. In 1962, President Kennedy had a bill introduced to authorize federal aid to higher education institutions in financing the construction of academic and related facilities. Although the bill was defeated in the House, the debate established the background for the passage of the Higher Education Facilities Act of 1963. Federal grants for construction, which reached a high of $467 million in 1966, and federal construction loans, which peaked at $200 million in the same year, were able to furnish a substantial supplement to state, local and private construction funds for building the facilities required by the phenomenal increase in college enrollments. Without federal funds it seems unlikely that the construction of facilities would have been adequate to provide for the great influx of students.

This tremendous surge in college enrollments resulted primarily from three factors. In 1945 the U. S. birthrate was 19.5 per thousand population. In 1946 the birthrate jumped to 24.1 per thousand. In 1947 it moved up to 26.6, then dropped in 1948 to 24.9 and remained above 24 throughout the 1950's. In 1950 there were eight million persons of high school age; by 1970 there were 16 million. Furthermore, in 1950 the number graduating from high school was equal to 59 per cent of all 17-year-olds. In 1960 the percentage was 65 per cent and by 1970 it was 78 per cent. In 1960 the percentage of high school graduates going on to college was 52 per cent. By 1970 it was 62 per cent. The higher birthrate, the larger percentage of youths graduating from high school, and the larger percentage of the high school graduates going on to college largely explain the surge in college enrollments from 2,285,500 in 1950 to 3,582,726 in 1960 and 7,920,149 in 1970.

A second step was to furnish support for the individual student. The Work Study Program of the Economic Opportunity Act of 1964 authorized grants to institutions of higher education to assist in the employment of students from low-income families. In 1964-65 the expenditure for Work Study was $23 million. This program was incorporated into the Higher Education Act of 1965 and greatly expanded to reach $112 million by 1968. It was reduced to $95 million in 1969, and thereafter combined with the Equal Opportunity grants that were authorized in Title IV of the Higher Education Act of

1965. These grants were to be used to assist students "of exceptional financial need who would be unable to obtain the benefits of higher education without such aid." By 1972 the expenditures reached $575 million. The Act also authorized low-interest insured loans to college students. On a much smaller scale the Upward Bound program of OEO furnished support for projects to provide special educational assistance to prepare disadvantaged minority high school students for entrance into college.

Recognizing that many low-income and minority students were enrolled in institutions with limited resources, Title III of the Act authorized the support of a Teacher Fellow program to furnish additional instructional services to these "developing institutions" and funds for cooperative arrangements under which they may draw upon the talent and experience of America's finest colleges and universities and on the educational resources of business and industry.

In addition to the federal programs, a number of private foundations made substantial grants in the 1960's to junior colleges and universities to assist in broadening their student bodies, and to aid minority students. It is possible to review the changes in minority enrollments that took place in the 1960's, but it is not possible to separate the several factors and programs influencing these changes, and to estimate the relative effect of each.

Successes and shortcomings

The major federal programs got underway in 1966. Thus, it is informative to compare enrollments in 1970 with those of 1965 to gain some indication of possible effects. Between 1965 and 1970, the proportion of white persons aged 18 to 24 who were enrolled in college increased from 26 to 27 per cent. During the same period, the proportion of blacks changed from 10 to 16 per cent. The black college population is still far short of the white enrollment, but substantial progress is evident. Comparable data are not available regarding the progress made by other minorities.

During this five-year period the enrollment of black students in the traditionally black colleges increased about 25 per cent. The largest increase in enrollment of black students was in junior and community colleges. They enrolled one third of all the black students and one half of all the black freshmen. Their development has contributed substantially to the increased college attendance of black students.

After 1966, about 200,000 students in serious financial need received Educational Opportunity grants annually, and more than nine million others obtained federally insured loans. Funds for these programs and the construction funds used to expand facilities without doubt had some influence in expanding minority enrollments.

Of the federal funds allocated for developing institutions, 56 per cent was granted to the traditionally black colleges. The total of these grants from 1966 to 1971 was nearly $100 million. A recent report of the federal Interagency Committee on Education states that the total support for these colleges from the federal government has increased from $108 million in 1969 to $242 million in 1972. Of this amount $165 million came from the Office of Education and $21 million from the National Institutes of Health. Since these colleges are those that black Americans can call their own, they are generally more responsive than others to the special needs of this minority group. Hence, the contributions to strengthen these institutions made by the federal government and private foundations are very significant. Their results will be more evident as time passes. They have been used to support faculty development, curriculum planning, and management seminars as well as to provide student aid.

Gaining admission to college does not guarantee that a student gets a college education. Some students find themselves unprepared to carry on the kind of learning activities that college faculties assign. The Upward Bound programs demonstrated with more than 3,000 minority students that special pre-college training experiences could help many of them develop the skills, habits, and attitudes required for success in the colleges in which they enrolled. But these programs reached only a small fraction of the minority students. Most of them gained college admission without special preparation because many colleges and universities recognized the need for broadening their student body and therefore admitted a wider range of students than before. But it quickly became apparent that unless this was coupled with a reexamination of educational practices, many of this new group of students would fail to get an education. The proportion of dropouts from a college varies greatly according to whether it admits a wider range of students than it did previously. For example, the City University of New York reports that dropout rates before the end of the first semester, 1970-71, after a policy of open admissions was adopted ranged from eight to 25 per cent on the different campuses. Those campuses that adopted remedial programs experienced a smaller proportion of dropouts. The dropout rate for the total university was 10.8 per cent, not greatly different from the dropout rates for years before open admissions, which was 11.2 per cent in 1968-69 and 12 per cent in 1969-70.

Another example of this dilemma was the California Educational Opportunity Program of that state's college and university system. This program was a special one designed for minorities and other disadvantaged students. San Jose State University reported that in the first year, 1968-69, the special freshmen students received much lower grades than regular students. Nevertheless, 71 per cent of the specials received satisfactory marks (a grade of C or better) and 67 per cent returned for the sophomore year. The report concludes that with a specially designed program the disadvantaged students "began slower, gradually caught up and attained creditable records although they did not outperform regular students."

Many other institutions are now seeking to develop curricula and teaching practices that are helpful to the new groups of students. But this will take time and experience. The reason for believing that helpful modifications will be made comes not only from the success some colleges have had in educating minorities but also from the experience of a century ago when the Land Grant Colleges were established to serve the youth from agricultural and mechanical classes. The college faculties at the time were faced with new kinds of students, but in the space of 20 years, curricula and practices were worked out that were quite successful.

Some of the present special programs emphasize remedial instruction in reading and mathematics. While these have proved helpful, three principles followed in the early programs of the Land Grant Colleges might also be useful in meeting this newer problem. The first is to use examples and assignments which apply the content of the course to the experience and interests of the students. The second is to begin a program with concrete materials and develop the abstract principles from the concrete. A third is to time each topic so that the students can master the essential material before moving to the next. The use of these principles helped the new students of a century ago. Their application to the present curriculum is one way of helping the new students of today to gain a college education.

Educating for the world of work

The Smith-Hughes Act of 1917 established a policy of cooperating with state and local schools in the support of vocational education in the public schools, but until the 1960's few changes were made in the law to reflect the profound changes in occupations. In 1961, President Kennedy asked the Secretary of HEW to convene an advisory body to review and evaluate the national Vocational Education Acts and make recommendations for improving and redirecting the program. This Panel of Consultants on Vocational Education made its report on November 27, 1962.

However, the Area Redevelopment Act (ARA) of 1961 and the Manpower Development and Training Act (MDTA) of 1962 were passed before the Panel's report was made. The ARA sought to reduce unemployment in depressed areas through attracting industry and jobs, and authorized the support of training for the new jobs to be developed. It made neither a large nor a significant contribution to vocational education. The MDTA's contribution was much larger.

By 1965, it provided appropriations of $400 million annually. At first, it concentrated upon the training of unemployed family heads, but in 1964, with the sharp rise in youth unemployment, the vocational training of young people accounted for about one quarter of the expenditures.

Both of these acts were designed to increase the number of persons with skills which were in demand and to reduce unemployment of persons who had been in occupations no longer in great demand or who had never been employed. These programs were to serve adults and out-of-school youths, not high school students. They differed from the Job Corps in serving persons within the community rather than in camps. Although the experience with these acts was both constructive and instructive, they were not intended to be comprehensive efforts to improve and redirect vocational education.

The Panel of Consultants found two principal failures in vocational education: lack of sensitivity to changes in the labor market, and lack of sensitivity to the needs of various segments of the population. Accordingly, it made five major recommendations: (1) Offer training opportunities to the 21 million non-college graduates who will enter the labor market in the 1960's. (2) Provide training or retraining for the millions of workers whose skills and technical knowledge must be updated, as well as those whose jobs will disappear due to increasing efficiency, automation, or economic change. (3) Meet the critical need for highly skilled craftsmen and technicians through education during and after the high school years. (4) Expand vocational and technical training programs consistent with employment possibilities and national economic needs. (5) Make educational opportunities equally available to all, regardless of race, sex, scholastic aptitude, or place of residence.

The Vocational Education Act of 1963 followed several of these recommendations. Its stated purpose was to make federal grants to the states in order "to develop an adequate vocational education system."

Prior to this Act, federal support of vocational education came from various specific pieces of legislation, and in 1962-63 reached about $50 million. In 1964-65, the first year of operation of the new Act, federal funds appropriated were $157 million, and by 1968 this had risen to more than $250 million. In addition, state and local funds furnished more than twice the amount granted by the federal government.

After three years of operation of the Act, the National Advisory Council on Vocational Education presented a comprehensive appraisal of the progress being made and the problems encountered. It found that there was a substantial increase in persons enrolled in vocational courses and some evidence of redirection of courses, but that the main emphasis was on the continuation of existing programs. The report pointed out that the number enrolled in health occupations and technical programs was extremely small in view of the potential labor needs, and that most new programs were being developed in post-secondary institutions, not in the high schools.

Progress made in serving new groups was also found to be very slight. The number of adults served increased 13 per cent, from 2.3 million to 2.6 million, while the number of high school students increased 43 per cent, from 2.1 million to 3.0 million, and post-secondary students 157 per cent, from 172,000 to 442,000. In contrast, the number of students with special needs amounted to 49,000, less than one per cent of the total enrollment. The Council concluded that progress in the first three years in developing a comprehensive program of vocational education was extremely slow.

In assessing the progress of vocational education from 1963 until 1970, the recommendations of the Panel of Consultants may serve as goals with which to compare progress. The first, that all 21 million non-college graduates who entered the labor market in the 1960's should receive training opportunities, is a reasonable goal only if the term training opportunities is broadly interpreted. The entering level of a very large number of jobs does not require special training beyond the short-term training commonly provided by the employing institution. On the other hand, if training opportunities are defined to include basic skills, attitudes, and habits, such as reading, speaking, listening, writing, computing, respecting others, working cooperatively, feeling responsible for tasks undertaken, meeting a regular schedule punctually, and the like, then clearly all persons entering the labor market need opportunities to learn these things. Many children and youths learn them through experiences in the home, the community, and the school without having a special vocational course, but those who have not learned them in this way should be provided with other opportunities.

Vocational training in the schools

Another kind of educational opportunity that should be generally available is occupational exploration. Many young people are uncertain about their ability to get a job when they leave school and their capacity to hold down any job they might get. This inhibits their selection of an area for training and reduces their motivation to learn what the program requires. Vocational education needs to furnish a closer connection between work and education, preferably cooperative education, in which students get actual experience on the job. A study of school-supervised work education programs made for the Office of Education in 1972-73 by System·Development Corporation found that "a cooperative education program is more likely than any other type of program to: provide students with job-related instruction in school; have a follow-up program for its graduates; have an advisory committee; provide job placement services; have a high rate of job-related placements; provide students with jobs that offer formal on-the-job training; help students in deciding on an occupation; provide students with jobs that fit into their career plans; provide students with jobs that have a high level of responsibility; provide students with jobs that afford a high degree of satisfaction."

Yet only a small fraction, less than two per cent, of high school students are in cooperative education or some other form of school-supervised work-study program. In this broader sense, vocational education is still far from the goal of reaching all who need it.

The Panel's second recommendation, that training or retraining be provided for the millions of workers who need it, is still very far from being met. In 1970, the number of workers being aided was only a small fraction of those who could benefit. Some progress, however, is being made. The several manpower programs as well as the vocational education legislation have established a precedent that is beginning to gain wide acceptance.

The third recommendation, that vocational education meet the critical need for highly skilled craftsmen and technicians, is being only partially met. The junior and community colleges have been more responsive to this need than the high schools. The skill centers of the Manpower Development and Training Act are commonly in the junior and community colleges. The apprentice training programs have made very few efforts to meet new needs.

The fourth recommendation was that vocational and technical training programs should be planned in terms of employment possibilities and economic needs. It has received a disappointingly inadequate response. The large bulk of the training programs continue to be ones that were offered in the past.

The study's final recommendation, that vocational educational opportunities be made available to all, has brought very little progress. Various manpower and poverty programs focused on the disadvantaged and achieved some success, but funds from the Vocational Education Act of 1963 have been used for very few programs aimed at providing services for those with special needs.

The slow progress in improving and redirecting vocational education can be accounted for partly by certain factors unique to vocational education and partly by those that are common to most educational programs. Foremost among the unique factors is the ambivalence of the American public toward vocational education. On the one hand, we value work and preparation for work, but on the other hand, we prize social mobility and do not want our children to take steps which might interfere with their getting to college. This ambivalence will continue to be a major obstacle unless a real transformation of the curriculum and patterns of schooling takes place. Sidney Marland, former Assistant Secretary of HEW, sought to stimulate this transformation through new programs of "Career Education," in which understanding of the world of work is a primary purpose of elementary education, exploration of career possibilities is a focus of junior high school programs, and planning for careers and preparation for them are emphases in the senior high school.

A second obstacle is the limited occupational orientation of most school personnel. They have had little first-hand experience with most of the job areas for which vocational education is provided; therefore, most have inadequate background for furnishing guidance to students or participating in program planning.

A third obstacle is encountered when the school seeks to offer vocational education to those in need of special services. Confusion between the school's role in sorting students and in educating them results in the rejection of those students who most need training on the grounds that they are not good enough for vocational education. The earlier Smith-Hughes courses were very selective, enrolling only about half of the students who wanted training. Vocational education also has a tradition of sex discrimination. Girls have not been enrolled in a number of occupational training programs. These attitudes and the corresponding practices are very hard to change.

A fourth obstacle is simply the geographic distance separating places where jobs are developing and the homes of those who seek employment. Until recently, the majority of children brought up on farms and in small towns in the Midwest and South eventually had to move to industrial centers in order to find employment as the demand for farm labor greatly declined. Many of the hard core unemployed are persons who had no opportunity in their rural childhood to prepare for work in an industrial center. Today, although rural areas still furnish more youths than can be employed there, the inner cities are increasingly a source of youths who can find employment only by going outside the neighborhood area in which they feel at home.

In a locally oriented school system, one cannot expect attention to be given to preparing youths for jobs that do not exist in the area. Only at the national or perhaps the state level can programs be planned that will make it possible for a student to obtain broad training with cooperative work experience locally, even if he must later move to a new location where his specialized training will enable him to obtain the type of job he seeks.

The goal of the Vocational Education Act of 1963 to develop an adequate vocational education system is still important, but greater and better-directed efforts are essential to attain it. Among the steps likely to improve vocational education are (1) an effort to help children gain a clearer understanding of the highly interdependent world of work in a modern industrialized society—what the functions of important clusters of jobs are, how they contribute to the nation's needs, what their conditions of work are, what abilities they require, what satisfactions they provide, how one prepares for them; (2) the provision of school-supervised work experience for most, if not all, high school students; (3) continuing development, with the aid of advisory committees, of realistic programs of occupational preparation in which the school supplements but does not supplant the training responsibilities of employers.

Desegregating schools and colleges

Although the Supreme Court mandated school desegregation in 1954 and the Eisenhower Administration began to enforce it, the process had not progressed very far by 1960. The enactment of Titles IV and VI of the Civil Rights Act of 1964 gave legislative authorization for several federal actions. Title IV directed the Commissioner of Education to conduct a survey concerning the lack of equal opportunities in education. The report of this survey, the Coleman report of 1966, documented both the seriousness of the educational disadvantages of minority groups and the relative ineffectiveness of the schools in overcoming them.

As mentioned earlier, the findings of the Coleman report are often misinterpreted. The study was conducted before concerted efforts were being made to educate disadvantaged children; therefore, it does not furnish information about the effectiveness of these efforts. It was concerned with differences among groups of students and used tests that maximized differences in academic ability and accomplishments. These tests do not focus on things that most students learn, but rather on those that schools do not emphasize. The National Assessment, however, shows that black students have typically been learning much less in school than non-blacks. Hence, the existence of serious disadvantage is firmly established. If the Coleman study had been conducted earlier, it would have furnished a better understanding of the complexity of the problems and would have given a sounder intellectual basis for improving the education of minorities and other disadvantaged children.

American educators have identified two major values to be sought in the desegregation of schools. The first is to provide an environment that children can perceive as representing the ideals of American society and where they can act as good American citizens. Respect for the dignity and worth of every individual, regardless of his color, race, ethnic origin, or income is a central ideal of America. Children need to be part of a school community in which this ideal is primary. A second ideal is appreciation for the varied contributions to America that are made by the many different persons and groups in American society. Children need to experience the ways in which other children, coming from different backgrounds, add to the life of the school.

The second value sought through desegregation is an environment which encourages and rewards the school learning of students who have had little opportunity for this kind of learning outside of school. The evidence from current studies indicates that the integration of a lower-class child in a predominantly middle-class school is likely to bring about a significant improvement in his school achievement, whereas, if he remains in a segregated school, his achievement will continue to drop in relation to the performance of middle-class children. The meaning of this evidence is often disputed, but the findings appear to hinge on the attitudes of both students and teachers. In spite of the heated controversies over school desegregation, these two values remain both important and worth the struggle required to desegregate many schools.

Title IV of the Civil Rights Act also authorized the support of short-term or regular-session institutes for special training of school personnel to deal effectively with educational problems occasioned by desegregation. These institutes appear to have had constructive results. More than 7,500 school teachers, supervisors, and counselors in the South attended them, and the knowledge gained and the attitudes affected by these experiences probably account for the fact that most desegregation plans carried out in the South were not impeded by the behavior of teachers and principals. Furthermore, a survey of teacher associations in 1971 showed a nearly unanimous sentiment in favor of desegregation. It seems clear that the preparation of school personnel for their roles in new situations is an important step in making a program effective.

Title IV also authorized the Attorney General to institute suits in the federal courts against school authorities who fail to comply with desegregation decisions. Although this authority was not often used, it probably served to encourage minority-group parents to bring complaints and school authorities to give serious attention to them.

Title VI specified that no person shall on the grounds of race, color, or national origin be excluded from participation in or denied the benefits of any program of activity receiving federal support. This has been an additional force to open college and university programs to minority persons. Since 1964, there has been a rapid desegregation of teacher institutes supported by the National Science Foundation as well as the many in-service programs supported by funds from the Office of Education.

In assessing the overall progress of school desegregation, both progress and problems are clearly evident. School personnel overwhelmingly support desegregation. A national sample of the general public in 1972 showed that 67 per cent supported school desegregation as a national objective, with only 22 per cent opposed. Interestingly, the percentage in the South of persons supporting desegregation was slightly higher than in the rest of the country.

However, although most schools in the rural areas and the smaller cities are now desegregated, the schools in the large cities are far from the desired goal. As tenant farming has given way to industrialized agriculture in the South, agricultural workers, mostly blacks, have moved to the cities to seek work. There they live in highly segregated areas, both in the South and in other parts of the nation. In 11 of the larger cities they comprise a third or more of the population. Desegregating schools in the larger cities has proved to be much more difficult than in smaller localities.

The desegregation problems still remaining in 43 Southern cities were studied by a group of private non-profit organizations and presented in a May 1972 report entitled, "It's Not Over in the South." This report identifies a number of serious difficulties which must be overcome before desegregation is a reality in these cities.

What we have learned

Six significant lessons can be learned from reviewing federal efforts in education in the 1960's. In the first place, the right problems were selected for national attention. The country as a whole suffers from the failure of nearly one fifth of our young people to learn what the schools are expected to teach them. The costs in unemployment, in the lack of constructive participation in society, and in inadequate rearing of children are a serious drain on the nation. Unnecessary restrictions in access to post-secondary education limit entrance into upper-status positions largely to a favored sector of American society, thereby creating a caste system that violates our national ideals and fosters resentment and conflict. Anachronistic vocational education programs place a costly drag on the development of a modern economy and reduce the chance that it will be able to respond to the growing demands for services in health, education, and recreation. The segregation of children and youths on the basis of race, color, national origin, or social class is a continuing denial of America's basic commitment to respect life and dignity of every human being.

These problems were very serious, and they were not likely to be solved by state and local efforts without federal assistance. In most cases, they were not even recognized as problems on the local level until the Congressional debates and the availability of federal funds brought them to local attention. Federal funds for all education during the period 1964-72 amounted to $64 billion. Furthermore, the amount of money required for mounting effective efforts to solve these problems was greater than the amount that could be furnished by states and localities under existing methods of financing education. The educational programs of the 1960's attacked serious problems that required federal assistance.

A second lesson was that a successful attack on an important educational problem requires a plan based on an analysis of the complex factors involved in the educational development of children. The school experiences of a student are interwoven with his experiences in the home and community, with friends and playmates, and with the mass media, particularly television. Some programs succeeded because they were based on an analysis of each problem that identified the serious malfunction of the educational process that caused the problem. This also enabled them to locate places where constructive leverage could be applied. The failure to do this in most initial programs led to fruitless projects.

The third lesson was that the school, home, and community organizations are stable systems, more static than dynamic. New programs usually require new conceptions, new attitudes, new skills, and new habits on the part of the persons involved, and provisions for the development of these are essential to the success of such programs. For example, in educating disadvantaged elementary school children in Detroit, teachers developed a program in which they conceived of the school as an environment in which each child could be engaged in a sequence of learning tasks that led to his being able to read independently. They learned to identify the assets of each child rather than his deficiencies and to design learning tasks that built on these strengths. They learned to manage a group of 35 children who were working on different tasks in the learning sequence. They found that no simple adjustment of their previous teaching methods was successful in stimulating and guiding the learning of seriously disadvantaged children.

A fourth lesson was that time is necessary both for individual development and institutional change. Crash programs did not work. Most of the legislation set time limits on the authorizations that were far too short to produce the changes desired. The delay in making annual appropriations was an even more serious handicap. If the federal government is to have a significant constructive influence on improving American education, it must authorize and support programs of long duration.

A fifth lesson was that fundamental changes in education would require the allocation, at least initially, of far more resources than were thought to be necessary when the programs were designed. In educating disadvantaged children, the more effective programs were those in which both federal and local funds were concentrated on a small enough number of children to make adequate support possible for whatever school and home activities were planned. When the funds were divided equally among all the disadvantaged children, only $150 per year was available in addition to regular expenditures for each child. But the more effective programs required $600 to $900 per child in additional funds.

A final lesson was the importance of comprehensive public information in building wide understanding of the nation's serious educational problems—their incidence, the factors that appear to be involved, the possible avenues of attack, the cost of alternative solutions, and the likelihood of success. This background did not exist when the programs of the 1960's were established. Hence, the political support for them was not adequate. More has been done in building public understanding of the health problems of Americans than of our educational ones.

The federal efforts in education during the 1960's not only furnished significant assistance to the schools in educating disadvantaged children, to higher education in broadening access for previously neglected youths, to schools and colleges in educating for the world of work, and to American society in seeking to eliminate racial segregation, but they also provided instructive experiences that can guide future federal participation in education.

10

Blacks
and the crisis
in
political participation

CHARLES V. HAMILTON

IT is significant that the decade of the 1960's opened with a debate in the country and the Congress over various provisions of a proposed civil rights bill dealing with the right to vote in the South. Three years earlier, in 1957, Congress passed and the President signed the first civil rights law in 82 years. The main provisions of that legislation pertained to voting rights. But that law was relatively weak and many people knew it would have to be strengthened. In many ways, the 1960's can be seen as a decade devoted to achieving the goal of full right of access to political participation. This seems a bit strange in a country that was assumed to have solved, or at least nearly solved, the problem of participation long before the 1960's. This optimism was reflected in the following statement by Professor Samuel P. Huntington: "The United States . . . pioneered in popular participation in government not only in terms of the number of people who could vote for public officials but also, and perhaps more importantly, in the number of public officials who could be voted on by the people."[1]

Huntington was more precise when he connected the expansion

---

[1] Samuel P. Huntington, *Political Order in Changing Societies* (New Haven, 1968), p. 94.

of political participation in America with lack of violence and relative stability. He identified the pluralist character of the American
polity as a main reason for this situation:

> Why did the early and rapid expansion of political participation fail to
> breed violence and instability in the United States? At least in part, the
> answer lies in the relative complexity, adaptability, autonomy, and
> coherence of the traditional political institutions which existed in Amer-
> ica in the seventeenth and eighteenth centuries. These institutions were,
> in particular, sufficiently variegated at the local, state, and eventually
> national levels so as to provide many avenues for political participation.
> The multiplicity of institutions furnished multiple means of access to
> political power. Those groups unable to influence the national govern-
> ment might be able to dominate state or local governments. Those who
> could not elect chief executives might still control legislatures or at least
> legislative committees. Those who were forever weak numerically might
> find support in judicial bodies anxious to assert their power and to
> locate a constituency. With rare exceptions most of the significant social
> and economic groups in American society in the eighteenth and nine-
> teenth centuries could find some way of participating in government
> and of compounding their influence with governmental authority.[2]

By the midpoint of the twentieth century, newly politicized
groups, especially black Americans, had emerged. They had left
the farms of the South and migrated to urban areas. Unfortunately,
they were moving into an economic situation where technological
changes had begun to make unskilled labor less and less marketable. Whatever the situation in the eighteenth and nineteenth centuries, it was becoming increasingly clear that the American polity
would have to accommodate the demands for participation of new
social and economic groups. Black Americans, certainly, (and Huntington was correct on this point) had relied on the judiciary to
protect their Constitutional right to vote. But this protection was
proving to be insufficient at best, and Huntington's failure to see
this insufficiency is the source of a major flaw in his pluralist
model.

Other institutions—the Congress, the Presidency, the political
parties—would be called upon to take a hand in dealing with the
growing problem of participation. Specific demands were couched
in legal and Constitutional terms (the Fourteenth and Fifteenth
Amendments to the U.S. Constitution were the focal points of debate). But because blacks were the objects of concern, and racial
discrimination the key problem, the issue was understood by many
as a moral one. Therefore, as the country entered the 1960's, the
attitude was widespread that progress toward political equality for
all Americans was necessary and possible. Yet despite this apparent consensus, the decade opened with intense debate over how

---

[2] *Ibid.*, pp. 128-129.

best to secure what most people seemed to want. And it was not until August 1965 that the Voting Rights Law was passed.

On the heels of this event came the war on poverty legislation. These social welfare measures mandated "maximum feasible participation" in decision making by those whom the programs were meant to help. The fact that this phrase meant different things to different groups and that its meaning remained a sore issue throughout the rest of the decade clearly indicated that this country was in the middle of its "battle of participation"—a battle that was inevitable, but one that had been deferred for many years. Professor John H. Strange has gone so far as to conclude: "Because of this single phrase and its implementation in the OEO and Model Cities Programs, the decade of the 1960's will most likely be remembered as the decade of participation."[3]

Thus, the stage was set in the 1960's for a challenge to traditional American optimism regarding the question of participation. Decades earlier, while England and other European countries were modernizing their political structures and grappling with problems of participation, the United States seemingly had solved them all. Only the modernization of its social and economic institutions was believed necessary.[4] The 1960's said to Americans that they now had to face a problem they had been spared for so long. As Professor Sidney Verba wrote in his 1967 article "Democratic Participation":

> The United States is one of the happy few nations of the world which have passed many of the traditional crises of participation—for example, the incorporation of most of the working class, through the spread of the franchise and the growth of mass political parties, and the incorporation of a multiplicity of ethnic groups into democratic politics. But the problems of participation are never solved once and for all. As societies change and new problems arise, issues of participation come to the fore again, as they do in the current racial crisis.[5]

Race and participation

In contrast to the way some observers have pictured it, the development of black political participation from Reconstruction on has not been either smooth, stable, or free of violence. In 1890, when many countries were extending suffrage, Southern states in this country began revising their constitutions with the purpose of excluding blacks from political participation. This fact is vital background for understanding the dynamic events of the 1960's. Black

---

[3] John H. Strange, "Citizen Participation in Community Action and Model Cities Programs," *Public Administration Review,* Volume XXXII (October 1965), p. 655.
[4] Huntington, *op. cit.,* p. 129.
[5] Sidney Verba, "Democratic Participation," *Annals,* Vol. 373 (September 1967), p. 54.

Americans had to risk life and job to exercise the franchise most racial and ethnic groups in the United States took for granted. It is a matter of historical record that they frequently lost both— lives and jobs—in the process. This story is too clear to excuse Huntington's and Verba's sanguine characterizations of the American participatory experience. America felt it had accommodated most if not all "significant" social and economic groups *only* because she had forcefully and deliberately denied the opportunity to blacks. Contrary to Huntington and Verba, it was the flagrant *abuse* of the pluralist model, not the operation of that model, that permitted this country to assume that it was dealing efficaciously with the matter of participation. Failure to grasp this inevitably will result in failure to understand the significance of the demands for participation in the 1960's.

The history of that demand during the 70 years from 1890 to 1960 was generally one of negative results. Court battles were usually ineffective; legislative efforts were unfruitful until 1957. In the South, at least, where most of the potential black voters were located, attention had to be paid primarily to *securing* the vote, not to its effective mobilization and utilization. Thus, instead of concentrating time and resources on being politically astute (mobilizing, bargaining, compromising), black leaders had to concentrate on being legally precise and Constitutionally alert. As useful as this training is in a political democracy, it is hardly the sort that prepares a constituency for viable *political* participation. In an important sense, then, an effective black elite developed keen legal skills (and in turn both influenced and encouraged the enforcement of American Constitutional law). But it was unable to develop those skills required for mobilizing masses and maneuvering in the political marketplace. Blacks, in other words, developed plaintiffs rather than precinct captains. And except for a few places in Northern cities like New York and Chicago, they developed legal warriors, not political ward leaders.

While other racial and ethnic leaders could spend time exploring the process of machine politics—learning how to recruit and deliver voters, and how to reward, punish, and bargain for benefits— blacks had to spend time checking legal precedents and filing lawsuits. There is a big difference between debating the meaning of the Fifteenth Amendment to the Constitution and learning the intricacies of a filing system established by local election laws.

This course of events had yet another consequence. As the 1960's opened, and as new activists appeared in the black communities, the need for expertise in political mobilization developed precisely at the time when judicial victories were being achieved, when legislative attention was being paid to the problems of black political participation, and just when the executive branch was becoming more responsive. Who would begin to organize and channel the newly enfranchised? That blacks were becoming increasingly politicized was evident. The combination of politicization and enfranchisement made the need for sophisticated political leadership that much more critical. The need now went beyond the traditional "civil rights leaders" who were skilled in legal battles and in mass demonstrations. But this was exactly what the existing black leadership had to offer: a political leadership of protest politics, a leadership that was atuned to taking to the streets or to the courts (two tactics that frequently went hand in hand).

Younger, more restless leaders—in SNCC (the Student Nonviolent Coordinating Committee) and CORE—wanted action; and more often than not this meant physical confrontation. They viewed the legal approach as too slow and too cautious. Attempts at negotiating and bargaining to them were simply stalling tactics on the part of the adversary. Compromise was regarded as a sellout. There was little reason to expect any other attitude. Precious little in their historical struggle would lend credibility to an approach that relied on *political* bargaining. Older leaders had the advantage of comparison; they could compare 1960 with 1940, and they could see meaningful change, albeit slow. But this kind of knowledge and attitude could probably only be appreciated through experience, and many of the younger leaders were in their pre-teens when Governor Faubus was resisting the desegregation of Central High School in Little Rock, Arkansas. Likewise, most of the younger people were not even born when A. Philip Randolph, using the Brotherhood of Sleeping Car Porters as his base, effectively threatened a mass March on Washington by blacks for jobs in defense factories, and wrested Executive Order 8802 out of a reluctant President Roosevelt in 1941. Therefore, the newer activists created their own agenda for social action, and it contained a heavy dose of accelerated protest politics. The mass rally, the mass march, the direct-action confrontation—these tactics not only suited their youthful style and energy, but also signaled more loudly and clearly the dissatisfaction of the demand makers. They had not personally experienced the earlier protest movements, but they were aware, if only instinctively, of rhetoric and its functions in arousing masses. It was not at all part of their background to even attempt to achieve results through mass mobilization of voters in the arena of electoral politics. This form of participation was not a part of the political heritage of blacks that older leaders could pass on to their younger successors. Again, the style was to protest and to sue; and in those isolated urban areas where blacks had voted for decades (Atlanta, Chicago, New York, Detroit), the gains made through the ballot box did not recommend it as a viable alternative.

It is accurate to say then that the best political participatory models that black leadership had in the 1960's were either lawyers or platform orators. There were no black success models in the manner of Tammany Hall, Boss Crump, or the Cook County Democratic political machine. The struggle pivoted around protest and crises, and it was clear, not least of all to Dr. Martin Luther King, Jr., that this approach, while functional to an extent, had severe limitations:

> Many civil rights organizations were born as specialists in agitation and dramatic projects; they attracted massive sympathy and support; but they did not assemble and unify the support for new stages of struggle. The effect on their allies reflected their basic practices. Support waxed and waned, and people became conditioned to action in crises but inaction from day to day. We unconsciously patterned a crisis policy and program, and summoned support not for daily commitment but for explosive events alone.[6]

Modernization deferred

Huntington has stated more clearly than anyone the differences between the United States and Europe in regard to the centralization of authority. In the process of political modernization, governments concentrate power in the center. Several countries on the European continent did this, during the emergence of monarchial rule that followed centuries of feudalism. England followed the same route ending up with parliamentary government. As the following comments by Huntington demonstrate, this pattern did not prevail in the United States:

> In continental Europe, as in most contemporary modernizing countries, rationalized authority and centralized power were necessary not only for unity but also for progress. The opposition to modernization came from traditional interests: religious, aristocratic, regional, and local. The centralization of power was necessary to smash the old order, break down the privileges and restraints of feudalism, and free the way for the rise of new social groups and the development of new economic activities. . . .
>
> In America, on the other hand, the absence of feudal social institutions made the centralization of power unnecessary. Since there was no aristocracy to dislodge, there was no need to call into existence a governmental power capable of dislodging it. This great European impetus to political modernization was missing. Society could develop and change without having to overcome the opposition of social classes with a vested interest in the social and economic status quo. The combination of an egalitarian social inheritance plus the plenitude of land and other resources enabled social and economic development to take place more or less spontaneously. Government often helped to promote economic

---

[6] Martin Luther King, Jr., *Where Do We Go From Here: Chaos or Community?* (New York, 1967), pp. 158-159.

development, but (apart from the abolition of slavery) it played only a minor role in changing social customs and social structure. In modernizing societies, the centralization of power varies directly with the resistance to social change. In the United States, where the resistance was minimal, so also was the centralization.[7]

Herein lies the crux of the problem faced by Americans in the 1960's. Because the country had been able to develop socially and economically over the centuries, it had not been forced to modernize its political institutions, i.e., to centralize political authority. All the elements considered significant had been accommodated in a political system that dispersed power. Blacks were not a political force to be reckoned with in the nineteenth and early twentieth centuries; therefore they could be ignored or their political progress delayed without discomfiture to the prevailing political order. This preferred American position permitted more than a few observers to assume that this country was a consensual society, destined to be spared the headaches of other societies. Indeed, the very presumption of cultural homogeneity gave the system its stamp of legitimacy. Professor Seymour M. Lipset has stated the case in the following manner:

> A major test of legitimacy is the extent to which given nations have developed a common "secular political culture," mainly national rituals and holidays. The United States has developed a common homogeneous culture in the veneration accorded the Founding Fathers, Abraham Lincoln, Theodore Roosevelt, and their principles. These common elements, to which all American politicians appeal, are not present in all democratic societies.[8]

This was a dangerous presumption at best. In fact, a careful examination of the history of the black struggle prior to the mid-twentieth century might have revealed signs that it was an unwarranted presumption. As noted earlier in this essay, judicial victories were being won painfully and slowly, but there was not an abundance of evidence to indicate that these victories were sufficient to assuage the desire of blacks for greater societal benefits. Indeed, such victories probably were adequate for those in the non-aggrieved class, but that group was not the correct barometer.[9] Too many racial problems persisted decade after decade, and this was laying the foundation for more serious ideological explosions culminating in the 1960's. Social scientists know, or ought to know at any rate,

[7] Huntington, *op. cit.*, pp. 125-126.
[8] Seymour Martin Lipset, *Political Man* (New York, 1963), p. 68.
[9] Herein lies one of the major weaknesses of those who prior to and during the crises of the 1960's were constantly admonishing that racial progress was being made. In one sense, they might have been right, but in another, they were irrelevant. It was not for them to pronounce, but for others to perceive that progress of a significant kind was being made.

something about this phenomenon, even if they fail to apply it to the United States. Lipset says:

> Resolving tensions one at a time contributes to a stable political system; carrying over issues from one historical period to another makes for a political atmosphere characterized by bitterness and frustration rather than tolerance and compromise. Men and parties come to differ with each other, not simply on ways of settling current problems, but on fundamental and opposed outlooks.[10]

With increased political fervor, blacks began in the 1960's to turn more and more to the national government for alleviation of their grievances. It is true that that level of government had always been more responsive to black demands than local or state governments. In fact, one major characteristic of the black political experience is the extent to which blacks have had to rely on the federal government. As those demands were accelerated, there was bound to be tension between what the demand makers felt to be their legitimate demands on the one hand and the preference of the system to limit centralized authority on the other. Blacks came face to face with the Constitutional argument of federalism.

The luxury this country enjoyed in its early years, one of having been spared the necessity of modernizing its political structures, had disappeared by the 1960's. An almost immediate response to a new dilemma was suddenly required, and under the worst of circumstances: crises and a widening ideological gap. In 1964, Burke Marshall pinpointed this problem in a series of lectures at Columbia University:

> Federal policy under Attorney General Kennedy has been to try to make the federal system in the voting field work by itself through local action, without federal court compulsion. Since the beginning of 1961 the Department has not brought a case or demanded voting records without first attempting to negotiate the matter with the local officials. The assumption has been, *even when there was very good reason to believe that it was not valid,* that state officials would correct any abuses which could not be defended on the facts.[11]

Federalism and legitimacy

This problem was presented in its starkest form in the South during the early 1960's and centered around civil rights efforts of SNCC workers. They were holding voter registration drives, marches, and sit-ins and calling on the U.S. Department of Justice to protect them against the brutality of the police and local white

---

[10] Lipset, *op. cit.*, p. 71.
[11] Burke Marshall, *Federalism and Civil Rights* (New York, 1964), p. 23 (italics mine).

citizens. Instances of violence were almost daily occurrences. The growing impatience of the young activists was pitted against the staunch resolve of the federal authorities not to contravene principles of Constitutional federalism. The civil rights forces tried constantly to involve the federal government in an ultimate challenge with the local authorities. James Forman, then of SNCC, described one meeting in the Spring of 1964:

> Sitting around the paneled room in the Justice Department were Burke Marshall, John Doar, Arthur Schelsinger, Jr., Steve Bingham, and his father, with Bob Moses, Lawrence Guyot, and myself representing COFO (Council of Federated Organizations). Burke Marshall pleaded with us to go slow on starting projects in the Third Congressional District; the Justice Department was trying to do some work in that area and it would take them time. We pointed out to him that all the United States Government had to do was throw one of the racist sheriffs in jail. This would prevent some of the brutality. We reminded him that the FBI had made one arrest in the Delta, indicating they had the power to make arrests if they wanted to. There was silence. We pressed the point and talked of the murders of James Chaney, Andrew Goodman, and Michael Schwerner.
>
> Burke Marshall replied in that trembling voice of his that they were not going to fight a guerrilla war in Mississippi and if they arrested a sheriff, they would have to fight this type of war. We stated vigorously that he seemed more concerned about Mississippi's whites than the safety of black people. We did not agree with his position that the whites would start a war, and, if they were capable of that, then the issue needed to be forced.[12]

Burke Marshall, in his Columbia lectures, discussed the federalism issue as it plagued national decision-makers. He was describing a series of incidents in the early 1960's involving arrests in sit-in demonstrations against racial segregation and countless police acts of harassment of civil rights activists.

> This has led in the past three years to the greatest single source of frustration with and misunderstanding of the federal government, particularly among young people. They cannot understand federal inaction in the face of what they consider, *often quite correctly,* as official wholesale local interference with the exercise of federal Constitutional rights. Apparently their schools and universities have not taught them much about the working of the federal system. In their eyes the matter is simple. Local authorities are depriving certain people of their federal rights, often in the presence of federal officials from the Justice Department. Persons doing this should be protected.
>
> What is wrong with this analysis? Is the federal government simply failing to meet a clear responsibility for enforcing federal law?
>
> The question embraces all the deepest complexities of the federal

---

[12] James Forman, *The Making of Black Revolutionaries* (New York, 1972), pp. 381-382.

system. It is surrounded by some basic constitutional notions which have worked, and worked well, in other contexts, preserving the dilution of powers intended by the framers of the Constitution, and at the same time protecting individuals against deprivation of their freedoms.[13]

Marshall missed the point, however. The fact that the institutions worked well under other circumstances and at a different time should not have been the basis for defending those institutions later —when time and circumstances had changed substantially. The 1960's presented very many of the conditions that earlier had caused other societies to move toward political modernization, meaning centralization of authority. The increased demands of blacks for participation became the vehicle for American political innovation and modernization. Marshall and others did not see it in that perspective; but comparison of events in the United States and the history of other countries demonstrates its validity.

The problem of access, of "entry into politics," indeed of participation—the subject of this essay—is directly related to the critical question of legitimacy. If some blacks became politically alienated in the 1960's and began to view the political system as illegitimate, it should not have been too surprising to knowledgeable social scientists. Many empirical studies have shown what happens under situations of sustained political exclusion. Lipset is very precise on this point, and it continues to be a puzzle why more American social analysts were unable to apply these findings to their own society in the 1960's.

> The second general type of loss of legitimacy is related to the ways in which different societies handle the "entry into politics" crisis—the decision as to when new social groups shall obtain access to the political process. In the nineteenth century these new groups were primarily industrial workers; in the twentieth, colonial elites and peasant peoples. Whenever new groups become politically active (e.g., when the workers first seek access to economic and political power through economic organization and the suffrage, when the bourgeoisie demand access to and participation in government, when colonial elites insist on control over their own system), easy access to the legitimate political institutions tends to win the loyalty of the new groups to the system, and they in turn can permit the old dominating strata to maintain their own status. In nations like Germany where access was denied for prolonged periods, first to the bourgeoisie and later to the workers, and where force was used to restrict access, the lower strata were alienated from the system and adopted extremist ideologies which, in turn, kept the more established groups from accepting the workers' political movement as a legitimate alternative.

> Political systems which deny new strata access to power except by revolution also inhibit the growth of legitimacy by introducing millennial hopes into the political arena. Groups which have to push their

---

[13] Marshall, *op. cit.*, pp. 49-50.

way into the body politic by force are apt to overexaggerate the possi-bilities which political participation affords. Consequently, democratic regimes born under such stress not only face the difficulty of being regarded as illegitimate by groups loyal to the *ancien regime* but may also be rejected by those whose millennial hopes are not fulfilled by the change.[14]

In the United States during the 1960's, new elites were making demands for political access and participation. The crisis was not seen by most decision makers as one requiring political moderniza-tion responses. Rather, the reaction was one of traditionally estab-lished norms and procedures. In spite of the fact that the Fifteenth Amendment to the Constitution was clear, the demand makers were required to go through the laborious judicial process. And even then, results were mixed.

Neither could one argue that this was at the time anything but a racial question. Middle-class blacks in places like Tuskegee, Ala-bama, were as effectively excluded from political participation as lower-class blacks in rural Georgia and Mississippi. The question of qualification was not one the resisters to change could raise with any degree of credibility.[15]

Challenging the status quo

The participation issue was shaped by this set of circumstances in the 1960's. The political struggles in the South involved large numbers of newly politicized individuals and groups, mostly young, white and black, from the North as well as the South. More than a few of the young white activists later returned to their Northern communities and college campuses and became insistent demand makers in those places. They had been schooled in the Southern struggles; some had experienced physical harassment, and their sense of political efficacy was wearing thin. To what many of them considered essentially a political and moral question, they had been presented with legal and Constitutional answers. It was only a short step from there to a conclusion that the status quo was being defended by resisters who saw their economic vested inter-ests threatened. Many of the new activists made that step and, as Lipset had warned, the ideological gap widened. The pattern was almost too perfect to miss. What was seen initially by many activists as a difficult struggle against local courthouse cronies got trans-lated into a struggle against capitalist, exploitative forces intent on maintaining control over black and poor people. What was under-stood at the outset as a racial—and largely regional—problem even-

---

[14] Lipset, *op. cit.*, p. 67.
[15] Charles V. Hamilton, *The Bench and the Ballet: Southern Federal Judges and Black Voters* (New York, 1973), pp. 215-216.

tually was interpreted as a national struggle of progressive elements against reactionary forces.

It would be easy but unwise to misunderstand the meaning of the statement issued by SNCC concerning the Vietnam war. The statement was issued January 6, 1966, and it indicates the growing alienation and widening ideological gap that was occurring at that time:

> We of the Student Nonviolent Coordinating Committee have been involved in the black people's struggle for liberation and self-determination in this country for the past five years. Our work, particularly in the South, taught us that the United States government has never guaranteed the freedom of oppressed citizens, and is not yet truly determined to end the rule of terror and oppression within its own borders.
>
> We ourselves have often been victims of violence and confinement executed by U.S. government officials. We recall the numerous persons who have been murdered in the South because of their efforts to secure their civil and human rights, and whose murderers have been allowed to escape penalty for their crimes. . . .
>
> We know for the most part that elections in this country, in the North as well as the South, are not free. We have seen that the 1965 Voting Rights Acts and 1964 Civil Rights Act have not yet been implemented with full federal power and concern. We question then the ability and even the desire of the U.S. government to guarantee free elections abroad. We maintain that our country's cry of "preserve freedom in the world" is a hypocritical mask behind which it squashed liberation movements which are not bound and refuse to be bound by the expediency of the U.S. cold war policy.[16]

Thus, some new activists saw the answer of federalism as an excuse for inaction on the part of central authorities. And after a point it really did not matter who was, in fact, right or wrong. What mattered was that significant numbers of new political actors *believed* the system was illegitimate. For purposes of this essay, *that* is the point to be made, not that contending forces were vehemently questioning each other's veracity.

From that point on, it was probably no longer sufficient to make the existing structures more effective, but rather what was needed was to begin, at least, to give serious consideration to restructuring the political institutions of the society. What the American society had been spared for over 170 years, it now had the burden of attempting—to embark on the process of political modernization. This meant it would have to reexamine its system of federalism, its method of recruiting new groupings into the political process, especially through the political parties, and its system of involving new significant groups in the governmental decision making process,

---

[16] Charles V. Hamilton, *The Black Experience in American Politics* (New York, 1973), p. 206.

particularly in the local areas of urban centers. This was the challenge of the participatory issue as it was raised in the 1960's, and it would not be an easy challenge to meet. It would be difficult precisely because the system was under stress.

Social institutions—religious, political, economic, educational—were under a virtual state of siege. Major cities were being firebombed periodically. Political leaders were being assassinated, and revolutionary rhetoric was plentiful. That history offered adequate precedent for such a state of affairs, can be seen in Huntington's discussion of seventeenth-century England:

> English harmony ended with the sixteenth century. Whether the gentry were rising, falling or doing both in seventeenth-century England, forces were at work in society disrupting Tudor social peace. The efforts to reestablish something like the Tudor balance broke down before the intensity of social and religious conflict. . . . In England, as in France, civil strife led to the demand for strong centralized power to reestablish public order. The breakdown of unity in society gave rise to irresistible forces to reestablish that unity through government.[17]

Old structures, new participants

The 1960's witnessed a major confrontation between the Democratic party and newly politicized forces attempting to exercise greater influence within that party. This confrontation began in 1964 and was still a serious issue in the early 1970's following party reforms and the 1972 Presidential election. The central question was who would participate and on what terms in helping to choose the party's Presidential candidate.

Following on the heels of the struggles in the South, especially in Mississippi, in the early 1960's, SNCC and other groups organized the Mississippi Freedom Democratic Party (MFDP). One of its goals was to challenge the regular state party delegates to the Democratic national convention in August 1964. The MFDP documented and charged that the white delegates were chosen by a process that deliberately excluded blacks in Mississippi. A legal brief was presented to the Credentials Committee of the national party, protest demonstrations were mounted, and the national party offered a compromise: the seating of all members of the regular party delegation willing to take the loyalty oath (to support the convention's nominee), the promise that black participation in party affairs would be mandatory in the seating of future delegations, and the acceptance of two MFDP delegates as delegates-at-large.[18]

---

[17] Huntington, op. cit., pp. 124-125.
[18] See Jennifer McDowell and Milton Loventhal, Black Politics: A Study and Annotated Bibliography of the Mississippi Freedom Democratic Party (San Jose, 1971).

The MFDP forces rejected the compromise, but not before intense debate within liberal, labor, and civil rights circles had taken place. The significance of the event for purposes of this essay is that it opened up a much needed discussion of the necessity for the traditional political parties to accommodate the participatory demands of newly politicized groups. That discussion was started, and four years later there were changes in the delegate composition of some Southern states. Bayard Rustin was partially correct when he concluded: "While I still believe that the MFDP made a tactical error in spurning the compromise, there is no question that they launched a political revolution whose logic is the displacement of Dixiecrat power. They launched that revolution within a major political institution and as part of a coalitional effort."[19]

One of the problems that had to be faced, however, was the cumulative impact such struggles and compromises would have on the new participants. The MFDP challenge was not an isolated event conceived in a vacuum. It reflected years of intense effort on the part of many blacks to open up a closed political system. Under such circumstances, the demand makers could reasonably conclude that they had every legal and moral, if not political, right to succeed. Indeed, *they* were the ones playing by the rules of the game; *they* were the ones willing to pledge loyalty to the party. And yet the violators of those rules and of the law were being pacified. If the new participants were bordering on cynicism and alienation, the burden of that result would be on the established forces. Notwithstanding the eloquent argument of Rustin and other liberals—white and black—that American politics required compromise, it is also the case that there are limits beyond which a theoretical political democracy cannot go and expect unswerving loyalty from those who perceive themselves to be the perpetual victims of the democratic process. The point is that there appeared to be insufficient attention to the possibility of growing alienation, and the same kind of disagreement described earlier between Burke Marshall and James Forman was recurring. As Professor David Apter has stated, societies that strive for the achievement of democratic, egalitarian polities are most susceptible to this problem:

Competition between politically equal units is the basis of the system, with competition in ideas reflecting competition of interests, the constellation of which represents the desires of the multitude. Such, briefly, is the ideal of Western libertarian government. It has a high commitment to rules and laws. When the discrepancy between theory and practice is great, individuals become lonely and divorced from the system. If too many withdraw from the political marketplace, a general condition of

---

[19] Bayard Rustin, "From Protest to Politics: The Future of the Civil Rights Movement," *Commentary*, XXXIX (February 1965), pp. 25-31.

alienation from the society results. . . . The theme of alienation runs through the history of secular-libertarian models.[20]

In a sense, this is the most serious problem presented by the participation struggles in the context of the racial situation of the 1960's. There is no question, as some establishment spokesmen have argued, that progress has been made in providing increased access to those previously excluded from political participation. The historical facts are too obvious to require extended debate on this subject. But in reality, the situation is not one of holding to the status quo with no change at all on the one hand and full, complete resolution of the problem on the other. The tension develops over pace and perhaps even process. In the American context, this issue becomes the crucial one around which the Lipset-type question of access and legitimacy turns. And how this issue is faced—again, not in a vacuum, but with years of history as background—becomes critical. It was not sufficient, then, to admonish the MFDP that they must become politically sophisticated, shed their naïveté and move from protest to politics. It may well be that too much damage had been done to the structure of the bridge to make it comfortably passable without major alterations.

The North and the national Democratic party

While specific protesters might not have been aware of the devious devices used by entrenched party interests to exclude or mitigate the effectiveness of new groups, they could hardly have escaped being aware of the overt consequences. And this applies to the North as well as the South. Thus, when James Q. Wilson describes party practices in New York City in the 1960's in the following manner, one must be aware that more than shrewd manipulation is being achieved:

> New York districts have been, and still are, divided into halves or even thirds for leadership purposes in order to find compromises between the competing claims of various ethnic groups residing in the district. Thus, a district containing significant numbers of Negroes, Italians, and Jews would be split into three parts, and each part given to a Negro, an Italian, and a Jewish leader. In turn, the single vote which that district had in Tammany Hall would be split into three one-third votes. This often worked to weaken the influence of Negroes even after they had captured a leadership.[21]

The instances of manipulation of electoral and representative processes have been too many and too well documented for an honest analyst to overlook them in studying potential consequences.

---

[20] David B. Apter, *The Politics of Modernization* (Chicago, 1965), pp. 30-31.
[21] James Q. Wilson, *Negro Politics* (Glencoe, Ill., 1960), p. 26.

For purposes of understanding the thrust of this essay, it is impera-
tive that intelligent and careful observers note the potential reper-
cussions of a practice in a Michigan city described by Professor
Lee Sloan. Entrenched political forces developed an electoral
scheme which permitted white voters the opportunity to determine
which among competing black candidates in a black district would
serve on the city commission. There were seven districts with a
commissioner being chosen in the general election to represent the
district on the commission. But in the primary election each district nominated two candidates who subsequently opposed each
other in the general election. Thus, while the primary election was
by district, the general election was at-large. This meant that the
dominant white electorate would choose the more conservative of
the two black candidates in the general election, as Professor Sloan
describes:

> Thus, white citizens of Lakeland can prevent the election of militant
> Negro leaders. At the same time, they can co-opt a conservative Negro
> leader. The Negro community will not be without representation but in
> the eyes of many Negroes, their representation will be unwilling to pro-
> tect or advance their interests.
>
> In the 1964 and 1966 general elections the two Negro districts were
> unable to elect the candidates of their choice. Merritt Reed, a conserva-
> tive Negro leader, won in both elections, despite his inability to carry
> his own District I.
>
> . . . Not surprisingly, many Negroes in Lakeland consider themselves
> to be disfranchised under the new electoral system. They are now
> denied the "right" to choose "their" representatives. In effect, the white
> electorate of Lakeland selects representatives for them, a pattern which
> characterized the accommodating leadership of the Old South. The fact
> that democratic procedures were used to take from them a "right"
> which was theirs under the old ward system leads many Negroes in
> Lakeland to view democratic government as but another form of white
> hypocrisy.[22]

These situations are more threatening to a viable society than
the more blatant forms of political exclusion noted in the South.
This is so precisely because the Northern variety has the pretense
of consistency of theory and practice, and when discovered to be
otherwise carries with it an aspect of deceit and disillusionment.
The resulting alienation is further ladened with intense distrust and
even hatred. It is in this sense that some blacks have been heard
to say that at least they felt more comfortable with the honesty
(if not the attitude and behavior) of white Southern racists.

In addition, one is led to believe that legal struggle and political
astuteness can, in fact, overcome Southern obstacles, while nothing

---

[22] Lee Sloan, "Good Government and the Politics of Race," *Social Problems*,
Volume 15 (1968).

short of violent struggles and violent-laden confrontations will suffice in the North. It should not be surprising then that the most violent and prolonged clashes in the streets during the summers of the late 1960's occurred primarily in the North rather than in the South—in the North, where the deceit was greatest and consequently where the developing hatred was thickest.

At any rate, violence and crises served as catalysts to open up the old participatory structures. The national Democratic party in 1968 again provided the case study. When other newly politicized groups (for the most part politicized around the issue of the Vietnam war) felt they were not being accorded adequate participatory opportunities in the 1968 convention, violence erupted. This led to moves to reform the party rules relating to delegate selection.

The McGovern-Fraser Commission on Party Structure and Delegate Selection developed a set of guidelines that operated in 1972. As part of an effort to correct what some perceived as abuses in the old system, these guidelines required state parties to encourage representation of minority groups, women, and youth in their convention delegates ". . . in reasonable relationship to the group's presence in the population of the state." The official interpretation was that this requirement was not to be understood to impose quotas, but the fact is that more than a few people took it to mandate just that. Thus, at the Democratic convention held in Miami Beach in 1972 only 17 per cent of the delegates had ever attended a national convention before. Many traditional party leaders were not included, and a bitter conflict developed between the "new" and "old" politics forces that carried over into the campaign, creating a wound that did not heal.

From the bloody and riotous streets of Chicago in 1968 to the convention floor in Miami Beach in 1972, there developed a political result that some people felt seriously crippled the chances of a major party to compete successfully. In the process of reforming to include previously excluded participants, the party had served to exclude older significant elements that would be needed if the party was to operate effectively. The issue of participation had by no means been solved.

Representative democracy and the "new politics"

After the 1972 election, a group of Democrats formed the Coalition for a Democratic Majority (CDM) to attempt to solve the party participation problem. This essay is not the place to discuss the detailed recommendations of the CDM, but it is important to note those parts of their report distinguishing between representative democracy and participatory democracy. The "new politics" people, the report said, had confused the two and consequently in their zeal to correct old abuses had created new problems:

> First, some participatory democrats did not confine themselves to assaults on those who were clearly unrepresentative of the Party's rank-and-file. Instead, their attack on the establishment was often directed against those who poll data and general election returns demonstrated did enjoy broad support among ordinary Democratic voters. This wing of the reform movement showed no small disdain for elected officials, party officers, mainstream labor leaders, and the more traditional spokesmen for minority, ethnic, and religious constituencies. To them, participatory democracy came to mean a process through which a minority of educated, often more affluent Party members and their allies sought to wrench Party leadership away from the representatives of more moderate, less active voters.[23]

The CDM argued rather effectively that the less affluent and less educated still did not participate in the "grass-roots" delegate selection process in spite of the rhetoric of the "new politics" people.

> Many of the leaders and representatives of these less affluent voters expend great effort to encourage them to participate more actively, but their habits of non-participation persist. . . . Yet some activists continue to justify a demand for full participatory democracy with the argument that their delegate selection rules will apply equally to all—college students with time on their hands and factory workers worn out after a day on the assembly line, upper-class housewives and their maids.[24]

This point is correct and well made, but its effectiveness is weakened precisely because the established mechanism appeared unable or unwilling or both to correct its obvious faults. The CDM began its report by honestly admitting that reforms were necessary: "They brought a belated end to the time when convention delegates could be selected at will by closed, narrow groups of party leaders, many of whom had acquired their posts well before the election period."[25] The unavoidable fact remains that seemingly little if anything would have been done to correct the abuses short of a violent confrontation and rather drastic reforms. Notwithstanding the fact that the American political system eschews violence, unfortunately it frequently appears unable to move on critical questions until a crisis is precipitated. Time and again one is led to conclude that insofar as motivation to change is concerned, *the catalyst must be the crisis, not the condition.* Thus, persons interested in correcting obvious wrongs are forced to create chaos before they are taken seriously.

---

[23] *Toward Fairness and Unity for '76* (A Report of the Task Force on Democratic Rules and Structure of the Coalition for a Democratic Majority), 1973, p. 9.
[24] *Ibid.,* pp. 9-10.
[25] *Ibid.,* p. 2.

This is a characteristic of the American political process that the CDM and others must be willing to recognize and admit. In addition, in some instances, their argument of "representative democracy" is seriously weakened when one studies the kinds of conditions described by James Q. Wilson and Lee Sloan. The CDM has to admit that the black elected officials chosen in that Michigan city under the system described by Sloan simply will not have the high credibility among the black constituents that their election would suggest. Thus, the CDM argument becomes rather simplistic and banal when applied to some cases. This is not so in every case, but certainly in some instances; and this fact means that more than lip service must be paid to the demands of those seeking to create new participatory structures.

Throughout the 1960's, one found the recurrence of a six-stage pattern of events similar to the following:

1. persistent condition of abuse
2. systemic protest
3. incremental response
4. crisis-precipitating protest
5. panic response
6. recoil-reaction.

This pattern was observed with black voter participation in the South as well as with the delegate selection process in the national Democratic party. Unfortunately, it is not a paradigm calculated to instill mutual trust and confidence, but rather one that exacerbates tensions among legitimate, contentious groups.

Central authority and demands for local participation

Sidney Verba has observed: "The more an individual perceives governmental activity as relevant to his own needs, the more likely he is to attempt political participation. . . . As the government becomes active in a particular field—culture or health, for example— it makes it more likely that individuals will define problems within that realm as having some political content and as needing governmental action."[26] This clearly was the case in the 1960's. Problems of poverty and urban deterioration became high agenda items under the Johnson Administration, and legislation was written that talked about the "maximum feasible participation" of those persons most directly affected by the new laws.

The government—meaning, here, the federal government—was called upon to assume an increasing role in the economic lives of poor people. Indeed, poor communities were fast becoming what I choose to call "public sector communities." In many instances, the

---

[26] Verba, *op. cit.*, p. 64.

major economies of such areas were the direct result of government funding. Thus, the central government was expanding its role at the same time that poor and previously non-active people were beginning to raise demands for "community control," "citizen participation," and "decentralization." At first, it would appear that these were diametrically opposed phenomena, and some of the local control advocates ultimately lost faith in their efforts precisely because they had to admit that there could not be decision making autonomy within a community as long as the federal government held the purse strings.

When the Economic Opportunity Act of 1964 was passed, there was only casual Congressional attention paid to the language of "maximum feasible participation." Consequently, this imprecise phrase was subject to varying interpretations by competing interest groups. There was disagreement over what the ratio of poor to non-poor in community action agencies (CAA's) should be. There was no agreement over the level of participation required: on the boards, in the professional staffs, or on advisory committees. In a short time, some groups began to equate blacks and other minorities with "the poor" and "target areas," thus leaving aside vast numbers of white poor and creating resentment among the latter in the process. In addition, so much time was consumed debating and deciding issues involving participation that the battle for political control appeared to be taking precedence over the specific economic aims of the federal programs. As a result, many CAA's suffered from restrictions imposed by the federal government, restrictions reducing local initiative funds. Above all, short-term funding seriously limited the capacity of CAA's to embark on long-term planning or to implement projects that had a life expectancy beyond one or two years.

Where local community agencies formed a coalition, "target area" residents had more influence on decisions. Frequently, however, representation followed neighborhood boundaries and this prevented some CAA's from taking more than a parochial view of their work. That is, neighborhoods tended to concentrate only on the needs of their own residents and failed to tackle poverty problems on a wider, more meaningful scale. Thus, some participatory structures contributed to a fragmentary, and therefore less useful, approach to problems. Obviously, this meant that some of the basic causes (rather than symptoms) of poverty would not be dealt with.

Short-term funding had another serious consequence. The board members and professional staffs of the CAA's had to spend an inordinate amount of time preparing reports in order to obtain future funding. In some instances, guidelines and deadlines became the major, continuing concerns. Because of this nearly constant distraction, it is hardly surprising that more attention was not paid to the substantive performance of many of the programs.

The CAA's were conceived in a time of crisis and were victims of the lack of a coherent, long-term conceptualization of what should be done. This constituted probably the worst kind of public policy formulation, coming at a time when the country could least afford to make mistakes.

The poverty program suffered from vacillation and high-level administrative instability. Persons in top decision making positions in Washington came for a while and moved on. In addition, during the first two years, it became quite clear that some local mayors and established political forces were fearful that a kind of Pandora's box had been opened. Whether in Mississippi or Chicago, it was certain that local community groups would be met by forces that were not prepared to make room for new decision making groups. Thus, the inattention displayed earlier by Congress to the language of "maximum feasible participation" changed to intense concern, and moves were made to restrict the development of new political groups. Title II (the community action section) of the legislation was the handiwork of a relatively small group of professional reformers in the executive branch and some university people sympathetic with their goals. These people had the support of President Johnson, who in turn had a very consensual political situation behind him. The professionals proceeded to fashion their own brand of social change, consulting neither the poor who, ostensibly, were to do the social changing nor the mayors and others who were destined to be affected politically by the changes in community power. This was hardly a situation that could long prevail. It was in fact a formula for intense political controversy.

All of this was aggravated by the fact that President Johnson began to spend much more of his time and energy on the war in Vietnam than on the war on poverty. The latter could not compete with the former for men, money, or the planning and policy analysis needed to direct and coordinate both successfully. The President's attention was diverted, and from then on it was certain that such politically controversial programs as the community action agencies would be the losers.

The dangers of procrastination

It is clear that the central government will play an increasing role in the welfare of the citizens and the economy of the society. This is so notwithstanding the current policy trend toward revenue sharing with its emphasis on local, county, and state agencies. The federal government will continue to be the major source of revenue. How those funds get distributed down to the lowest levels of government in order to provide the best possible services with the fullest kind of citizen involvement will be a critical question of the 1970's. If available funds are distributed according to traditional formulas of privilege and preference, the problems of political efficacy and legitimacy will not be solved. They will be aggravated. The time to deal with these issues is now, before another series of crises develops causing another round of panic responses. The American political system is probably at its worst when it has to respond to crises, and yet it constantly puts itself in that position by procrastinating and giving inadequate responses at earlier stages. In other words, what some pluralist advocates have perceived to be a major strength of the system—slow, protracted progress—might well be viewed in the 1970's as a crippling weakness.

Panic responses always lead some other groups to feel that the protesters have been coddled and a "backlash" (recoil-reaction) sets in. It is this phenomenon that one observed among ethnic groups in the early 1970's. They came to feel that the system was being blackmailed by black protesters, and remained quite unaware of or indifferent to the conditions that had sparked the protestors' outrage. Such an attitude is hardly conducive to the enlightened resolution of problems.

There will not be a viable atmosphere for working out solutions as long as local participatory structures are manipulated to dilute (if not to exclude) the influence of newly politicized groups. Unfortunately, very little attention has been paid to reforming local electoral systems in order to avoid situations similar to those described by Wilson and Sloan. Virtually no attention has been given to the need to modernize structures in order to create more efficacious relationships between local community groups and the central government. And the only discussion one hears about the possibility of encouraging metropolitan (or regional) government is in the context of efficient administration, the dilution of the growing inner-city vote, or the desire to serve more privileged suburban residents.

The public sector as a steadily increasing source of employment for blacks and poor people is an established fact. Yet such policies as the Hatch Act (and its state counterparts) serve to depoliticize those who pursue public employment. This means that some of the most intelligent, sensible, and articulate elements of the new political groups are denied the opportunity to contribute to political action, except by indirection and periodic voting. Their leadership skills are unused, and the field is left to a relatively small cadre of private sector elites or to social action entrepreneurs. Although Verba recognizes that government activity serves to activate people, he fails to recognize the impact of this in terms of the constraints imposed on those who increasingly will become employed in the public sector. This is an important area of public policy vis-à-vis public sector communities that needs further analysis. It directly connects participation with a developing economic trend.

Economics and the need for political access

The relationship between economics and political participation has always been important. As new groups enter the system, they find it necessary to participate in order to obtain, secure, and then develop a particular economic status. This was true of the European immigrants who began coming to this country in the nineteenth century, and it was the case with farmers and factory and craft workers in organized unions. This opportunity is no less necessary for new groups in the 1970's as the federal government is called upon to play a more direct role in the economic lives of citizens. The connection between economics and politics is not an obscure one. Like all other elements in society, minority groups must turn increasingly to the public sector, and this fact alone will raise the stakes of participation.

There is sufficient political behavior data to show that those persons with a higher socio-economic status participate more in the political process than those with a lower status. But for those groups who must rely increasingly on the public sector to raise their socio-economic standing, it is not sufficient to await the occurrence of one condition before the implementation of the other. The two must coincide. Thus, while it is true, as stated in the beginning of this essay, that the 1960's opened with a debate on the right of blacks to vote in the South, there was little attention paid to the economic dependency of blacks who would eventually exercise that right. Now that problem must be met. And as the government is called upon to deal with it, an increased exercise of central authority over state governments and the private sector will be necessary.

The United States can no longer afford the luxury of the Tudor-type political structure that Huntington correctly described. The societal stresses that this country escaped for two centuries are now upon us, calling for more effective central government. The loose, fragmented system of an earlier time will no longer suffice. Demands for local participation must not be seen as disruptive centrifugal forces aimed at establishing local, isolated islands of autonomy. Rather, they must be viewed as representing a new opportunity to create one viable entity. The demand is not for absolute hegemony, but for inclusion into structures that are perceived to be legitimate. For a long time, America has had the rhetoric, but not the reality.

The task might seem insurmountable, but that is probably because too many traditionalists have assumed for too long that there really was not a problem. Some of the literature produced by our leading socio-political analysts from the post-World War II period into the 1960's was at best misleading. We are now faced with the challenge of political modernization—a challenge which requires both the centralization of authority and, at the same time, a broadening of the base of political participation.

11

Some
lessons
of
the 1960's

ELI GINZBERG & ROBERT M. SOLOW

I N this brief concluding essay, our intention is not so much to summarize as to distill. The individual articles in this symposium are, after all, themselves summaries. Each provides a sketch of a range of complicated policy problems, and of a tangled variety of half-coordinated attempts to solve them. We can hope to extract two kinds of lessons from this history. One has to do with the general process of social reform in a middle-class democracy, or at least in this middle-class democracy. A second has to do with the specific legislative programs that made up the Great Society. We do not have much to add to what our colleagues have said about the nature of particular problems and the successes and failures of individual programs in responding to them, so we will concentrate our attention on the more general implications of recent experience for social intervention and social reform.

It seems to us that no one who reads the evidence in the preceding essays can seriously subscribe to either of the extreme, simple, fashionable dogmas: that social legislation is merely a sham, aimed at camouflaging, not solving, problems; or that all major political intervention in social problems is a mistake, bound to fail, and better left to local government, private charity, or the free market. Contrary to these dogmas, the evidence seems to show that the problems are real, that the political pressure to do something about them is often irresistible, and that many partial, but genuine successes have been achieved.

Often, though not always, the intended beneficiaries of social legislation do benefit. There are sometimes unintended and unwanted side effects; and some public programs simply don't work or prove too costly. But there is nothing in the history of the 1960's to suggest that it is a law of nature that social legislation cannot deal effectively with social problems, or that state and local governments or private enterprise will always do better than the "Feds." We can find no support for such sweeping generalizations. Our own conclusions are more modest, and leave much more room for case-by-case judgment.

Goals

A first lesson is that the public will accept large-scale programs of social intervention only at long intervals. One measure of time is the generation that elapsed between the New Freedom of Woodrow Wilson and the New Deal of Franklin Roosevelt, and again between the New Deal and the Great Society. There is nothing inherently cyclical about such a pattern; but only special circumstances—like the breakdown of the economy in the Great Depression or the rise of the civil rights movement and the political awakening of the black population—with an assist from strong leadership can set the stage for major social reform. At other times, a piecemeal approach is the only kind possible.

Indeed, we would go further. Social progress in a democracy depends on its ability to recognize and respond to challenges which require government intervention in the interests of economic performance and social justice. If the government avoids piecemeal remedial action when and where the facts warrant, it is likely to be forced later on to mount more ambitious programs of social intervention when the constraints of time, resources, and tolerance will be more painfully binding. Prolonged neglect is costly. Most social problems do not fade away. They become more acute when neglected.

Piecemeal reform is not easy either. The public has limited tolerance for reform at any time. More often than not, it is the quiet life that appeals to the Congress and to the voters. In a democracy whose political and economic systems are functioning reasonably well, the disadvantaged—those who can expect to gain directly from political or economic or social reform—will usually be a minority, and generally a weak or powerless minority. Social legislation needs a constituency larger than its direct beneficiaries. A larger public must share the goals of social intervention before political reform becomes possible. In the American system of government, that makes the President a key figure. No one else is likely to be able to fashion the required public consensus on goals and to get and maintain the required Congressional support—especially on those occasions when the situation calls for major reforms on several fronts.

Even a President who can successfully use all his arts of persuasion and all his instruments of power to induce his countrymen to change their values, attitudes, and behavior toward the disadvantaged must reckon with intrinsic limitations. Even a President who begins with a smashing electoral victory—as Lyndon Johnson did—will find that he has only a finite stock of political capital to spend, and as he runs into opposition, he depletes it. A President who takes the lead in a broad program of social reform must anticipate mounting opposition from groups who balk at paying the price for progress, especially the progress of others. He must also reckon with increasing frustration among the potential beneficiaries, whose expectations are likely to outpace the improvements in their circumstances.

In the case of Lyndon Johnson and his Great Society, there was another factor. More than anything else, the Vietnam war was the main enemy of the Great Society. We shall point out later on that the war stole resources that might otherwise have gone to finance social programs on a scale sufficient to show results. But here we want to emphasize that the bitterness, hostility, and disillusionment generated by Johnson's prosecution and escalation of an unpopular war destroyed the consensus on social goals that he had earlier managed to create. And the problem was compounded by the fact that the natural anti-war constituency was also the natural constituency for social and economic reform.

Promises

It is hard enough for a reformist government to set realistic goals. It is almost impossible for it to limit itself to realistic promises. Here the social engineers of the 1960's clearly failed. The Administration's spokesmen promised to undertake and win the war on poverty, to assure every American family an adequate home, to relieve old and poor people of the financial burdens of illness, to widen the educational opportunities of poor children, to speed the integration of the black community into the mainstream of American life, to provide skill training so that men and women on the periphery of the economy could get better jobs. A democracy with a two-party tradition is inured to exaggerated promises and claims, especially in an election year. But the mid-1960's saw the President, his advisers, and the Congressional leadership wantonly blur the distinction between campaign promises and legislative commitments. From one point of view, the Great Society programs were doomed from the moment of their enactment: There was no prospect that any government could deliver on such ambitious promises, certainly not within the time limits that an impatient public would allow.

It is easy to see how damaging this kind of puffery can be to the good name of sensible social policy. It will not be easy to kick the habit. One has the impression that nothing less than a Crisis can any longer attract political attention. The Urban Crisis, the Environmental Crisis, the Energy Crisis are only the latest in a long line. If verbal overkill were merely a device to attract attention, that would perhaps not be so bad. But the distortion goes deeper. One can hardly respond to a Crisis with small-scale experimental programs that will test out the nature of the problem and accumulate some knowledge that can ultimately lead to the design of better policy. A Crisis has to be met on a grand scale. But of course, before one Crisis has been resolved the next Crisis is on the scene, and each is blown up so as to demand all available attention and resources. This sort of atmosphere is hardly conducive to the rational allocation of public funds and administrative capacity.

We conclude, then, that especially if the issues are complex, and especially if they have been ignored or minimized earlier, it is important that the leadership's promises of results from intervention be realistic rather than extreme. A public which has been encouraged to expect great things will become impatient, critical, and alienated if the progress that is achieved falls far short of the rosy promises. A wise leadership is careful to promise no more than it feels reasonably sure it can deliver within a reasonable time.

Knowledge

The social problems requiring remedial action by government are usually complicated. Their causes are not understood in their entirety and the proposed cures are of uncertain efficacy. There is likely to be no firm body of knowledge and experience to tell us how to shape manpower programs, carry out a war on poverty, or insure that children in the ghetto will learn to read—certainly not at the moment when the problems gain visibility and attention and the demand for action becomes irresistible.

Our selective review of the Great Society's social interventions exhibits a wide range in the quality of the intellectual base on which programs have been erected. The Social Security Administration provided what turned out to be realistic estimates of the increased utilization of hospitals resulting from Medicare. But the same experts were far off the mark when it came to estimating unit costs. As a result, Congress and the public had the unpleasant experience later on of having to cover the much enlarged costs of the program through higher payroll taxes and larger co-payments. Since Medicaid legislation was enacted with even less study and discussion, it is not surprising that its open-ended commitment of federal funds for health care for the poor did not stand up for more than two years before Congress chose to limit eligibility.

The operation and administration of public programs, as well as their design, require a base of knowledge and experience that may well be lacking at the start. It took several years, for instance, for the U.S. Office of Education to recognize that much of the money it was allocating to states and localities for compensatory education was not being spent on the targeted population, and then to correct the situation. And it took even longer for the educational authorities to learn to distinguish between attractively packaged programs which would later prove ineffective and the less exciting but more productive approaches to improving the learning skills of poor children.

To take one last but very important example: The course of welfare reform would have been much smoother had expert knowledge been able to foretell the massive welfare drift of the early 1960's. As things turned out, the modest reforms of 1962 and 1967 were simply obliterated by the rise in the welfare rolls. This unexpected result certainly contributed to the inability of any more substantial reform program to capture a working majority.

Almost by definition, a new social program is likely to be hobbled at first by the lack of knowledge and experience of those charged with its design and operation. A sensible public and its legislative representatives will allow time and resources for knowledge and experience to be accumulated. But if the new programs do not command sufficient support, or if the initial enthusiasm which led to their enactment is dissipated, the minimum essential stability and learning time may not be forthcoming. As a consequence, the President, those charged with administering the program, and the legislators who control its finances will be caught up in a public relations charade in which the rules of the game are continually changed so that it is impossible to keep score. In the manpower arena, the White House has sought each year to launch "exciting new" programs by repackaging the funds which had been appropriated a year earlier. This is no way to run a railroad, much less a manpower program.

The conclusion to be drawn is not that our government should delay action in critical areas until it has all the knowledge and technique to fashion a successful solution. In the first place, the required knowledge can be generated only by action, at least on an experimental scale. Moreover, a democracy really has no option but to act while it learns. It must run risks to meet the needs and desires of its citizens as best it can. The most one can say is that a responsible leadership will proceed with caution in areas where it lacks adequate knowledge and experience, in the expectation that second efforts at social intervention will be improved by what is learned from the initial experiments. We do not know if the idea of the frankly experimental public program can be made politically viable. It is worth a try. But there is an important corollary: Social problems must be tackled early. By the time a breakdown in the system has become acute and acquired an important constituency, the pressure for a remedy cannot be put off by talk of experimentation and learning. The time for putting together a base of knowledge is earlier. But there is correspondingly less reason even for conservatives to oppose experimental programs of social intervention, except perhaps on the overriding principle that nothing new should ever be tried.

Resources

In judging the record of the 1960's, it is useful to keep in mind that a social program is usually better defined by its budget than by the language of the enabling legislation. The earlier essays give examples of programs in the fields of health, education, and manpower that never commanded resources commensurate with their expressed goals. When this occurs, it is not necessarily an accident or a miscalculation. When Congress feels pressure to do something about which it is skeptical, or in which it is uninterested, or toward which it is ideologically hostile, one tactic it often adopts is to pass a bill with high-sounding language, establish an agency, and starve it for funds. Thus, one can say about many a program of the Great Society what G. B. Shaw said about Christianity: It has not failed; it has never been tried.

In some cases, underfunding is just a concomitant of overpromising. When a program has been puffed up beyond reason as the cure for everything, its appropriation is bound to be too small. Here the habit of Crisis-mongering is an important part of the difficulty: When every problem is blown into a Crisis, the government must promise to do everything in order to be permitted to do anything. And the budget can never be sufficient for doing everything.

The dangerous habit of underfunding has longer-run consequences. New programs can be started modestly, but it is dangerous and often fatal to hide from the legislature and the public the scale of resources that will be required if significant progress is to be achieved. Unless the resources required are stated realistically, a multiplicity of programs may be encouraged; and if, as is likely, each of them is undernourished, their eventual failure is assured.

In the case of the Great Society, the Vietnam war was an independent cause of underfunding for social programs. As we pointed out in our Introduction to this symposium, the increase in military spending was large compared with the allocation of resources to new social programs. President Johnson apparently refused to ask Congress for a tax increase to finance the war in the fear that the request for higher taxes would erode support for an already unpopular war. In the end, he financed the adventure by inflation. So convoluted did this commingling of politics and economics become that when a large group of academic economists tried to drum up support for an anti-inflationary tax increase, they were opposed by others who did not disagree with their analysis, but argued that a tax increase would only make it easier for the Administration to continue the war. And in turn, this argument was rebutted by the contention that failure to increase taxes would only lead to the sacrifice of more of the budget for social programs on behalf of the military.

One of the by-products of a policy of tackling emergent social problems early, with frankly experimental programs, is that it would yield better information about the cost side of a benefit-cost analysis. There could still be errors in extrapolating the costs of small-scale pilot programs to full-scale social intervention. But we would certainly be on firmer ground.

Administration

Among the scarce resources necessary for the success of any complicated enterprise, private or public, are organizational and administrative talent and will. In a federal system of government like ours, much of what happens in the public domain happens through the cooperation of state and local governments. Even where the federal government initiates and finances, day-to-day planning and operations will often be in other hands. In area after area, in such diverse fields as education, manpower, welfare, and housing, there is relatively little that the federal government can do on its own. It is not able to deliver services to large numbers of citizens in their home communities. It can, we know, mail checks to beneficiaries of the Social Security program, or to the recipients of one or another type of educational grant or loan. But when it comes to organizing a Head Start program or establishing and operating a skill-training center to assist employable people on the welfare rolls to move into productive employment, the federal government must work through state and local agencies and, to a lesser extent, through contractors in the private or non-profit sectors of the economy.

The last decade has demonstrated that the strengths and weaknesses of the intermediaries through which the federal government must operate determine in considerable measure the success of its program efforts. It is clear that the best-conceived federal program will falter or fail if the agencies charged with implementing it lack initiative or competence. And the sorry fact is that most state and local governments—with some notable exceptions—are poorly structured and poorly staffed to carry out new and innovative tasks. They have a hard time even meeting their routine commitments.

We must in fairness add that the record of performance of govern-ment's contractors in the private and non-profit sectors also leaves much room for improvement. The runaway inflation in medical care costs after the passage of Medicare-Medicaid does not reflect much credit on either the voluntary hospitals or on the health professionals, though it must be said that the legislation helped to provide perverse financial incentives to patients and suppliers. The best that can be said for the manpower programs that engaged private employers is that the performance record is mediocre. The firms that accepted performance contracts to teach the hard-to-teach have folded their tents and slipped away. There are many reports of sharp practices, shoddy workmanship, and outright fraud involving real estate brokers and builders working with federal funds to provide housing for poor families.

The Nixon Administration, committed to the doctrine that any-thing is better than the interference of a too-large federal government in the affairs of the individual citizen, has opted in favor of general and special revenue sharing. The stated objective is to encourage state and local governments to play a larger role in determining program priorities and in operating those that are found worthy of funding.

Decategorization and decentralization of federal programs in edu-cation, manpower, health, urban development, and other areas are attractive goals once one realizes the inherent incapacity of the federal government to be directly involved in the delivery of services to millions of beneficiaries. But if the transfer of responsibility is a matter of political convenience and ideological rectitude, the weight of recent evidence should not be ignored. Most state and local govern-ments must be substantially strengthened if they are to discharge their expanded functions effectively. In the meanwhile, and perhaps in perpetuity, the federal government must continue to insist on certain priorities, exercise surveillance over the execution of pro-grams, and maintain financial control. It is the height of political naïveté or cynicism to assume that those who effectively control state and local governments will look out solicitously for the interests of the designated beneficiaries of federally financed programs in the absence of a check by the federal government. It would be an even bigger mistake, in our view, to take it for granted that state and local governments will care as much for the redistributional design of social programs as the federal providers of the funds would wish.

The record

As we review the record of the 1960's, we cannot fault President Kennedy's efforts to embody advances in economic knowledge in policies designed to speed the country's growth and reduce its excess unemployment. (It goes without saying that there may have been errors of detail.) It would be hard to argue that his modest initiatives in the areas of manpower training, welfare reform, or civil rights were focused on issues better left alone, or that the remedies he sought were extreme. It was generally felt at the time, and has since been amply confirmed by historians, that the first Kennedy Administration, whatever its other strengths and weaknesses, was characterized on the domestic front by caution and restraint. The enthusiasts promised much broader action for the second Kennedy Administration.

While several of the Great Society programs had their roots in staff studies initiated during the Kennedy years, it was President Johnson's leadership which turned these modest beginnings into legislative realities, primarily in 1964 and 1965. Once again, as we review the details, it is difficult to argue that Johnson's decisions were unreasonable with respect to the problems he singled out or the legislative reforms he recommended.

With respect to Medicare, we need only recall the sudden and dramatic shift from their long-time opposition by Wilbur Mills and the American Medical Association to appreciate the strength of the accumulated forces demanding remedial action. Congress had to act. If an error was made, it was not in passing Medicare but in adding Medicaid as an afterthought.

Nor do we disagree with the executive and legislative decision to put special funds into elementary and secondary schools to provide compensatory education for the hard-to-instruct. Over the years, the federal government had made funds available to accomplish high-priority national educational objectives. Hence it was a logical next step for it to help raise the educational achievement of children from low-income families. It is true that this effort was both administratively and substantively inadequate. But time and experience have seen many weaknesses removed, although no educational system has as yet designed an effective remedial program. It is a fair guess that in the absence of a federal initiative we would today be much farther from the solution. This is clearly a case in which it is better to have tried and failed (and learned something) than never to have tried at all.

Of all the Great Society programs, the war on poverty is most open to criticism. The promises were extreme; the specific remedial actions were untried and untested; the finances were grossly inadequate; the political structuring was so vulnerable that it had to be radically reformed within a few years after the program was launched. Yet despite these weaknesses, we cannot argue that poverty is not a subject worthy of national concern and federal intervention; that many components of the specific OEO legislation from the Job Corps to Operation Mainstream were not sensible first efforts; that without Presidential leadership and Congressional support for social intervention the nation would today be better off. The prolonged economic prosperity of the 1960's helped to lift many families out of poverty, but this longest boom in the nation's history also proved that economic growth is not the answer for all who lack an adequate income.

With respect to federal efforts in housing and urban development, the record is mixed. Much that was attempted succeeded, such as facilitating home ownership by the middle class. On the other hand, suitable housing for low-income families remains a serious challenge. Even more difficult has been neighborhood preservation in urban centers, since large numbers of minority-group members must have access to housing which was formerly not available to them. The specialists agree that the federal government has an important role to play in housing and urban development. They differ only about the approaches the federal government should follow. But as is frequently the case in complex arenas of societal change, there are no right or wrong answers; there are only cautious or radical experiments, the outcomes of which must be assessed before the next round of plans and policies is implemented.

We come to the last of the major interventions directed to improving the position of the black minority. While the Kennedy Administration made a few moves on this front, it was Johnson's leadership that brought about major improvements in race relations. Even today, a decade after the effort was mounted, there is no agreement about what he ventured and what he accomplished. But a few facts are incontrovertible: The black population has made striking gains in occupational status and in income, in political participation and as office holders, in the options that black people have to determine how and where to live, in the way in which they are treated by the law enforcement authorities and in the courts. Blacks remain a disadvantaged minority suffering from the cumulative effects of more than three and one-half centuries of racism, segregation, and exploitation. But the gains over the last decade have been large and give promise of being sustained. And here in particular, Presidential leadership played a critical and constructive role, even though some believe that President Johnson did not go far enough and others are convinced that he lost his followers because he moved too rapidly.

The record of the Great Society is one of successes mixed with failures, of experiments that proved themselves at least partly successful and experiments whose returns do not appear to have justified the effort. In other words, it turned out about as any sensible person should have expected.

Index